CROSSBILL GUIDES

Provence
and Camargue
FRANCE

Crossbill Guides: Provence and Camargue – France
First print: 2020

Initiative, text and research: Dirk Hilbers, Constant Swinkels, Albert Vliegenthart
Editing: Dirk Hilbers, John Cantelo, Brian Clews, Kim Lotterman
Illustrations: Horst Wolter
Maps: Constant Swinkels, Dirk Hilbers
Type and image setting: Oscar Lourens
Print: Drukkerij Tienkamp, Groningen

ISBN 978 94 91648 16 8
© 2020 Crossbill Guides Foundation, Arnhem, The Netherlands

This book is produced with best practice methods ensuring lowest possible environmental impact, using waterless offset, vegetable based inks and FSC-certified paper.

All rights reserved. No part of this book may be reproduced in any form by print, photocopy, microfilm or any other means without the written permission of the Crossbill Guides Foundation.
The Crossbill Guides Foundation and its authors have done their utmost to provide accurate and current information and describe only routes, trails and tracks that are safe to explore. However, things do change and readers are strongly urged to check locally for current conditions and for any changes in circumstances. Neither the Crossbill Guides Foundation nor its authors or publishers can accept responsibillity for any loss, injury or inconveniences sustained by readers as a result of the information provided in this guide.

www.crossbillguides.org
www.knnvpublishing.nl
www.saxifraga.nl

KNNV Publishing  SAXIFRAGA foundation

CROSSBILL
GUIDES
FOUNDATION

This guidebook is a product of the non-profit foundation Crossbill Guides. By publishing these books we want to introduce more people to the joys of Europe's beautiful natural heritage and to increase the understanding of the ecological values that underlie conservation efforts. Most of this heritage is protected for ecological reasons and we want to provide insight into these reasons to the public at large. By doing so we hope that more people support the ideas behind nature conservation.
For more information about us and our guides you can visit our website at:

WWW.CROSSBILLGUIDES.ORG

Highlights of Provence

1 Set aside several days for the Camargue, one of Europe's top birdwatching destinations (routes 1-7).

2 Explore the many calcareous scrub and grass lands of Provence's interior with its swathes of orchids and clouds of butterflies (e.g. routes 15, 16, 18, 19, 22, 23).

3 Take a boat trip over to Île Port-Cros, a completely unspoilt island with one of the most intact submarine ecosytems of the Mediterranean (route 12).

4 Climb the Mont Ventoux and discover its unique flora and fauna (route 24).

HIGHLIGHTS OF PROVENCE

5 Immerse yourself in the purple sea of lavender on the plateau of Valensole, with its remarkably rich birdlife of dry fields (route 21).

6 Descend into the sublime depths of the Gorge du Verdon or Gorge de la Nesque, or stay on their lip and watch the vultures and eagles fly by at an arm's length (routes 19 and 20).

7 Discover the verdant hills and orchid-rich plain of Maures, the acidic crystalline massif that is the oldest in entire Provence.

8 Find the rare birds, plants and insects of the steppe plain of La Crau (routes 8 and 9).

ABOUT THIS GUIDE

About this guide

 boat trip or ferry crossing

 car route

 bicycle route

 walking route

 beautiful scenery

 interesting history

 interesting geology

This guide is meant for all those who enjoy being in and learning about nature, whether you already know all about it or not. It is set up a little differently from most guides. We focus on explaining the natural and ecological features of an area rather than merely describing the site. We choose this approach because the nature of an area is more interesting, enjoyable and valuable when seen in the context of its complex relationships. The interplay of different species with each other and with their environment is simply mind-blowing. The clever tricks and gimmicks that are put to use to beat life's challenges are as fascinating as they are countless.

Take our namesake the Crossbill: at first glance it's just a big finch with an awkward bill. But there is more to the Crossbill than meets the eye. This bill is beautifully adapted for life in coniferous forests. It is used like a scissor to cut open pinecones and eat the seeds that are unobtainable for other birds. In the Scandinavian countries where pine and spruce take up the greater part of the forests, several Crossbill species have each managed to answer two of life's most pressing questions: how to get food and how to avoid direct competition. By evolving crossed bills, each differing subtly, they have secured a monopoly of the seeds produced by cones of varying sizes. So complex is this relationship that scientists are still debating exactly how many different species of Crossbill actually exist. Now this should heighten the appreciation of what at first glance was merely a plumb red bird with a beak that doesn't seem to fit properly. Once its interrelationships are seen, nature comes alive, wherever you are.

To some, impressed by the "virtual" familiarity that television has granted to the wilderness of the Amazon, the vastness of the Serengeti or the sublimity of Yellowstone, European nature may seem a puny surrogate, good merely for the casual stroll. In short, the argument seems to be that if you haven't seen some impressive predator, be it a Jaguar, Lion or Grizzly Bear, then you haven't seen the "real thing". Nonsense, of course.

But where to go? And how? What is there to see? That is where this guide comes in. We describe the how, the why, the when, the where and the how come of Europe's most beautiful areas. In clear and accessible language, we explain the nature of Provence and Camargue and refer extensively to routes where the area's features can be observed best. We try to make the region come alive. We hope that we succeed.

HOW TO USE THIS GUIDE

How to use this guide

This guidebook contains a descriptive and a practical section.
The descriptive part comes first and gives you insight into the most striking and interesting natural features of the area. It provides an understanding of what you will see when you go out exploring. The descriptive part consists of a landscape section (marked with a red bar), describing the habitats, the history and the landscape in general, and of a flora and fauna section (marked with a green bar), which discusses the plants and animals that occur in the region.
The second part offers the practical information (marked with a purple bar). A series of routes (walks) is carefully selected to give you a good flavour of all the habitats, flora and fauna that Provence and Camargue has to offer. At the start of each route description, a number of icons give a quick overview of the characteristics of each route. These icons are explained in the margin of this page. The final part of the book (marked with blue squares) provides some basic tourist information and some tips on finding plants, birds and other animals.
There is no need to read the book from cover to cover. Instead, each small chapter stands on its own and refers to the routes most suitable for viewing the particular features described in it. Conversely, descriptions of each route refer to the chapters that explain more in depth the most typical features that can be seen along the way.
In the back of the book we have included a list of all the mentioned plant and animal species, with their scientific names and translations into German and Dutch.
Some species names have an asterix (*) following them. This indicates that there is no official English name for this species and that we have taken the liberty of coining one. For the sake of readability we have decided to translate the scientific name, or, when this made no sense, we gave a name that best describes the species' appearance or distribution. Please note that we do not want to claim these as the official names. We merely want to make the text easier to follow for those not familiar with scientific names. When a new vernacular name was invented, we've also added the scientific name.
An overview of the area described in this book is given on the map on page 12. For your convenience we have also turned the inner side of the back flap into a map of the area indicating all the described routes. Descriptions in the explanatory text refer to these routes.

 interesting flora

 interesting invertebrate life

 interesting reptile and amphibian life

 interesting mammals

 interesting birdlife

 site for snorkelling

 interesting for whales and dolphins

 visualising the ecological contexts described in this guide

Table of contents

Landscape	11
Geographical overview	12
Geology	15
Climate	23
Habitats	25
The coast – dunes, cliffs and islands	27
Salt marshes and lagoons	31
Rice paddies, freshwater marshes and the Rhône river	36
La Crau – a unique stony plain	41
Low ranges and plains	44
Cliffs and plateaux – Haute Provence	54
Montane forests and the Mont Ventoux	59
History	62
Nature conservation	70
Flora and Fauna	75
Flora	77
Mammals	89
Birds	92
Reptiles and amphibians	103
Insects and other invertebrates	107
Practical Part	117
Camargue, Crau and Alpilles	118
Route 1: Mas du Pont de Rousty	119
Route 2: The northern Camargue	121
Route 3: Around Saintes-Maries-de-la-Mer	125
Route 4: Étang de Scamandre	129
Route 5: The Eastern Camargue	131
Route 6: Along 'La Digue'	135
Route 7: Via La Palissade to the coast	137
Route 8: Crau – Peau de Meau reserve	140
Route 9: The Wet Crau and Marais de Vigueirat	143
Route 10: A walk in Les Alpilles	147
Additional sites in the Camargue-Crau-Alpilles area	151
Côte d'Azur	154
Route 11: The saltpans of Giens	155
Route 12: Île Port-Cros	158
Route 13: Massif des Maures	162
Route 14: Plaine des Maures	166

TABLE OF CONTENTS

Route 15: Mont Sainte Victoire — 171
Route 16: Massif de Sainte-Baume — 174
Route 17: Along the Endre river — 177
Additional sites in the Côte d'Azur — 180
Haute Provence — 184
Route 18: Plaine de Calern — 185
Route 19: Grand canyon du Verdon – a first exploration — 189
Route 20: Grand Canyon du Verdon – Sentier Martel — 194
Route 21: The Valensole Plain — 198
Additional sites in Haute Provence — 201
Vaucluse — 203
Route 22: Car route through the Vaucluse — 204
Route 23: Walking in the Montagne du Luberon — 209
Route 24: The summit of the Mont Ventoux — 213
Additional sites in the Vaucluse — 217

Tourist information and observation tips — 221
Acknowledgements — 239
Picture and illustration credits — 240
Species list and translation — 241

List of Text boxes
Mistral misery — 24
Lavender trivia — 57
Papal power problems — 66
The Marseillaise, a song for everyone — 68
The Camargue horse: fact and fiction — 91
Flamingos – Camargue's pink pride — 95
The Provence five — 109
La Cigale, the mascot of Provence — 113

LANDSCAPE

Rows of lavender encircling an old stone shed. Bright yellow sunflowers against a deep blue sky, as beautiful and radiant as in a van Gogh painting. A little square in a medieval hilltop village. A country lunch in a small family restaurant. Chequered table linen with sun spots from the filtered light beams through the leaves of a tall Plane Tree. The food is delicious – directly from the land from a recipe that was in the family for years. And the wine – *Oh-lah-lah!*
These are some of the classic images of Provence, so celebrated in magazines all over the world. If there is one place in the world that embodies the romance of country life (and food), it is this wonderful area in southeastern France. Provence embodies the dream of many hard-working city folks of a rural retreat for recharging and reconnecting with a beautiful, pleasant nature.
Everything about this romantic image is true.
Perhaps because of this Arcadian rather than wild image, Provence is less popular with adventurous naturalists than it ought to be. This was different in the two previous centuries, when first train travel and then cars became available to an increasing number of people. Naturalists in search of sun and warmth discovered the region and came home with the most fantastic stories of wild mountains and marshes, of colourful Bee-eaters and Hoopoes, of Flamingos against a setting sun. They raved too about flashy Two-tailed Pasha butterflies gracefully flying over hillsides covered in wild cork oak forests, and about all those country roads with thousands of wild orchids in their verges. That family restaurant was there too – it had a Praying Mantis in the geraniums, geckos on the walls and you heard the Scop's Owl calling all evening long. In short, the Camargue and Provence represented an exotic flora and fauna that was as unfamiliar as it was enchanting.
And everything about that was true as well. In fact, it still is.
Then in the '70s, 80s and '90s, people started to take the plane to go on holiday and discovered Spain, Greece and then destinations outside Europe. Southern France's status as an exotic destination for naturalists was usurped. At least that's our explanation for the relative low popularity for the region among birders and naturalists today. It is astonishing, because there are few European destinations with a more diverse flora and fauna than Provence. Ranging from dunes and saltmarsh via steppes and forests to Alpine meadows, it has an enormously varied landscape. It is a

View towards Sault in the Vaucluse – this is the classic image of the picturesque Provence.

GEOGRAPHICAL OVERVIEW

hotspot for wildflowers (especially orchids), butterflies, reptiles and birds. We found 170 species of birds on a spring trip that wasn't even aimed specifically at birdwatching!

So, it is time to (re)acquaint yourself with Provence and Camargue and to discover that it hasn't lost its exotic charm. This guidebook explains to you why the region is so blessed with wildlife, provides you routes to find them and will help you rediscover Provence's delights.

Geographical overview

Provence is a region whose borders are not strictly defined. It is not administrative entity such as a province (which is ironic as the word 'province' stems from Provence).

Speaking in a general sense, Provence is the region in the southeast of France bordered in the west by the river Rhône, in the north and east by the Alps and in the south by the sea. It comprises the coastal strip (known as the Côte d'Azur; another region without a clear boundary) and interior plains, hills and mountains, the 'classic' Provence. This is also roughly the region we describe in this book, with the addition of the Rhône Delta,

Overview of Provence with the location of the routes that feature from page 117 onwards.

GEOGRAPHICAL OVERVIEW

known as the Camargue. More specifically, this guide covers the wedge between Nice in the east, Orange in the northwest and Montpellier in the south-west.

Provence's topography is highly diverse, almost chaotic. It has many wild mountain ranges separated by unexpectedly gentle or even flat terrain. But there is a general pattern. Overall, the ranges have an east-west orientation and slope down from the Alps in the east to the Rhône valley in the west. Taking the perspective of a giant, Provence then is somewhat like a flight of stairs – starting from sea level you step over the first mountain range up the first plateau, over the next range (a bit higher now) onto the next, more elevated plain, and so on.

Dunes, saltmarsh and shallow lagoons in the coastal Camargue.

The lowest parts of our area is the Camargue and la Crau (the former estuary of the Durance river; see page 42). This is an area with many towns and villages, such as Arles and Avignon.

Following the coastline east of the Camargue, it doesn't take long before you reach, near Marseille, the first mountains. This range extends all the way to Fréjus in the east, is broken up into various parts. In the west lie the ranges of les Calanques and Massif de la Sainte Baume, which consist of young limestone. Further east are the Massif des Maures (including the islands of Port-Cros and Porquerolles) and Esterel, which are made up of acidic schists. Separating these ranges is a small plain that stretches out between Toulon and Hyères in the west and Fréjus in the east. North of these ranges, where the landscape is flatter, lies the main east-west motorway A8 that connects Montpellier to Nice and goes further into Italy.

North of the A8 lies another mountain range, which is very wide and high in the east, but becomes narrower in the west, where it forms the Mont Saint Victoire near Aix-en-Provence and finally the low but rocky Alpilles, just east of Arles.

Northeast of the Alpilles flows the Durance, Provence's largest river, beyond which lies the the province of Vaucluse. The Vaucluse stretches out between the Luberon mountains in the south (the small towns

LANDSCAPE

GEOGRAPHICAL OVERVIEW

of Cavaillon, Pertuis and Manosque are the main centres here) and the Mont Ventoux in the north. The Vaucluse a lovely region, famed for its wines, lavender, its historical villages and of course the Mont Ventoux with its unique wildlife. As you cross the Vaucluse from west to east, you'll notice that the western part is more densely inhabited,

The Valensole plain with the Verdon mountains in the background (route 21). This mix of rolling plains and wild mountains is typical of Provence.

warmer and at lower elevation, and you gradually enter a higher, wilder and less populated terrain as you proceed east.

There you meet the Durance again. East of the river, the land rises to a flat plateau on the edge of the high mountains. This is the area of the Plaine de Valensole (famous for having the largest lavender fields and an attractive birdlife) and Plaine de Canjuers (a superb wildlife region, but under military supervision so is difficult to access). Directly bordering this area lies, as an extension of the Alps (albeit one covered in this guide), the monumental Grand Canyon du Verdon – a spectacular deep gorge where the Verdon cut through the limestone mountains, which reach an altitude here of over 1400 metres.

Rivers from the Alps cut deep ravines in the limestone ranges of the Haute Provence. The Gorge du Verdon is the most famous of them (bottom).

GEOLOGY

Geology

The combination of plains and limestone mountains is Provence's scenic hallmark, but once you start to explore, it won't take long before you discover that the region is much more diverse. There are sea cliffs, dramatic gorges alternating with windy plateaux, friendly, rolling hills cheek by jowl with the lagoons and dunes whilst the ochre soils of Roussillon form. There are beautifully coloured badlands and even an area that looks like a Mediterranean version of fjords, *les Calanques* (site B on page 180).
This geological diversity makes it difficult to read the geological history of the landscape. The geological oddities seem scattered randomly across the region. This is the result of a long and complex history of tectonic movements, and the ever-changing influence of the sea.

The oldest rocks of Provence
Much of Provence consists of limestone ranges, recognisable by their greyish, blond or white colour. But they are not the oldest part of the region. In fact, the limestones are geologically a rather young addition to the landscape. Much older is the small area that stretches out from Cape Sicié just south of Toulon to Cannes in the east. This is the *Crystalline Provence* – an area that comprises the Massif de Tanneron, Estérel and, most importantly, the Massif and Plaine des Maures (routes 13 and 14). The islands of Port-Cros and Porquerolles are also part of this area of Hercynian bedrock, as are large parts of the islands of Corsica and Sardinia.

View towards the Hercynian mountains near le Roquebrun. This is the old core of Provence.

LANDSCAPE

GEOLOGY

Bedrock from the Hercynian orogeny (mountain building phase) is amongst the oldest of Europe. It dates back to the Carboniferous Period, 370-290 million years ago, before the Atlantic Ocean existed and Europe and America collided. It was also long before the Pyrenees and Alps existed. The Hercynian mountains must have been formidable; a very long range of incredibly high mountains. Today, remains of the Hercynian Chain (which has an American counterpart in the Appalachian Mountains) form a broken belt across Europe, from southern Portugal through Spain, western France (e.g. Massif Central, Brittany, Vosges, Ardennes) through to the Norwegian mountains. A large area from the southern Provence and the Tyrrhenian islands (Corsica and Sardinia) also belong to this range, and deep underground, buried by the more recent limestone, it is still present in much of Provence.

After the Hercynian orogeny, during the Permian, erosive forces gradually ground down these mountains and deposited the debris in large plains around the mountains. Positioned at the edge of a tectonic plate, the area also became volcanically active. The Earth spewed large amounts of rhyolite, an acidic form of lava. This created the Estérel range between Fréjus and Cannes, which is famous for its red rhyolite rock, that seems to glow in the evening sun.

The difference in landscape between the crystalline and the limestone Provence is enormous. The granite, gneiss and amphibolite rocks of the old Provence are not as dramatic as the rest of Provence. Rather the topography was smoothened over the years to form a more gentle, hilly terrain. The bedrock retains water much better than the porous limestone, and therefore the land is overall more verdant. Last, but certainly not least, the bedrock is acidic and supports a different flora (see page 80).

The limestone Provence – Pyrenean mountain building phase

Limestone dominates Provence. The mountain ranges are the result of a four stage process: first marine sedimentation, then tectonic upheaval, a subsequent folding of the layers and finally riverine erosion and deposition.

At the end of the Permian Period (299-251 million years ago), much of today's Provence was part of a shallow sea. Shellfish, mostly microscopic, sank to the seafloor when the animals died, leaving the calcareous shells on the bottom. This biological littering, because that is what it was, built up at a rate of about 1 mm per year. As the number of layers grew, and the pressure they exerted with it, the sediments were compressed into limestone. Even in this compacted form, 0.2 mm of limestone still

GEOLOGY

White limestone cliffs are typical of most mountain ranges. This is La Caume in the Alpilles (route 10). In the background lies the plain of the Durance river.

corresponds with one year of marine deposits. Hence, over the deep epochs of geological time, a limestone belt was formed that is in many places several kilometres thick. In it are countless fossils of larger marine animals, mostly shellfish.

Under tectonic pressure, the seafloor rose, surfaced and folded to form the limestone mountain chains we see today. This process didn't happen once, but several times as the sea levels ebbed and flowed, which is one of the reasons why the geology of Provence is both rich and complicated.

The first time limestone emerged was during the Triassic Period (251 – 200 million years ago). At this time the Iberian microplate (a 'crumble' of the great American-Eurasian plate that broke into an American and European plate), became squashed between Africa and Europe (see page 19). The Iberian plate was pressed against the European and created a large mountain range that consisted of the Pyrenees and several ranges in the present-day Massif Central and Provence. The Alps didn't yet exist at that time.

During the formation of the Pyrenees (around 50 million years ago), the mountains of Mont Sainte-Victoire, Sainte-Baume and the Mont Ventoux rose from the seabed. Although today, they seem like forerunners of the Alps, they were actually formed together with the Pyrenees.

Subsequent cycles of thaw and frost eroded the mountains to rocky crests. The generally soft limestone is very susceptible to erosion. As rain water is naturally somewhat acidic, it dissolves the limestone. Water that seeps into the cracks and expands when it freezes easily pries into the cracks and

LANDSCAPE

GEOLOGY

The fabulously coloured ochres of Le Colorado (site C on page 217).

widens and deepens them – a process that you can see on the limestone plateaux, such as on the Plaine the Calern (route 18).
The Alps formed a little later than the Pyrenees, and the period in between these events was important for Provence. The land mass of Corsica and Sardinia, which was attached to Catalonia and southern France, broke loose and drifted to its current location, opening the western Mediterranean. This affected Provence considerably. Suddenly, the region wasn't part of a collision zone. Instead, the pressures were reversed and the earth crust was stretched. The surface sank and the old Rhône basin dropped below sea level, as did large parts of the coast and of the current Vaucluse. The sea was back! It was in these warm, shallow coastal seas that the young limestones of Provence were formed – those that would later become the plateau of the Vaucluse, the Luberon, the Alpilles, les Calanques and the Nerthe (west of Marseille).

The limestone Provence revisited – Alpine mountain building phase

Around 24 million years ago, the Alpine mountain building phase finally began – a process with tremendous force and incredible slowness that continues up to this day. Not only the Alpine arch was formed, but the entire region rose up, lifting the former seabed up to a highland plateau. Many of the jagged ranges in the west, such as the Alpilles and the Luberon, are examples of this. The older limestone ranges of Pyrenean origin received an extra push.
As soon as slopes formed, rivers followed and carved out their valleys. Up in the mountains, the water created deep gorges in the limestone, (e.g. Gorge du Verdon and Gorge de la Nesque (routes 19-20 and 22 respectively).
The steep mountain slopes meant that water ran off with great force. This became even more apparent in the Quaternary period, between 1.8 million and 11,500 years ago, the period of the glacials or 'ice ages'. In these cold

GEOLOGY

Geology of Provence in five maps
(The red dot is Provence; the red arrows indicate tectonic movements)

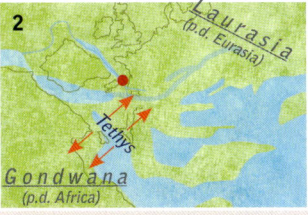

1 - Map of the world around 350 million years ago, when all the world's landmass was concentrated in one supercontinent – Pangea. The Hercynean mountain range is shown. Parts of this range still surface in the Massif des Maures and surrounding areas.

2 - Around 200 million years ago, the continent was gradually breaking in two – the southern Gondwana and the northern Laurasia being divided by the Tethys sea.

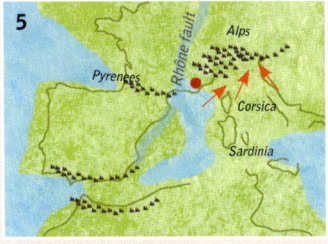

3 - New rift valleys separate the Iberian Peninsula from France, making it an island. Note the long peninsula attached to Iberia, from which many parts of Provence as well as Corsica and Sardinia originate.

4 - Iberia tilts and the African plate presses it against southern France, pushing up the Pyrenees.

5 - Corsica and Sardinia drift to their current position and Provence is subdued and becomes inundated by the sea. Later, as the African plate collides with the European, the Alps are formed and the whole of Provence, still partly under sea level, is pushed up.

LANDSCAPE

GEOLOGY

The plateau of Calern (route 18) is one of many karst plateau in the central and north-eastern part of Provence. Typically, the soils are thin, dry and rocky and the plateaux are riddled with craterlike dolines – fertile depressions that are the result of collapsed caves.

periods, the Alps were a world of ice. Only in the height of summer did the snow melt so that an entire winter's worth of melted snow fed the streams that rushed down the mountains. The high, snow-capped mountains had, like today, a torrential regime – for a short time in spring, an enormous volume of water rushed down the valley, taking with it lots of sand, pebbles and even rocks, which were deposited further down to form plains.

One spectacular limestone range was formed in this Alpine mountain building period that today attracts visitors from around the world: les Calanques, south of Marseille. Here, the workings of the rivers created numerous steep valleys, which were later, when the sea level rose, partially flooded, leaving many canyons filled with crystal-clear sea water. These bays look a bit like fjords, although the latter have a very different geological history.

The plains

Rivers with such an episodic runoff typically form wide, flat riverbeds that are largely dry for much of the year. Today, you can see this in the Durance river valley (see page 47).

Over time the Alpine rivers deposited enormous layers of sediment that filled the valleys, leaving only the highest crests sticking out of the deposits. This odd landscape is what you encounter when you explore the western Provence, around Les Alpilles (route 10) and further down to Saint-Martin-de-Crau or up to Avignon or Cavaillon. Heavily eroded, rocky crests engulfed by a level, fertile land.

GEOLOGY

Some of these ranges, such as the Luberon, can still be called mountains and are several hundred metres high. Others are more like very rocky hills, like the Alpilles (the name literally translates 'Little Alps'). But there are also 'ranges' that don't protrude more than 5 or 10 metres, such as the 'hill' you cross when you go from Saint-Martin to Maussane-les-Alpilles (site E on page 153).

As noted earlier, the rise of the Alps was (and is) a slow process. The lowland river plains rose with the entire region as tectonic pressures grew. The lowland became upland, from which new rivers gouged their way down to the lowland. The sedimentary plains started to show a vein-like pattern of small river valleys. The Plaine de Valensole (route 21) is a perfect example of this – more or less level, with the mountains in the background. However, as you travel across the area, you frequently drop down into a V-shaped valley, cross a brook and climb up again to the flat world. This soil type at these altitudes offers the perfect conditions to grow a specific type of plant that would make Provence world famous: lavender (see page 57)!

Further to the west there are younger plains built up with the sediments of rivers and the sea, mostly sand and clay. When mixed together and put under pressure, these metamorphised to a clayey type of sandstone stained reddish by the iron in the sediment. The brittle sandstone is known as ochre, already a valuable mineral in Roman times. Perhaps the most spectacular ochre layers are found in the Colorado de Rustrel (site C on page 217). This is an old ochre mine, where the spectacularly coloured, iron-rich, loamy sandstones surface in odd shapes.

La Crau and the Camargue

La Crau is also a river plain, which may come as a surprise, as there is no longer a river to be seen in this dry, semi-desert environment. The Crau plain is especially interesting as it was formed by the Durance, which now bends to the northwest near Cavaillon, but formerly took a southern course and formed a sea delta, laying the foundations of today's Crau plain (see page 41). In fact, it wasn't until the end of the Würm glacial (18,000 years ago) that the Durance abandoned the Crau plain and took its current course to flow out in the Rhône river south of Avignon. The river brought down the boulders that are so typical of the dry Crau, and also brought down sediments, which cemented together to form an impenetrable layer. The winter rains run off quickly and leave a very dry and thin soil in summer, effectively making it a semi-desert.

The Camargue is the geologically youngest part of the area described in this book (and is officially part of Bouches-du-Rhône and not Provence).

GEOLOGY

Some geological highlights of Provence

Hercynian sites
1 Massif des Maures: soft hilly landscape with acidic rock (route 13,14).
2 Estérel: Rhyolite cliffs.

Limestone sites
3 Calern: dolines, poljes and karst landscapes (route 18).
4 Verdon: one of Europe's most spectacular limestone gorges and plateaux (routes 19 and 20).
5 Calanques: limestone bays, karst plains and underwater source (site B on page 180).
6 Gorge de la Nesque: karst plain and gorge (route 22).
7 Alpilles: Young limestone ranges, surrounded by plains with riverine and marine sediment (route 10).

Riverine and marine sediments
8 Valensole: old river plain on molasse (route 21).
9 Ochre of Rustrel: old marine sediments with sand and clay, creating spectacular colours. (site C on page 217).
10 La Crau: old riverbed, impermeable and thereby creating extreme, desert-like conditions (route 8 and 9).
11 Presqu'île de Giens: double tombolo, connecting the Hercynian 'island' of Giens with the mainland (route 11).
12 Camargue: dunes, coastal lagoon and saline-freshwater gradient (route 5, 6 and 7)

It is a textbook example of an estuary, where the interplay between currents of saline seawater and fresh river water, each with its own sediments, created the landscape. In a way, the Camargue is like the Alps a collision zone, but not one of land masses, but of water currents. Where these currents meet, they come to a halt, and the suspended sands settle to form mud flats and sand banks which then develop into a sand spit with low dunes. The sea regularly breaks through this barrier, after which new sediments 'patch up' the breach. In 1859, the Camargue coastal barrier was consolidated with 'La Digue' (route 6). Behind it on the land side, the river water stagnates and forms a coastal lagoon, the huge Étang de Vaccarès.

Most of the time, the river flow keeps the sea at bay, but during storms and at high tide, the seawater pushes inland, creating channels and salt marshes, and filling the lagoon with salt water.
River and sea together produce a maze of gradients of saline, brackish and saltwater marshes. In the Camargue, these water flows are regulated in channels, but the overall pattern of saltwater *sansouieres*, brackish *pelouses* and freshwater marshes and paddies is still clearly visible.

Climate

Overall, Provence has a typical Mediterranean climate with hot and dry summers and wet and mild winters. However, the close proximity to the Alps and the varied topography means that the both climate and actual weather conditions vary strongly from place to place.
There is a clear difference between the climate of the western and the eastern part of the coast. In the east, the strip of land with a true Mediterranean climate is narrow and confined to the Côte d'Azur. Just a little inland, the mountains are already so high that the temperatures go down and the precipitation up. The high mountains do however shield the Côte d'Azur from a very typical climatic feature that plagues the western coast: the Mistral. This is a cold, in winter even freezing, wind from the north, which often takes on the character of a storm that can last for days (see box on next page).

	average summer high	average winter low	precipitation
Nice	23.9 °C	9.2 °C;	733 mm/y
Avignon	24.0 °C	6.0 °C	494 mm/y
Sault	18.2 °C	1.3 °C	855 mm/y

The differences in climate are clearly shown in the precipitation and temperature graphs of Avignon (in the Rhône Valley), Nice (on the coast but close to the Alps) and Sault (at the foot of the Mont Ventoux). Nice has of these the most Mediterranean climate, with hot summers and mild winters. Rain falls in autumn and winter. Avignon has an overall drier climate with similar summer temperatures, but colder winters; the result of the mistral wind (see next page), which blows around 140 (!) days of the year with an average wind speed of 90 kms an hour. Very different again is the climate on the plateaux of the Vaucluse and High Provence. Here, the precipitation is not so clearly restricted to the autumn and winter, but spread out over the year. The summer temperatures are only a bit lower than those of the two other Mediterranean cities, but the winter temperatures are considerably lower than on the coast.

CLIMATE

Mistral misery

The mistral is a fascinating, often very frustrating, and quite literally striking aspect of Provence's climate. It is a fierce, localised wind that comes straight down from the mountains in the north. When it breathes its icy blast, people stay indoors and birds plunge their heads deep into their feathers and stay huddled on the ground or deep in shelter. Those who are foolish enough to take to the air anyway are turned into origami projects. Legs and necks are folded into unhealthy-looking configurations and toes and tips are jerked to all points of the compass.

The mistral wind blows for over a third of the year. The fiercest mistrals are in winter and early spring. Speeds of 135 km per hour have been recorded, which is officially hurricane force. In summer, the Mistral is little more than a strong breeze and a welcome relief from the Mediterranean heat.

The mistral is a so-called *katabatik wind* – a local air circulation system that occurs in valleys just outside of large mountain ranges. The mountains function as a reservoir of cold air, which spills over the upland plateau and plunges down into the valley. In the case of the mistral the effects are especially dramatic because the air rushes down from both the Massif Central in the west and from the Alps in the east. The narrow Rhône valley funnels the air and works it up to high speeds that scour and scourge the open Camargue and Crau plains and the lowlands further east. To make matters worse, regular winter depressions near Sardinia pulls the air south. All these factors together account for the impressive wind speeds.

The mistral winds flog the open landscape, blowing up tongues of briny foam over the bunds that line the lagoons of the Camargue (top) and picking up entire table sets as if they were tumbleweeds (bottom).

HABITATS

Habitats

The Camargue and Provence combined support a wide array of habitats that range from coastal flats to sea cliffs and from lowland plains to subalpine meadows. Some of these habitats are typical for the Mediterranean, others are more typical of the temperate and Alpine regions. Provence lies on the crossroads of these three biomes (see page 76).
Add to this the erratic topography with mountains, plains and plateaux scattered over the area, and you encounter a landscape that appears to have been put in the blender: most habitats can be found, fragmented, in many areas of Provence. There are Alpine plateaux quite close to the coast and Mediterranean scrublands far inland. Nevertheless, the conditions in which these habitats occur, are fairly well defined, which is shown in the illustrations on this page and the following.
In the Camargue (below image) the presence of water and salt are the defining elements. On the coast there is a narrow row of dunes, behind which salt marshes and saline lagoons dominate. Further inland, the river water becomes dominant, supporting reedbeds, freshwater meadows and rice paddies. Naturally, there is a wide range of intermediate habitats of brackish meadows and marshes. In the field, a complex system of channels and dams have created rather strict borders between the fresh and saline environments (which you see so well on routes 1 and 2). Further away from the river, there are the steppes of La Crau and the hot mountains of the Alpilles.

Idealised cross-section of the habitats of the western lowlands. The sea and the Camargue are on the left and the Alpilles on the right.

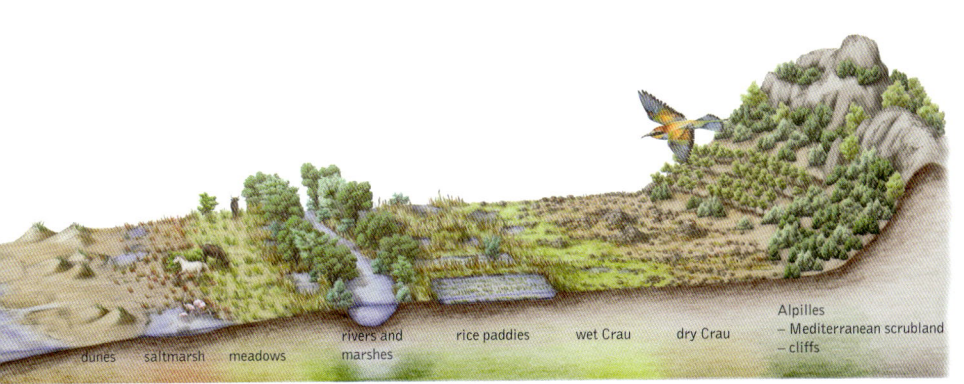

dunes saltmarsh meadows rivers and marshes rice paddies wet Crau dry Crau Alpilles – Mediterranean scrubland – cliffs

LANDSCAPE

HABITATS

In Provence proper, the situation is more complicated. On the coast, there are both limestone cliffs (very dry and shrubby) and acidic rocks, covered in more luxuriant Mediterranean forests. Most villages and agricultural lands are on the lowland plains, which is where you find that lovely Provençal patchwork countryside with the vineyards, the sunflowers and the lavender fields, separated by woods, hedges and scrublands.

The limestone mountains are mostly oriented east-west, which means that there is a north and a south slope which vary strongly in climate and vegetation. On the south slope, Mediterranean scrubland and higher up Downy Oak woods dominate. On the north slope, Downy Oak and Austrian Pine grow in the lower parts, while Beech woods can be found higher up. Many mountains rise to a rocky plateau, covered with flowery, steppe-like grasslands, interspersed with scattered Box bushes and pines. While some of these places are wild and deserted, others are used for the growth of lavender. These uplands are riddled with deep ravines with cliffs and gorge forests.

Finally, towards the Mont Ventoux, the Alpine character becomes more pronounced. There are dense forests on the slopes (first Downy Oak, then Beech and subsequently pine). Above the treeline, bare limestone remains with scattered junipers.

The next chapters describe these habitats and their flora and fauna in more detail.

Idealised cross-section of the habitats of the eastern Provence. The cliff coasts are on the left and the forerunners of the Alps (such as the Mont Ventoux) on the right.

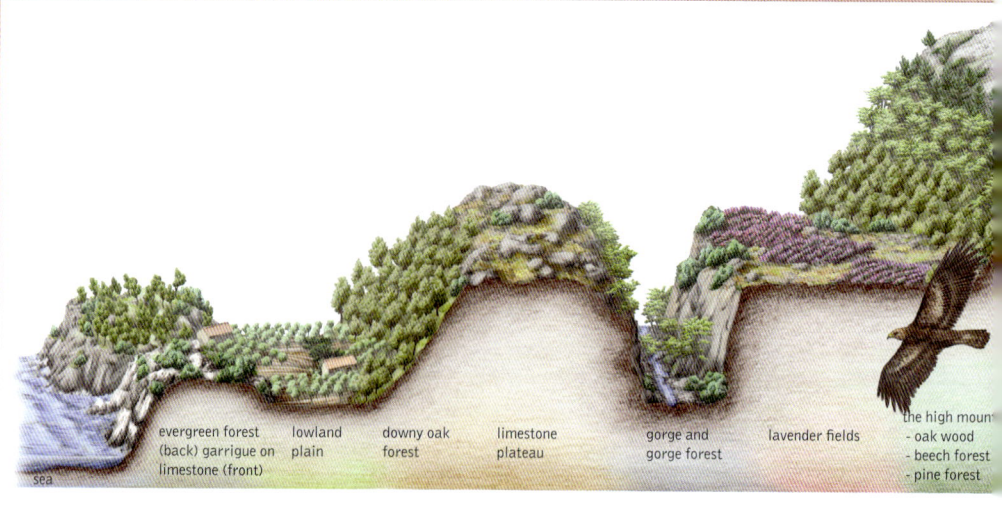

sea | evergreen forest (back) garrigue on limestone (front) | lowland plain | downy oak forest | limestone plateau | gorge and gorge forest | lavender fields | the high moun - oak wood - beech forest - pine forest

THE COAST – DUNES, CLIFFS AND ISLANDS

The coast – dunes, cliffs and islands

Sand dunes feature on routes 6, 7 and 11. Limestone coastal cliffs are spectacular on sites B, C and D (see page 180-182). Acidic cliffs and islands are present on routes 11 and 12, plus site A on page 180. The sea life is best discovered on route 12 and sites A and C on page 180-181.

The coastal strip of Provence is one of contrasts. The western part is relatively flat, with saltmarshes and dunes on the coast. These wild places belong to the *Réserve Naturelle Nationale de Camargue* and surrounding reserves. Further east, ports and industrial areas dominate between Fos-sur-Mer and Marseille.

Marseille is the gateway to the other part of the coast, known as the Côte d'Azur. This one is rocky and wooded with deep blue bays and coves, a deep blue sea, expensive boats, posh restaurants and jet set. It's been the retreat for rich and famous for centuries and in their wake, masses of tourists crowd the seaside towns and villages on the coast in summer. Therefore, the Côte d'Azur is perhaps not the first region that comes to mind when selecting your wildlife sites to visit.

That would be a mistake though. Since the coast is so rough and mountainous, many parts have escaped from development and are now protected nature reserves, including two of France's seven National Parks: les Calanques and Îles Port-Cros and Porquerolles.

The scenic diversity of the Côte d'Azur is enormous. Les Calanques have high limestone cliffs, white and as bare as bones, towering over the perfect blue sea. Elsewhere, old, dense Mediterranean forests on acidic hillsides take over (near the Massif des Maures and Estérel for example). In between are smaller ranges, plains and several small but highly attractive marshlands.

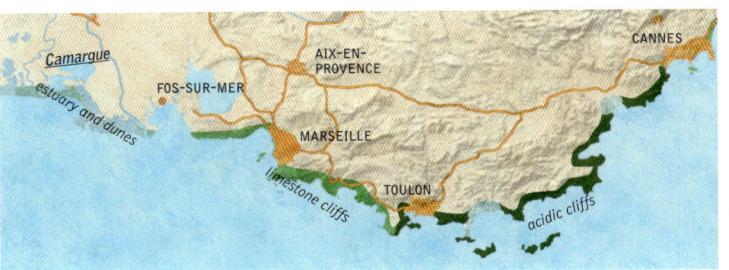

Position of the different types of coast of Provence. Dunes, estuaries and salt marsh are light green, the bare limestone cliff coast is a darker shade of green, while the wooded, acidic cliffs are dark green. Each of these have a different ecology, flora and fauna.

LANDSCAPE

THE COAST – DUNES, CLIFFS AND ISLANDS

The dunes

Start in the west, the first habitat type you encounter is the frail Mediterranean dune strip of the Camargue. Dunes are not commonly found in the Mediterranean basin as the sea does not transport much sand. Where dunes did form, people were quick to develop the site for tourism, thereby degrading the habitat. Seen in that light, it is a wonderful surprise to find the dunes of the Camargue have been spared such a fate. They are amongst the least disturbed and best-preserved dunes in the Mediterranean. Here the natural processes of erosion and sand deposition, which are so vital to intact dune ecosystems, are still occurring.

These processes create a mosaic habitat with eroding and growing dunes. In general, the seaward side of the dunes is more dynamic and exposed to the elements. The plants that grow here are highly adapted to these specific conditions and are strictly bound to the coast. They are drought-resistant plants, specialised in withstanding the constant influx of sand and salt. Some of them are familiar species further north like Sea Rocket and Sea Bindweed, but others have a Mediterranean distribution, like Sea Medick and Sea Daffodil.

The land side of the dunes is more sheltered and stable, allowing a taller and more diverse vegetation. Here the first small shrubs can be found, offering shelter for other flora and fauna.

The dunes of the Camargue (top) are rather low but beautifully preserved and very flowery. Sea Bindweed (bottom) is one of the attractive wildflowers that is exclusively found in the dunes.

Bare limestone cliffs

When we follow the coastline eastwards, past the ugly industry of Fos-sur-Mer and the city of Marseille, we encounter the stunning limestone cliffs of the *Parc National des Calanques*, established in 2012 and the

CROSSBILL GUIDES • PROVENCE

THE COAST – DUNES, CLIFFS AND ISLANDS

The barren limestone coastal cliffs of les Calanques are popular among hikers (top). The rocky coast, both limestone and crystalline, are the exclusive haunt of the rare European Leaf-toed Gecko (bottom).

youngest National Park in France. A *calanque* is an old river valley in the limestone landscape which has filled with seawater. Les Calanques are extremely rugged with steep cliffs which make a spectacular scenery. The *Falaises Soubeyranes* are the highest sea cliffs in the Mediterranean, reaching 394 metres. The cliffs are breeding sites for some birds that are rare or absent elsewhere in France, like Pallid Swift, Cory's and Yelkouan Shearwaters. The vegetation type here is known as *garrigue*, consisting of low, dispersed, often thorny shrubs which are well adapted to the dry, sunlit condition of the limestone cliffs. The shrubs all have deep roots that explore the cracks in the porous bedrock for underground aquifers as there is no surface water. Plants found here are often aromatic and include Cistus species, Kermes Oak, Phoenician Juniper and many herbs like Thyme and Rosemary. Reptile species profit from the open habitat and include the rare Leaf-toed Gecko, Montpellier Snake and Ocellated Lizard.

Wooded acidic cliffs

Further east, around Hyères, the limestone cliffs give way to a more acidic soil, belonging to the 'Crystalline Provence', the geologically oldest part of region (see page 15). Here we find the Presqu'île de Hyères, a peninsula with small dunes accompanied by some saltmarshes.

THE COAST – DUNES, CLIFFS AND ISLANDS

The well-known Îles d'Hyères, which are offshore fragments of the Massif des Maures, are famous for their sea-life, unspoilt vegetation and special flora and fauna of the 'Tyrrhenian' ecoregion (i.e. Corsica, Sardinia and surrounding islands and coast). Some species found here can hardly be found anywhere else in France like the Leaf-toed Gecko, Tyrrhenian Painted Frog, and the shrub Jupiter's-beard, closely related to the vetches.

These islands and the adjacent coastline are much greener than the limestone cliffs of les Calanques – a result of the hydrology and the different bedrock (see page 52). Dense Mediterranean forest and tall *maquis* with large Holm Oaks, Cork Oaks and Strawberry Trees can be found here. Their size is remarkable, when you factor in the salt, strong gales and burning, all of which slow down tree growth. The well-developed Mediterranean forest found on the Îles d'Hyères is indeed extremely rare and valuable.

The most ecologically intact of the islands is Port-Cros (route 12), which has no roads and only a handful of inhabitants. It is a National Park and rightfully so. Next to the old Mediterranean forest with its rich flora and fauna, its most visible feature is not apparent at first sight: the sea surrounding the island also belongs to the National Park. Because of the gradual slope of the land into the sea, the very clean water and low disturbance, a wealth of flora and fauna has developed here. Around 500 species of marine algae are found here and around 180 species of fish. Cold-water coral reefs are another feature. One of the Mediterranean's last Neptune Grass barrier reefs (a reef with seagrasses) is found near Île Port-Cros.

The Îles d'Hyères archipelago is very popular with divers and day-trippers and therefore visits are regulated, but very much worth the effort (see page 158).

The landscape of the crystalline part of the coastline is covered in splendid Mediterranean forest (bottom). One of the typical plants here is Jupiter's-beard, which is a large bush related to the Kidney Vetch (top).

SALT MARSHES AND LAGOONS

Salt marshes and lagoons

> Salt marshes, saline and brackish lagoons are present on routes 3, 5, 6, 7, 11 and site F on page 183. The *pelouses* (brackish to fresh meadows) are a feature of 1, 2, 3 and 7, plus site F on page 183.

The bird-filled salt marshes and lagoons of the Camargue work like a magnet for naturalists and birdwatchers. In the open landscape of distant horizons, Flamingos look like animated blobs of candy floss while waders fidget around them like ants. Terns and Slender-billed Gulls patrol the lagoons and in any bush on the coastline a migrant might take shelter. Another treat is the special flora that perseveres under the blazing sun and saline conditions. The wide vistas, the low sun and a lone Camargue horse completes the picture of this exotic habitat.

The salt marshes and lagoons can indeed be seen as the beating heart of the Camargue. They attract hundreds of thousands of migratory birds each spring and autumn and provide breeding grounds for still more. If you take a closer look, you'll see that the salt marsh consists of a patchwork of shallow saline lagoons, glasswort steppes (known as *sansouires*) and rough brackish meadows (known as *pelouses*).

The lagoons are found in the lowest parts, bordered by the *sansouires*. The almost steppe like *pelouses* are found on higher, less saline ground. These natural salt marshes have been converted into salt pans in the eastern part of the Camargue.

Europe's largest population of Greater Flamingos is found in the Camargue.

LANDSCAPE

SALT MARSHES AND LAGOONS

Lagoons

The warm shallow waters and nutrient rich soils of the lagoons form the perfect nursery for shrimps, molluscs and algae. Here they prosper and reach staggering numbers. They occur just as much in the mud as on it, and the invertebrates are food for the many birds that arrive every spring and autumn. After a long and exhausting journey, this 'all-you-can-eat' buffet is just what these migrants need.

Sansouire is the local name for saltmarsh (bottom). One of the conspicuous birds here is the Black-winged Stilt with its impossibly long legs (top).

The Camargue functions as one of western Europe's prime stop-overs for migrating shorebirds, which rest and regain their strength before continuing to their breeding grounds in the north in spring and then back south again in the autumn.

For some of them, the Camargue is the end of the journey. They join the resident birds to breed or winter. The most striking bird of the saline lagoons are present throughout the year – *Les Flamants Roses* rely upon this habitat completely.

The lagoons also play a major role in the water regulation of the area. Ever since humans started living in the area, floods were a major concern. The lagoons, especially the largest and most well-known, Étang de Vaccarès, form the principal component of the water management in the area, which is made up of a complex network of sluices, dikes and ditches. This network ensures that during peak discharge of the Rhône river, the adjacent lands are not flooded, whereas during the drier periods it retains sufficient water to irrigate the land.

Because of this network, most of the water from other parts of the Camargue and the Rhône river will pass through the lagoons. The Étang the Vaccarès is markedly less saline where fresh

water enters the lagoon in the north. This gradient of brackish to saline and the shallowness of the Étang (it is nowhere deeper than two metres) makes it such an important wetland for a large variety of birds.
The influx of fresh water is also a concern for nature conservation, as it makes the Étang sensitive to pollution upstream of the Rhône river or in other parts of the Camargue. Recent studies show that toxins are accumulating in fish tissue. In time this could also have adverse effects on birds living and foraging in these lagoons.

Sansouires

Moving from the saline lagoons onto the land, you first encounter extensive flats, dominated by glassworts. These succulent plants are some of the toughest on the globe. They are able to deal with enormous amounts of salt, while simultaneously facing extreme heat and sunshine. You could maybe compare this with the equivalent conditions of two deserts at the same time; extreme evaporation and absence of freshwater.
In the wettest and most saline parts on the edge of the lagoon, glassworts are the only plants, scattered over the muddy plain. Salt crystals colour the mud white. During summer the soil is 'cracked' as a result of the extreme heat. When the soil is not bone-dry, it is most likely flooded or very muddy. The most spectacular feature of the *sansouire* manifests itself during autumn, when the glassworts turn bright red. Enhanced by the setting sun, the glassworts set the October landscape on fire.
Because the sansouires are flat, it may come as a surprisinge that it is the altitude that determines the variety in this ecosystem. The difference between the low and high sansouires is a matter of centimetres, but these make all the difference in the world. The low sansouires (and the lagoons into which they seamlessly fade) are the places with the high concentrations of food. The higher parts are a lot less saline, as rain water is saved, forming a thin lens over the saline ground water.
For plants, conditions in the high sansouire are less harsh. As salt concentrations decrease, plant cover increases, which in turn catches the sand that is blown in from the coast. The denser vegetation is appreciated by birds like the rare Spectacled Warbler. In places where the influence of the salt groundwater diminishes further, rushes and tamarisks take over and the transitions starts towards either the *pelouses* or freshwater marshes.
Flooding in the high sansouires takes place only in very rare, extreme weather conditions. These higher spots are essentially like islands in the low sansouires, which makes them very attractive for breeding birds. The high sansouire is the place where the bulk of the waders, gulls, ducks and

SALT MARSHES AND LAGOONS

terns breed – safe from floods and unreachable for foxes and other land predators. The birds often breed in large colonies, which are fragile and therefore strictly protected. The birds themselves though, you can see everywhere in the lagoons and sansouires.

One thing the colonial birds dislike is when the vegetation grows too tall. Grazing by Camargue horses, sand blown in by the wind or other 'disturbances' can actually be beneficial for colony breeders. The rare Collared Pratincole for example, prefers to breed in grazed salt marsh, even though the birds do get stressed when the livestock comes too close to the nest.

Experiencing these subtleties of the sansouires and understanding the struggles of its inhabitants requires more than a few five minute stops on the side of the road. The most 'Camarguian' way to do this is of course on the back of a white Camargue horse. Alternatively, a walk over *la Digue* (route 6) on a quiet, sunny day is just as good to feel the sun burning on your head and the salt crystals biting in your lips.

Pelouses

Imagine a sunset on a clear day. A Camargue bull slowly making its way through the golden grasses in the evening sun. On the horizon, a big flock of Starlings fly out of the tamarisks. Temperatures are warm and grasshoppers are chirping. This may as well be Africa, but it's not. This is the zone of brackish meadows in the Camargue, or *pelouses*.

The *pelouses* are found at the least saline end of the lagoon–sansouire–pelouse complex. Superficially rooting plants only need to tolerate slightly brackish conditions to grow, but due to the persisting salt in the deeper soil, the habitat is not suited for trees. With a little help from the grazing cattle and horses, the pelouse remains an open landscape, where tamarisks are the tallest plants.

Grasses and rushes dominate these meadows, making them ideal pasturelands. They have traditionally been grazed by the Camargue horses and bulls, but always in low numbers, leaving plenty of room for wildflowers. (see page 77). The flowers and the bulls and horses attract insects, which in turn make the pelouse a fine habitat for birds. The Cattle Egrets riding horseback only strengthens the Savannah feel, as do the colourful Bee-eaters and Hoopoes.

With its free-roaming black bulls and its Cattle Egrets, the *pelouses* of the Camargue have an almost African feel.

SALT MARSHES AND LAGOONS

Saltpans

Thusfar, the description of the delta is one of natural habitats. Lagoons, *sansouires* and *pelouses* are natural or largely natural landscapes (setting aside grazing and haymaking) and fade into one another with a changing hydrology. Wet or dry? Saline or fresh? These are the landscape-defining questions. However, in the eastern Camargue (just west of the Grand Rhône; routes 5 and 6) and again on the Presqu'île de Hyères (route 11) you find a completely artificial variety of the lagoons: salt pans. They are no less impressive though. Shining white and pink basins, separated by straight dikes, stretch out towards the horizon. You would almost think you were looking at a land art version of a Mondrian painting.

Salt production in the Camargue goes at least as far back as the Greeks and Romans, who brought prosperity to the region through this industry. The routes along which the salt was transported were so important they bore the name routes du sel or salt roads. Today the salt pans are still one of the major tourist attractions and almost in every giftshop in and around the Camargue you can buy the famous *fleurs de sel de Camargue*.

The salt pans are also interesting to naturalists. They consist of a chain of shallow basins, connected by small channels. The process is straightforward: salt water flows into the basin, some of it evaporates, saltier water flows out to the next basin and so on until all the water has evaporated leaving behind only the salt. Between basins there is a gradient from saline water to extremely salty brine.

Nature-wise, the basins at the beginning of the chain are the richest. This is where the large breeding colony of Flamingos is found, and they are the best place to see Slender-billed Gulls, Little Terns and Kentish Plovers. The saltier the basins become, the less life remains. Eventually, only salt-loving bacteria are able to survive, and do so in enormous numbers. There are so many of them that they turn the entire basin pink.

The viewpoint of Salin de Giraud (route 7) overlook the pink, hypersaline basins of the Camargue saltpans.

LANDSCAPE

Rice paddies, freshwater marshes and the Rhône river

> The lowland river habitat is not easy to explore. Routes 2, 3, 7 and 9 explore elements of it. Fine reedbeds and freshwater marshes are found on routes 1, 2, 3, 4 and 9, of which Étang de Scamandre (route 4) deserves special mentioning. Also activity C on page 152 visits reedbeds. Rice paddies are a prominent feature on routes 1 and 2.

Woodland along the Petit Rhône (route 3; top).
Simplified map of the Camargue with the freshwater zone in green, brackish marshes in olive and saltmarsh in red (bottom).

The Rhône is a truly majestic river. Starting in the snowy heights of the Alps, it travels down, through the vibrant city of Lyon with its splendour achieved through silk and trade, then nourishing some of the most important vineyards of France, past Avignon where half a bridge is enough to be famous, and on to Arles, the gateway to the Camargue. Here the river splits into a *Petit* and a *Grand* branch.
Half of the Camargue is fed by fresh water from the River Rhône; the rest is under the influence of the sea. Together with the riverine marshes of the Durance (a tributary to the Rhône; see page 47), it forms the most important freshwater wetland in southern France. Along the river,

there is a belt of tall riverine forests, where Golden Orioles sing their tropical tones and herons find shelter. In countless lakes and marshes where the water has come to a standstill, there are massive reedbeds (some of the largest in the country), which provide a home to huge numbers of birds. Part of these marshes have been transformed into rice paddies. Although not as rich a habitat as the lagoons and reedbeds, they form a good secondary habitat for waders, herons, gulls, terns and Glossy Ibises. An advantage of the paddies is that birds are much easier to see than in the dense reedbeds.
Close to the coast, things start to change. The sea gains influence and salt water mixes with the river flow. Reed give way to rushes, Glossy Ibises are replaced by Flamingos and Ash and Poplar forests make room for tamarisks.

CROSSBILL GUIDES • PROVENCE

RICE PADDIES, FRESHWATER MARSHES AND THE RHÔNE RIVER

The Rhône river arms

Up until the 18th century the Rhône was flanked by areas of tall, dense forests of White and Black Poplars, Alder, Narrow-leaved Ash and Downy Oak; trees that are capable of withstanding frequent floods. The rich soil was much coveted by the farmers, but since there were no proper dikes to prevent the delta from flooding, cultivation came late to the delta. Only in 1869 the river was encased in a system of dikes and the land was free from strong changes in water levels and floods. The forest was soon cut down and converted into rice paddies. Another wave of deforestation followed after the construction of a network of drainage ditches just after WWII. Nowadays only a fragment of the large forests remains, mostly as a ribbon along the river channels. However, there are some patches of forest left at La Capelière and Vigueirat (routes 5 and 9). From a distance, the riverine woodlands are beautiful. The trees are very tall and sport majestic crowns. After all, the river sediments are very fertile, there is plenty of fresh water and the climate is warm enough for trees to grow almost throughout the year. However, the riparian woodland is not the best place to search for wildlife. It forms a wild jungle of Brambles and Nettles, impossible to explore since there are no trails, other than the river embankments themselves. The locals often use the forest as an illegal rubbish dump, which is a great shame as it stains an otherwise beautiful forest. The canopy nevertheless forms an important breeding site for birds, such as Golden Orioles, Green Woodpecker, Hobby, Turtle Dove and Night Heron. Kingfishers perch on low hanging branches and migratory use the forest as a leafy highway.

The riverine swamp forest is in many places rather degraded, but locally there are some beautiful patches left, such as in the Marais du Vigueirat (route 9; top). These forests are teeming with wildlife. One typical animal here is Aesculapian Snake (bottom).

LANDSCAPE

RICE PADDIES, FRESHWATER MARSHES AND THE RHÔNE RIVER

A stroll along the dikes (which are closed for motorised traffic) is more than just about birds. Many tall flowers and flowery herbs grow on the sides of the dikes; Common Birthwort, Smearwort, Crown Vetch, Danewort and lots of crucifers and umbellifers paint a wild and colourful landscape. These plants escape the shade of the forest, but still enjoy the high nutrient load in the soil. The warm and damp conditions are ideal for Tree Frogs, of which there are thousands along the river. The Aesculapian Snake is another inhabitant of the riverside forest that is frequently seen on the dikes, basking in the sun. Furthermore, the tall vegetation is used as perches for masses of dragonflies, particularly in late summer.

Marshes and ponds

Although much smaller than the vast swamps that once covered the delta, the freshwater marshes of the northern Camargue are still impressive. Most of them lie north of the Étang de Vaccarès, or close to the river arms, such as the marshes of Capelière, Vigueirat and the Étang de Scamandre, the latter west of the Petit Rhône.

This is the world of massive reedbeds, beds of bulrush and Yellow Iris, the latter flowering impressively in spring. The vegetation is dense, but in many places, there are smaller and larger lagoons with submerged and floating water plants.

The reedbeds and lagoons form a rich ecosystem, with a large number of species (birds in particular), often occurring in good numbers. The base of the food chain is mostly invisible to us. The warm and muddy waters are like a soup of nutrients, in which all kinds of tiny invertebrates float freely, nurturing themselves with tiny algae or minute fauna. They in turn feed the carnivorous insects like dragonfly larvae, fish and amphibians, which in turn are food for birds.

It is difficult for us to see this underwater micro-cosmos. Vice versa, what happens above the surface remains a mystery to

The Camargue harbours the largest reedbeds in France.

the aquatic fauna too. For the frogs and sticklebacks, the world must be like a Greek tragedy, ruled by the demons from above. Fate is a dagger-like bill from the heavens, spearing its victim with pinpoint precision. The Gods are Purple, Grey and Great White; they are the Night and Squacco Herons, Little and Great Bitterns that all hunt for fish and large invertebrates in the water. With endless patience they wait until something comes within reach. By contrast, Little Egret, Glossy Ibis and Spoonbill are more active hunters, chasing their mostly invertebrate prey, snatching, prying or sifting them out of the mud or water.

In contrast to grasslands, scrublands or forests, reedbeds form dense stands of slender, relatively tall plants. They are very hard to penetrate for animals that are not used to manoeuvre in this dense jungle – hence they are excellent safe retreats for those species that are adapted to live in this environment. The reedbed ecosystem is one of specialists, and no group illustrates this better than the birds. Almost none of the widespread birds are found in reedbeds, but the Reed, Great Reed, Moustached and Savi's Warblers, Reed Buntings, Bearded Tits and the herons and the bitterns, the Water Rails and Purple Gallinules – they are found in reedbeds and (almost) nowhere else.

One species not well adapted to exploring the hidden world between the stalks is *Homo sapiens*. For us, the trails and boardwalks through the reedbeds are the only way to get close to this habitat, but to really immerse in it is virtually impossible. Fortunately, the Camargue is blessed with many boardwalks and nature trails, some of which penetrate deep into marsh.

Rice paddies

Rice paddies are square, inundated fields, separated by a small bund, sometimes fringed with a channels with some reeds. Birdwatching in the paddies with the short rice plants is much easier than in the reed marshes.

Although rice has been cultivated in the Camargue since at least the late 16th century, rice paddies were only widely created after WWII, when an elaborate system of ditches and bunds was constructed. This network feeds the paddies with the required fresh water, according to the unnatural water regime needed for the production of rice. Whereas a normal water cycle will have high water levels and floods in winter and low water levels or drought during summer, for the rice production, this is reversed. The paddies are dry fields in winter and flooded during the summer months, when the rice grows. For the farmer it is worth it though. Because rice is the only crop capable of withstanding the high salinity of the Camargue soil and thus the only option for food production here.

RICE PADDIES, FRESHWATER MARSHES AND THE RHÔNE RIVER

The conversion of the marshes into rice paddies was undoubtedly disastrous for local flora and fauna. The rice paddies today offer no interesting flora, and only few invertebrate species, albeit ones that occur in large numbers. For the birds, it turned out to be a bargain. Now that in spring and summer the rice paddies are submerged, they provide food in a period in which normally there was a shortage. Rice paddies are perfect foraging grounds for long-legged birds like Black-winged Stilt and Glossy Ibis (whose spread in Iberia and subsequently France owes much to rice cultivation). The paddies are also great places to observe Squacco Heron and Little Egret. Especially in spring, Mediterranean gulls and Gull-billed Terns also profit from the abundance of food.

In spring, the rice paddies are perfect places to look for herons, ibises and waders, such as Wood Sandpiper (top left) and Black-winged Stilt (bottom left).

The observant visitor might notice that some paddies draw hundreds of these birds, whereas others are completely deserted. Rice paddies are one of the clearest examples of the importance of organic agriculture for wildlife. The unvisited paddies are loaded with tons of chemicals (fertiliser and pesticides), whereas the organically managed paddies are free from such a chemical load making them of tremendous ecological importance, as illustrated by the amount of foraging birds.

CROSSBILL GUIDES • PROVENCE

La Crau – a unique stony plain

Routes 8 and 9 and site B on page 151 visit La Crau.

Granted, the flat, stony plateau of the Crau with scattered weeds is not everyone's favourite landscape. Even if you happen to be among those people who recognise the beauty in desolate areas, you'll probably find the infrastructure and large factories on the horizon an unforgivable blot on the landscape. Still, La Crau is one of the great natural treasure troves of France – one that couldn't be in starker contrast than the adjacent Camargue.

The dry, stony plateau of La Crau is called the *coussoul*. Drought is law here, and the burning sun its enforcer. Due to these environmental conditions, the flora and fauna is often described as the most northerly and isolated outpost of the Maghreb, otherwise a habitat of North Africa. Between the rocks and grasses, excellently camouflaged birds like Pin-tailed Sandgrouse, Stone Curlew and Little Bustard find shelter. When inspected carefully, rare flora and insect life can be found. The Crau is unique in that several endemic species occur (species which occur nowhere else in the world), like the Crau Grasshopper and the Crau Buprest* (a beetle).

Although drought is what defines La Crau, there is no great difference in annual rainfall when compared to 'wetland' Camargue. The semi-desert

The dry plain of La Crau with the Alpilles in the background.

LANDSCAPE

LA CRAU – A UNIQUE STONY PLAIN

condition of La Crau is not courtesy of a climatic cause. Rather it is be explained by its geology. La Crau is the old delta of the Durance river. After the Durance changed its course about 18,000 years ago (see page 21), it left a wide plain with sediment layers close to the surface, which the French call *Poudingue* – a mix of calcareous 'cement' and pebbles. The *poudingue* is so dense that plant roots can't penetrate it to reach the ground water. Drought-resistant herbs and superficially rooting dwarf shrubs are able to survive, but trees can't root, leaving the plain open and bare, with no shade. Add to this the dessicating mistral, and you have all the ingredients for a semi-desert plain.

On the edges of the plateau and places where the soil is a little deeper, there are fields with alfalfa and grain, which are highly appreciated by birds. In spring they are, for instance, among the best places to find the Little Bustard.

The *poudingue* is slightly tilted, with the lowest part in the west. The layer is also thinner here, allowing calcareous seepage water to reach the surface. Within a short distance, the yellow and brown stony plain gives way to green, permanently moist meadows. This is the wet Crau, a part of the region that is a lot less known. The meadows are full of wildflowers with, locally, an abundance of orchids. It is one of the best places to find the Loose-Flowered Orchid and the rare Meadow Orchid* (*Anacamptis palustris*). In addition, there are many sublime places to find rare dragonflies and birds like Roller and, at least until recently, Lesser Grey Shrike.

Two of the showcases of Crau wildlife: the Pin-tailed Sandgrouse has its only French population in this area (top). The Crau Grasshopper is a true endemic – it occurs nowhere else in the world but in La Crau (bottom).

CROSSBILL GUIDES • PROVENCE

At its very western edge, the Crau slowly transforms into riverine forests and wet marshes as influence of the Rhône river increases, with the beautiful Marais de Vigueirat exactly amidst this transition.

Sheep shape La Crau

The landscape, flora and fauna of La Crau is further influenced by herders and farmers. The specific conditions on the plain make it suitable for little else but rearing sheep. Plants grow best in La Crau in winter when temperatures are lower and rain is frequent. This is when the large flocks of sheep roam the plain. In autumn, they graze the wet meadows and in winter, they are moved to the *coussouls*. In summer, when there is insufficient food, the sheep are brought to the grasslands in the mountains, where the growing season is in the warmer months. Hundreds of years of grazing resulted in the extremely open vegetation and accompanying wildlife that we now highly value.

In many parts of Provence, indeed in much of the Mediterranean region, traditional sheep rearing is in decline. Fortunately, La Crau is an exception to this trend. With 120,000 sheep annually visiting La Crau, the transhumance system with its seasonal grazing cycle is still largely intact. Any visitor to the area between, roughly, March and June will see flocks of sheep, a shepherd and his dog on the coussouls. For the preservation of the unique flora and fauna of the area, this grazing regime is vital.

A conspicuous landmark of La Crau are the piles of stones you find scattered over the steppe. They are of great importance for the fauna, providing breeding spots for Little Owls and Lesser Kestrels and a favoured hide-out for Ocellated Lizards. The history of the stone piles is an interesting one: they were all created in WWII to prevent military planes from landing on the otherwise perfectly flat land.

Modern agriculture and industry is today's greatest threat to La Crau. By drilling through the *poudigue*, farmers tapped into the underground water sources for irrigating crops on an industrial scale. Companies and infrastructure supporting the nearby industrial port of Fos-sur-Mer forms another important 'player' in the development (or destruction) of this unique landscape. The military also occupies part of the *coussouls* (and counter-intuitively is arguably the least damaging). Currently, about 80% of the total area of the Crau semi-steppes has disappeared. Fortunately, since 2001 the last remaining patches are a protected natural area, the *Réserve Naturelle des Coussouls de Crau*. Here you get a taste of the glorious old Crau – the sun blazing, the wind blowing over the open plain and a unique flora and fauna (described on pages 87 and 97).

LOW RANGES AND PLAINS

Low ranges and plains

> The scrublands, woods and flowery grasslands of the lowland plains are the goal of routes 14, 17, 22 and sites A to D on pages 217 to 218. The Mediterranean limestone ranges feature on routes 10, 15, 16, 22 and 23 plus sites D and E on page 153, and B and E on pages 180 and 182. The lush, wooded ranges with acidic soils are present on routes 12, 13 and 17 plus site A on page 180.
> Site E on page 219 is a good place to enjoy the Durance river, while the much smaller but very fine Endre river is the goal of route 17.

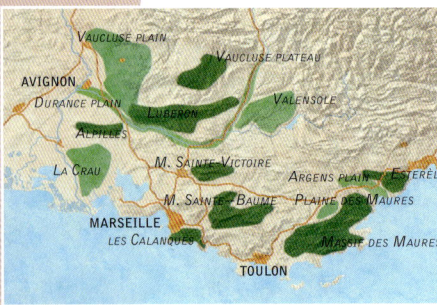

Position of the plains (light green) and low mountain ranges (dark green) in Provence.

Lowland Provence is like its wine: colourful, festive and immediately pleasing for those who taste it for the first time, yet also layered, complex and highly intoxicating for the connoisseur. Once you've imbibed your full share of the scenery, it's easy to get lyrical about its beauty and diversity. But when you sit down and try to get to grips with the ecology, it is all, to be honest, a bit of a mess. Nothing is clearly defined. A forest is never just a forest but also a scrubland with some pastures; pastures are invaded with scrub or interspersed with rocky slopes that seamlessly give way to cliffs. Gone are the neat divisions between habitats and their ecological drivers like

The classic landscape of the plains of Provence – a pleasant mix of fields, vineyards, woodlands and farmsteads.

salinity and the presence of water that make Camargue and La Crau such 'readable' places. To stick with the metaphor, the low ranges and plains are rarely white or red, but consists of a thousand shades of rosé, of which the region is deservedly famous.

On the edge of the Mediterranean

The lowlands of the coast and the Rhône valley are dominated by habitats that are unique to the Mediterranean region. Also, on the hot south-facing slopes of the lower mountain ranges, the flora and fauna consist of typically Mediterranean species. All that lives here is adapted to extremely hot, sunny and dry summers and winters that bring relief in the form of milder temperatures and life-giving rainfall.

However, it doesn't take much to disturb this climatic spell. If you move a little higher in altitude or onto a mountain slope that runs west or north then you find yourself in a place where the extremes of the Mediterranean climate are evened out. The habitat has turned to a 'sub-Mediterranean one' – a rosé of temperate and Mediterranean biomes. Mountain slopes that face away from the sun are covered in much more verdant bushes or forests of Holm Oaks and pines. Frost-sensitive plants are gradually replaced with more hardened species at higher altitudes. This position on the edge of the Mediterranean is one of the reasons for the high biodiversity in the lower Provence.

Another one is the region's complex geological history (see page 15). Provence is gifted with a large number of more or less isolated ranges from various different mountain building phases. The plains in between are equally varied; some are the result of tectonic shifts along a fault line, whereas others are old or current river floodplains.

Each mountain range has its own character. Some have bare rock close to the surface and are therefore much drier than others. The Alpilles, Calanques and Montagne Sainte-Victoire fall within this category. The Luberon and Montagne Sainte-Baume are more wooded, while the Vaucluse plateau contains a mix of both, but, due to its more northerly position, is not as hot and dry as the other ranges. The Massif des Maures and Estérel are very different from all of these, because they are not made up of limestone, like the others. This makes such a difference that we describe them in a separate chapter on page 52.

The plains consist of a mixture of river sediments and bedrock of ancient sea floors that rose above the surface due to tectonic pressures. They too are very different from one spot to another. The Durance and Rhône lowlands are lush and fertile; parts of the Vaucluse are covered with seaborn,

LOW RANGES AND PLAINS

Abandoned fields and pastures in the hills are beautiful in spring and early summer. The limestone soil and warm temperatures are perfect for wildflowers (including many orchids) and butterflies.

nutrient-poor and iron-rich sandstones (the famous 'ochres'; see page 21 and site C on page 217). There are many patches with karstic limestone, while the lowlands near Le Luc are of acidic sandstones. Finally, there is the human factor, both present and historic. Husbandry, sheep rearing in particular, has shaped Provence in the past (see page 70). Today, the flocks have largely disappeared and vast areas of former pastureland are abandoned. Much of the land is currently in transition from grazing land to bushes or woodland, which explains the many in-between habitats. Succession is pushing many areas in Provence towards forest cover, but increasing numbers of forest fires are denuding the hillsides again. Many local differences in vegetation are the result of historic events like fires, agriculture and grazing.

All this together explains the occurrence of so many different species and the paucity of sites with a very clear, well-defined habitat.

A true forest, a typical scrubland, a neat field or clearly bordered pasture is the exception rather than the rule.

Variation in landscape begets diversity of flora and fauna. In these lowlands, there seems to be a spot for plants and animals of every inclination. There are, indeed, many different species to be found, but there is a catch. Many of a naturalist's target species that adorn the seemingly endless list of possibilities are local or in low densities. It is very possible to spend a full day in the field without seeing the bird, plant or butterfly on your wish list. Fortunately, a batch of other great surprises or breath-taking observations usually makes up for this. This makes exploring the lowlands so fulfilling, yet it rarely satisfies completely. There is always a plant or animal (and usually quite a few) that failed to show itself. Thus every trip promises an excellent excuse for a future visit! Broadly speaking, lowland Provence consists of four different habitats: the rivers, the plains (mostly dominated by agriculture), the mountain ranges with their scrublands and cliffs, and the acidic plains and mountains of the Plaine and Massif des Maures.

LOW RANGES AND PLAINS

River valleys

Besides the Rhône, there are several important rivers in Provence. The Durance is the largest of them and the only one that originates in the Alps. It springs up at 2,390 metres, just below the *Sommet des Anges*, a little east of Ecrins National Park. The river snakes its way through various narrow valleys and enters 'our region' at Dignes-les-Bains, after which it flows through a wide valley. The Verdon River joins the Durance just south of Manosque. The river then continues, first on the south side of the Luberon mountains, before squeezing itself through the gate between the Alpilles and Luberon. Its last stretch is over to Avignon, where it flows into the Rhône.

Over much of its length (as you can see when driving over the A51), the Durance has the look of a very long construction site – mostly bare, with heaps of pebbles. A disproportionally small stream makes its way through large fields of debris, snags and puddles.

This is all natural though. The Durance is a classic example of a braiding mountain river, with extreme differences in water discharge. In early spring, when a winter worth of snow melts on the Alpine slopes, the Durance becomes a wild, thunderous river. This also explains the large amount of pebbles in the river bed; they all are transported down from the Alps, mostly locked in the melting ice.

As a result of this unstoppable force, the floodplain of the Durance largely escaped cultivation. Although the river has been dammed to some extent and sheep and cattle graze the floodbed grasslands, most of the original habitats are still intact. The large gravel banks form quiet and safe breeding sites for birds (e.g. Little Ringed Plover, Common Sandpiper). The pebble banks also support an interesting flora of rare pioneer plants that benefit from the open habitat. Most of them flower in summer, as they can only germinate after the spring floods.

When gravel banks are high or distant from the main river channels (typical of braided rivers is that the channels change position constantly),

The Durance is a braided river, with many islands, shingle banks, shrubby and grassy patches and even woodlands.

LANDSCAPE

LOW RANGES AND PLAINS

The shy Yellow Clubtail (top) is a true river specialist and occurs along the Durance River. On hot days, the banks of this river attract the shiny Lesser Purple Emperor (bottom).

they become overgrown with grasses and bushes. Such places are again very attractive for wildflowers, including, in some places, masses of orchids. Shrikes, Bee-eaters and a large variety of songbirds perch on the bushes, feeding on insects. The Bee-eaters are largely dragonfly eaters here, as the braided river is very rich in them.

In the parts of the river bed where the river hasn't flown for decades, there are patches of old riverine forest. Elm, Ash, Poplar and Willow grow here – roughly the same as along the Petit and Grand Rhône, but not as tall. The inaccessibility of these forests is appreciated by tree breeding herons, Golden Oriole, Hobby and Turtle Dove.

The other rivers in Provence are much smaller and have a different character. The Endre, the Nesque, the Argens, the Real Martin, the Arc and the Var are fed by local sources and run-off water. All of them are green ribbons in an otherwise hot and dry landscape. Many streams are lined with Alders, Ashes and Willows, with decorative sedges and Royal Ferns growing on the banks. All in all, this creates shady and cool retreats next to the more open, sunlit sections. This combination of shade and sun with the clean, oxygen-rich water is ideal for dragonflies and damselflies (see page 110). Large Tortoiseshell, Lesser Purple Emperor and Southern White Admiral are typical river valley butterflies, but the wet patches beside the river and wildflowers in the adjacent meadows attract many more species. In such places, tens, even hundreds of blues, fritillaries and skippers of a dozen or more species can congregate to drink and take up minerals from the mud. Among the Bee-eaters, Kingfishers, herons, Sand Martins and Grey Wagtails, you may find Dipper and Red-rumped Swallow. The latter is increasing in numbers but nevertheless an uncommon bird, that mostly breeds underneath bridges.

All in all, these smaller rivers are superb places for naturalists, partly because there are flora and fauna present that occur mostly or exclusively

LOW RANGES AND PLAINS

here, but also because the wildlife of the surrounding dry hills frequently comes down to take advantage of the water and food that is available in or around the river. That said, all these rivers differ again in what can be found – the particular run-off regime, the presence or absence of trees and cliffs, the soil type through which the river flows (limestone or acidic) makes a big difference in what lives in and around a particular stretch of river.

The plains

The rivers and streams also play an important role in the formation of Provence's landscape as we know it today. Through time they carved their way through the mountains and deposited sediments from the Alps. Eventually this led to the formation of valleys and plains in the region. These are often highly fertile, as the river provided a continuous supply of nutrients through the deposition of sediments. This is where you find the vineyards, olive groves and fields of artichoke and sunflowers.

The lowlands abound in small country roads, the one even more picturesque than the other. Many of them are lined with plane trees.

However, not all of the low plains in Provence are formed by river sediments. The larger parts of the Vaucluse plateau, the valley of Aix-en-Provence, the plains of the Maures and Cuers and the lowlands of Salon-de-Provence have tectonic origins. These are former sea beds that rose above the water level when the Iberian and later the Italian sub-plates crushed onto the European plate. The Plaine des Maures consists of ancient sediments of now withered Hercynian mountains, dating back many million of years (see page 15). These parts of the plains are frequently rocky and dry, covered in *maquis* or woodland and contrast sharply with the fertile riverine soils that are close by. You see these differences wonderfully when exploring the Vaucluse (route 22) and the region around Les Alpilles (route 9 and site D an E on page 153).

It is this combination of soils and relatively level terrain that make the valleys and plains of Provence such ideal places

LANDSCAPE

LOW RANGES AND PLAINS

The raptor of the lowlands – the Black Kite.

to live and to grow crops. As such, this has become the ultimate example of *la douce France*; the land of painters where the weather is always nice, the landscape pretty and where each idyllic village has its rustic square where some locals quibble over a game of *Petanque*.

With the exception of the Plaine des Maures (see page 166), there are no large nature reserves in these lowlands. Nevertheless, they are still highly attractive for naturalists. Above all, the scenery is wonderful, with the Plane tree lined lanes, the fields of lavender, sunflowers, poppies and grapes, and the views of the mountains in the background. In the roadsides and in the small woodlands and fields, you'll find large numbers of orchids. The list is impressive, from warm-temperate European species like Lady, Man and Lizard Orchid to southern specialties such as Drome, Black Spider and Champagne Orchid – you can find them all. But again, what grows in one spot is likely to be very different from what is found in the next. The same goes for the butterflies and other insects and the reptiles.

What lags behind somewhat is the birdlife. Granted, there are Cirl Buntings, Buzzards and Black Kites galore, but on average, the plains seem to hold few birds. They are there though, the Rollers, the Bee-eaters, the Hoopoes, the Woodchat and Red-backed Shrikes, the Stone Curlews and Short-toed Eagles. Just in very low numbers. The changing land use and intensification of agriculture is the main cause of the decline of these sensitive birds (see page 96).

The low mountain ranges

Much of mainland Provence is made up of low mountain ranges, such as the Alpilles and the Mont Sainte-Victoire. They are among the showpieces of Provence: scenic, with a wide variety of flora and fauna and a fine network of walking trails to explore them to the full.

Most ranges are clothed in woodlands on the northern slopes (mostly open pine forest, Holm Oak and, high up, Downy Oak) and *maquis* on the rocky south-facing parts. Near the summits and along the river valleys, there are extensive areas of cliffs.

In spring, the Mediterranean scrubland is swathed in pink, white and yellow flowers while the scent of Rosemary and Thyme is everywhere.

LOW RANGES AND PLAINS

The Mediterranean scrublands are some of the most biodiverse areas in the world. In particular wildflowers occur in dazzling variety, which in turn allow for a rich insect life. It may take several walks up and down the same path before you have a good idea of what lives in a particular place.
Although the scrublands are in full flower in spring, there are wildflowers around throughout the year. Paperwhite Narcissi, Rosemary and Shrubby Globularias are true winter flowers, indicating that even then it is warm enough for insects to pollinate them.
Drought is, together with grazing animals, the greatest challenge to the vegetation. All plants display some sort of adaptation to drought and grazing. Some have very thick or hairy leaves to prevent evaporation of precious water and others have poisons, needles or thorns to dissuade grazing. Some species avoid the heat by flowering in the cooler months, or escape the jaws of goats and sheep by growing in or underneath thorny bushes.
The young limestones are particularly porous and dry. Just how porous they can be is best shown around Les-Baux-de-Provence (site D on page 153), where you can find the most bizarre rocks, sculpted by water into formations that look a lot like Emmental cheese. As rain water is naturally acidic, it dissolves the soft, basic limestone. Karstic rocks, monoliths and cliffs are the result.

Warm flowery grasslands and roadsides have a superb insect life. The Broad-bordered Bee Hawk-moth (top) and Knapweed Fritillary (bottom) are just two of many beauties in such places.

As you can imagine, cliffs form a peculiar habitat which presents a unique set of opportunities and challenges to its flora and fauna. There is almost no top soil for plants to root in, water runs off immediately and surface temperatures are often extreme. However, plants that do find a crack in the rock, may find a permanent source of water in its depths and, with no competition from other plants and beyond the reach of goats and sheep, life is suddenly easy. The number of cliff-dwelling plants is surprisingly high (there is even a word for plants adapted to living on cliffs – *chasmophytes*). Common *chasmophytes* on the limestone cliffs are Phoenician Juniper, Shrubby Globularia, Red Valerian and Broad-leaved Snapdragon* (*Antirrhinum latifolia*).
The crevices are interesting places for reptiles and birds as well. It is the kind of place where

LANDSCAPE

LOW RANGES AND PLAINS

Pretty Les Baux looks down over the plain of La Crau (site D on page 153).

geckos dwell. Among the birds, the swifts stand out. Three species can be found together: Common, Pallid and Alpine. On the cliffs, there are no terrestrial predators. Additionally, the warm air rising up from the bare cliffs makes them a perfect spot from which broad-winged birds can take off. This is why many raptors are cliff dwellers: Bonelli's Eagle, Egyptian Vulture, Peregrine and Eagle Owl are the typical ones in Provence.

Plaine and Massif des Maures – Hercynian Provence

The description thusfar pertains to the limestone ranges. The plain that lies in the arch of Toulon, Cuers, Le Luc, Le Muy and Fréjus, the mountains to the south of this area and the islands of Porquerolles and Port-Cros are very different. This is the geologically oldest part of Provence (see page 15) and consists of a variety of acidic bedrocks. Perhaps more important than the acidity of this soil is that water doesn't soak away so easily, making it more readily available for plants. Oak forest and *maquis* rather than open pinewoods and garigue, is dominant here. There are only few areas with bare rocks, giving these hills a much more verdant and friendly appearance.

Calcareous or acidic rock types are to plants what football teams are to many people; you either support one team or the other, never both. The flora of the acidic hills is radically different from that of calcareous soil. Cork Oaks, Tree Heath, Strawberry Tree, Manna Ash, French Lavender and Sage-leaved Cistus are among the dominant plants here. In the hills,

LOW RANGES AND PLAINS

Sweet Chestnuts are grown and traditionally form an important crop in the Massif des Maures.
The only protected lowland plain (other than Crau and Camargue) is the *Reserve Naturelle de Plaine des Maures*. This plain of about 17,000 ha escaped large-scale transformation to agriculture because the soil is too poor. A low *maquis* of dwarf shrubs with scattered Umbrella Pines and Cork Oaks creates a beautiful, wild landscape. The area harbours endangered reptiles like Ocellated Lizard and Hermann's Tortoise, rare butterflies like both species of festoons and Two-tailed Pasha. The bird life is equally exciting, with Red-backed and Woodchat Shrikes, Dartford Warbler, Roller, Nightjar, Short-toed and Golden Eagles.
The winter rains create puddles and temporary streams in winter, which dry up in the course of spring and form a unique 'micro'-habitat. Besides a collection of rare dwarf plants, there are tens of thousands of tongue-orchids, which are spectacular sight in April and May. At least five species occur, often in large mixed populations. Among them are masses of the highly localised Scarce Tongue-orchid (see page 86).
Just south of the Plaine des Maures lies the Massif des Maures with its enormous stands of Cork, Holm and Downy Oak and Chestnut. The forests of Massif des Maures appear fully natural, but that is not the case. The harvesting of cork, foraging of pigs in the forest, the use of wood for fuel, bee-keeping and the harvest of chestnuts were the main economic pillars of the inhabitants of Massif des Maures. It gives this region its own cultural identity, next to being scenically and biologically different from all other mountain ranges.

Unlike the other plains, de Plaine des Maures is largely natural, with low scrubland and scattered Cork Oaks, pines and Strawberry Trees.

LANDSCAPE

Cliffs and plateaux – Haute Provence

> Limestone plateaux and cliffs go hand in hand, and both are found on routes 10, 15 and 22 (in the low Provence) and 18, 19 and 20 plus sites A, B and C on page 201-202 (in the high Provence). The finest cliff forests are present on routes 16 and 20, plus site B on page 201. The plateau of Valensole and Sault (routes 21 and 22 respectively) have spectacular lavender fields.

'The sun beats down relentlessly on the plateau, tormenting the meagre box scrub. A lone vulture silently drifts by, its silhouette distorted by the heat haze.' This may well be your first impression of the High Provence. But it could also be very different one: 'The wind howls over the plateau, tormenting the meagre box bushes. Along the cliffs, a lone vulture is balancing between the jet streams that round the cliffs.' Or perhaps: 'a sudden bolt of lightning rips the ashy skies. A few second later, hail the size of ping-pong balls crash down on the plain, tormenting the meagre box bushes and the lone vulture sitting on a ledge of the cliff.'

All are truthful images of the wild uplands of Provence, where the variable weather creates wildly different atmospheres that unite only in one thing – the harshness of the environment.

The spectacular cliffs of the Gorges du Verdon are a raptors' paradise. Golden Eagle (top) are a frequent sight among the numerous Griffon Vultures (bottom).

The plateaux are indeed worlds of extremes. They are close enough to the Mediterranean to be influenced by the dry and hot summer weather, but sufficiently high for temperatures to drop rapidly at night. Being on the doorstep of the Alps, clouds build up easily, resulting regularly in extreme storms, hail and in winter even snow. Another factor is the summer drought. Water disappears into the limestone and sinks away so deep that only long-rooted plants can reach it.

Between the plateaux, rivers carved out deep canyons where the situation is the exact opposite. Here, the world is under the spell of constant moisture and shade. Rain and snow accumulate. The water that sinks into the limestone of the plateau, emerges from the canyon walls in numerous small springs that unite with the river in the depths below. They provide a constant source of water that allows trees to grow to enormous dimensions. For them, it is the light for which they must struggle, not water, nor the nutrients in the soil. Their canopies shield the gorge from extreme precipitation, keeping more of the dampness within and the light out of the gorge.

Box, Pine and Angel's Hair – the plateau ecosystem

Paradoxically given the harsh environment, the plateaux are brimming with life. The flora is overwhelmingly rich, with masses of Grape Hyacinths, various greenweeds, milk-vetches, White and Hoary Rockroses, Wild Tulips, daffodils, fritillaries and orchids, often growing by the thousands. The typical grass of these flower-rich grasslands is the Feather Grass, or rather more lyrically *Cheveux d'Ange*, Angel's Hair. It is a classic steppe grass (in Eastern Europe it dominates sand and loess steppes) that gets its typical graceful appearance from very long flexible awns ¬– long soft white hairs which light up in the early morning and evening sun. From mid-May to the end of summer, it gives the plateau its sun-bleached appearance. Although trees have a hard existence, the plains are not naturally treeless. It is the herds of sheep that make them barren. When left un-grazed, as is more and more the case these days, Box and Downy Oaks (on the lower plains) and Austrian

From mid-spring onwards, the Angel's Hair grasses wallow gracefully in the wind on the upland plateaux.

LANDSCAPE

CLIFFS AND PLATEAUX – HAUTE PROVENCE

Late April on the Plaine de Calern (route 18) – thousands if not millions of Grape hyacinths, Green-winged Orchids, Early-purple Orchids and Meadow Saxifrages burst into flower on the karst plateau.

Pines (higher up) take over. This is a gradual process, with Box invading first and pine following later. These woodlands are generally open and light, and most of the wildflowers occur here in the grassy patches, or in the rocky grasslands between the Box bushes.
The same goes for the insects, of which there are many on the plateaux. Butterflies are particularly numerous and diverse, with lots of fritillaries and blues. Among the special butterflies are Apollo (on the higher plateau), Spring and Autumn Ringlets and Great Sooty Satyr. In summer, the rapid flying owlflies (ascalaphids) buzz around by the dozens (see also page 114).
The plateaux have an interesting birdlife too. Among the more common songbirds are Subalpine Warbler, Serin, Mistle Thrush, Crested and Coal Tits, Bonelli's Warbler, Woodlark and Tree Pipit in the more wooded areas, while Rock Thrush, Skylark and Wheatear occur on the open, rocky plains. The frequent presence of Short-toed Eagle indicates a high density of snakes and large lizards, its preferred prey. Among them is a rare species – the Meadow Viper, a species that has a scattered occurrence in steppe-like environments and mountain plateaux of southern Europe.
In many places on the plateau, you'll find smaller and larger depressions with dense green grass and, in spring, drifts of Pheasant's-eye Daffodil. These are dolines, naturally fertile hollows in the karst plateau. If wildflowers and butterflies are an interest, explore the slopes of these dolines; these sunny, wind-sheltered environments often hold special species of plants and insects.

Cliffs and gorge forests

Some of the finest forests in Provence are found in the steep gorges, such as the Gorge du Verdon. Too deep and complicated to access, they were not suitable for exploitation, so foresters never showed any interest. The forests remain wild and fully natural. Typical of the gorge forest is the

CLIFFS AND PLATEAUX – HAUTE PROVENCE

Lavender trivia

The beauty of the lavender fields of Provence is world famous. The lavender industry itself is a typical feature of Provence. Around 70% of the lavender fields in France are found in the Vaucluse and Valensole plains.

There are around 20 species of Lavender, but only one is grown: the 'true' Lavender is the Narrow-leaved version, *Lavandula angustifolia*. In French it is called *lavende*, which is not to be confused with *lavendin*, which is a cross between Narrow-leaved Lavender and Wide-leaved Lavender. and is also cultivated. A third species, French Lavender, is not grown, but occurs naturally in acidic lowlands, such as the Plaine des Maures.

The native range of lavenders is from the Canary Islands to the Middle East. The Narrow-leaved Lavender most likely originates from Persia (present-day Iran). Its cultivation goes back millennia, to at least the ancient Greeks. Lavender was brought to Provence by the Romans, grown in greater amounts in the Middle Ages but didn't become an agricultural industry until the 19th century.

Like today, it was the scent (coming from etherical oils in the flowers) that was the plant's great virtue in ancient times. Originally it wasn't just the pleasantness of the scent that was appreciated, but also its medicinal qualities. It chases away lice (bringers of diseases) and has anti-bacterial qualities. Add to this the wonderful smell and it is no wonder that lavender was added to soap to wash clothes. In fact, the name *lavendula* stems from *lavare*, to wash. Even today, lavender is used in soaps, perfumes and in small quantities as a herb to give flavour to meats and cheeses.

People are not alone in their appreciation of lavender. The plants form a wonderful source of nectar for insects. Butterflies, moths and bees have an unstoppable attraction to the flowers. However, this doesn't mean that the lavender fields are necessarily good butterfly habitats. Lavender is not a larval food plant for them. The butterflies you find in the lavender fields come from nearby grasslands, woodlands and scrublands.

During the last decade or so, the industry has been under threat from a small, cicada-like insect, whose larvae feed on lavender. They eat the roots, while the adults feast on the leaves. More problematic however is the fact that this *Cicadelle* is a vector for bacteria that festers in the plants sap channels, causing it to die down. A remedy for this problem has yet to be found.

The Lavender fields flower from late June to mid July, depending on the altitude. They are very photogenic and in recent years, an increasing number of Asian tourists have discovered the fields as a place for photoshoots.

LANDSCAPE

large variety of different trees and the great differences in size. There are woodland giants growing in places with plenty of moist soil (mostly low down) and stunted dwarfs where the soil is dry and thin, or where trees have only the cracks in the rocks to root in. The familiar rule of thumb that small trees are young and tall ones old goes out of the window here. The environment dictates the size. And, also, the species.

Deep down in the gorge, the conditions are permanently damp and the soil is rich. Here you'll find willows, alders, maples and ashes, often of an impressive size. In the more Mediterranean realms, elms and Montpellier Maples are often present. Higher up on the slopes, there are Beech trees and in drier areas, Downy Oaks and pines. However, since the gorge is so narrow, all these different trees grow in close proximity to one another.

On the steepest slopes, there is no forest at all, just cliffs and crags. They form the habitat for a range of attractive birds, all of which are strong flyers that profit from the lack of predators, for which the cliffs are too steep. Swallows, swifts and martins are especially well represented. Both Crag Martin and House Martin breed here in large numbers, as do Common and Alpine Swifts. Large raptors prefer cliffs to breed as well. The colonies of Griffon Vultures of the Gorge du Verdon are famous, but also the rare Egyptian Vulture prefers this habitat, as do Golden Eagles and Eagle Owls. Short-toed Eagles breed on both cliffs and trees, while Black Vulture prefers the tall tree canopies of gorge and slope forests. Other typical cliff birds are Rock Thrush, Raven, Red-billed Chough, Black Redstart and, in winter, Alpine Accentor and Wallcreeper.

The birdlife of the cliffs is not randomly distributed along the gorge. South and east-facing cliffs with plenty of cracks and hollows are much more interesting than smooth or north-facing slopes. The southern aspect means warm, rising air, which greatly assists the broad-winged birds when taking off. The highest zone of the cliffs, well above the woods is best for cliff birds, which in practice means that watching cliff birds is usually most rewarding from viewpoints on the edge of the plateau, rather than from the gorge itself.

The Gorge du Verdon

Montane forests and the Mont Ventoux

> Explore the cool mountain Beech forests on routes 16, 20 and on your ascent to the Mont Ventoux (route 24). Also the ascent to the Plaine de Calern (route 18) and site A on page 201 visit Beech forests.

You don't need to climb very high to escape the fierce sun and enter the balmy, shady world of the deciduous Beech forest. Above 800-1,000 metres, the sub-Mediterranean Downy Oak woods give way to, for northern Europeans, familiar Beech woodlands. There are many beautiful Beech forests on north-facing slopes in the high northern and north-eastern part of Provence. In the south, it is a rare habitat. One exception of a southern Beech forest is the superb pristine forest on the north slopes of the Sainte-Baume massif (route 16).

The Beech, more than any European tree, builds its own environment. The tree only grows in moderately damp, cool and shady conditions – quite the opposite of what the Mediterranean climate has to offer. More than any other deciduous tree, it creates these conditions for itself. The canopy shields the forest floor (and the sensitive bark) against direct sunlight and keeps the moisture in. The leaves it sheds are naturally acidic and create an environment where very few plants can thrive, except... the Beech. This

From the Vaucluse plateau (route 22) you have wonderful views of the Mont Ventoux, with its oak woods at the base, followed by Beech, Scotch Pine and bare rock at the top.

LANDSCAPE

MONTANE FORESTS AND THE MONT VENTOUX

Although Beech forests are a feature of the northeastern part of the Provence. Some of the finest old stands are found in an isolated spot on the north slopes of Massif de Sainte-Baume (route 16).

is why so many Beech forests have a poor undergrowth.

In Provence however, all areas with a climate favourable to the Beech happen to be on limestone. This soil neutralises the acidity of the leaves, allowing for a much richer flora (and thereby fauna) than you'd find in the Beech woods on acidic soils in many places in northern Europe.

A walk through the Beech forests is especially attractive in spring, when Liverleafs, Wood Anemones and a variety of other spring flowers carpet the forest floor. Red Deer, Wild Boar, Badger, Pine Marten and other mammals find a retreat in these generally quiet places.

Higher still, coniferous trees, mainly Scots Pine and Silver Fir mix in and eventually take over from the Beech. This forest allows much more light to penetrate, particularly on the south slope. In sunny spots and clearings, the forest floor is covered with wildflowers and grassy patches, which attract a score of butterflies and other insects. As you move up, these open areas increase and form the rocky steppes of the limestone plateau, described on page 54.

The pine-fir forest has a rich birdlife, which includes Black Woodpecker, Firecrest and Coal and Crested Tits, Short-toed Treecreeper and Nuthatch. The forests of the Mont Ventoux support even more birds.

Mont Ventoux – something special

The *Géant de Provence*, the peak of the Mont Ventoux, is unique within the region. The limestone summit bears a superficial resemblance to the karst plateau, but it is much higher and colder than any of the other high points of Provence. Comparisons with the Alps fail as well, as the Mont Ventoux is drier and barer than Alpine peaks of similar altitude. The top of the Ventoux is so dry, that the naked limestone seems almost devoid of

MONTANE FORESTS AND THE MONT VENTOUX

vegetation. From a distance, one could make the mistake of thinking it is covered in snow (which it is in winter).
In terms of flora and fauna, the Mont Ventoux sits between the Alpine meadows and the upland karst plateau. The ecological conditions are different from either as the mountain stands isolated from other peaks of this height. Accordingly, it boasts its own unique wildlife and flora. In the same small area where hordes of cyclists reach the final stretch of their battle with gravity, the naturalist strolls around in delight, faced with so many special species. The Mont Ventoux has something for every taste – birdwatchers enjoy Alpine Accentors and White-winged Snow Finches in winter and Golden Eagle and Citril Finch throughout the year. There are masses of very rare and local wildflowers present (see page 85), which is remarkable because the peak looks at first glance devoid of vegetation. Just about every leaf or blade belongs to some special high mountain flower. Apollos and other typically Alpine butterflies gracefully dance over the slopes. There are even Chamois who find enough to graze on these slopes to survive. Even among the reptiles, the Mont Ventoux has a star species, namely the rare and localised Meadow Viper.
You get the picture – in what is in the end just a very small area – between the tree line and the peak – there is a wealth of flora and fauna. This is a world which has no equal, neither inside nor outside Provence.

The Mont Ventoux is snow-covered in winter and early spring.

LANDSCAPE

History

The first signs of habitation in Provence go back far into pre-historic times. For the Romans and throughout the Middle Ages, the region was of huge strategic importance. It was the route for crossing the Alps from Italy to western Europe and vice versa. For any civilization that wanted to trade with western Europe, Provence was their gateway. However, the strategically and economic important areas remained restricted to the coast and the Rhône valley. The hinterland always remained somewhat of a backwater. So much in fact that the term for rural backwardness, the disdainful term 'provincial' is directly derived from 'Provence'.

The Provence mountains with the snow-capped Alps in the background, seen from the Mont Ventoux. One of the easiest places to cross the Alps was near Provence, which made it a region of strategic importance already in Roman days.

The dawn of time

In multiple places across France, cave drawings and primitive stone tools have been found, the oldest of which (from Lézignan-la-Cèbe just outside Provence) date back to about 1.5 million years ago. Interestingly, many drawings were found in les Calanques, in caves that are now over 37 metres under water(!), as the sea level was so much lower at that time.
Tools were found that were used to scrape meat off the bones of, for instance, Bison and Rhinoceros that may have first fallen prey to Sabre-toothed Tigers, Cave Lions and Panthers, that roamed Europe at the time.
Since then, two ice ages have come and gone, during which people moved in and out of the region. Around 11,000 BC the last glacial ended, the climate improved and the sea rose to its current level. The large animals from before the ice ages had disappeared. The local tribes now hunted Wild Sheep. Eventually, around 6,000 BC, the first sheep were domesticised in Provence (and Europe). This led to the first sedentary tribes.

HISTORY

Towards civilization – the Greeks and Romans

Around the eighth century BC the Celts came to the region, where they clashed with the Ligurian inhabitants at the time. Celto-Ligures eventually shared the territory of Provence, each tribe in its own valley, each with its own king and dynasty. They left the first remaining marks on the landscape in the form of (now largely degraded) hilltop fortresses. They also constructed *bories* – dry stone huts for farmers and shepherds. Bories are somewhat of a Provence tradition. Most of them, though, date from the Middle Ages or even later.

The Ligurians worshipped nature and established sacred woods. One of these is the forest of Sainte-Baume (route 16), a forest that throughout history maintained its spiritual significance. Mary Magdalene is said to have retreated in a cave on this mountain. The Ligurians were also the first known to have used the Rhône River to trade. They shipped iron, silver, alabaster, marble, gold, resin, wax, honey and cheese to other tribes in Gaul. Etruscan traders from Italy began to visit the coast. Slowly Provence started to become a trading centre in Europe.

Later, seafaring Greek merchants started to visit the area regularly. They came from the island of Rhodes and named the river *Rhodanos*, which eventually became *Rhône*. Later they founded Provence's first permanent Greek settlement known as *Massalia*, the modern-day Marseille, later followed by the cities of Nice (*Nikaia*), Monaco (*Monoicos*) and Saint-Tropez (*Athenopolis*). Massalia became one of the major trading ports of the ancient world. It traded with people throughout Europe and at its height, in the 4th century BC, it had a population of about 6,000 inhabitants and had a huge influence on the rest of Provence. The Massalians developed a civilization in classical Greek style, with villas, temples and outdoor public meeting areas. They also established the first olive groves and vineyards in the area. The most famous citizen of Massalia was the mathematician, astronomer and navigator Pytheas, who first connected the moon cycle to the tides, and devised exact measurement tools for determining latitude.

In 218 BC, the rising Roman Empire and the Massalians allied to stop (unsuccessfully) the march of Hannibal on Rome, and did so again in 207 BC when another Carthaginian army set out to level Rome. With various threats between 200 BC and 100 BC, the Massalians reached out to the Romans for help multiple times. Roman influence gradually increased in the region. In 49 BC, Julius Caesar made Massalia and Provence Roman provinces. He also founded Arles. Having the only bridge over the Rhône river, this became a major city in the area.

LANDSCAPE

HISTORY

A restored collection of bories in the Luberon mountains (route 23). Although most of stone shepherd huts were built from the late Middle Ages onwards, the first date back to the Celto-Ligures, centuries before the Roman empire.

In 14 BC the Romans drove out the final Ligurian tribes, which announced the beginning of the Pax Romana, a period of peace that lasted over three hundred years. During this period, all of Provence had the same language, administration, currency and culture for the first time in history. Residents of Provence felt secure enough to give up their fortified hilltop settlements and move down into the plains. The landscape changed, especially in the fertile valleys, where prosperous farms produced grains, olives, grapes and artichokes, which were sold in the cities or shipped to other parts of the empire. Agriculture thrived not in the least because of some ingenious feats of engineering, like aqueducts (famously found in Arles and the Pont du Gard, just west of the Rhône). In Fontvieille, just outside Arles, lies a huge complex of 16 water-driven mills to grind wheat. It is considered the largest concentration of mechanical power in the ancient world.

The Romans founded city after city. Avignon, Apt and Orange and many other places have triumphal monuments, amphitheatres and arenas still reminding us of their Roman origins. The Romans connected these cities with solidly built and regularly maintained roads, a novelty in the area. Eventually, Provence became the showcase of Roman wealth, culture and power. Monuments, theatres, baths, villas, fora, arenas and aqueducts were constructed throughout the region, many of which still exist.

In the fourth century AD, Emperor Constantine made Christianity the leading Roman religion. The first churches and monasteries date from that period.

Early Middle Ages

In 257 the Pax Romana ended with an invasion of Germanic tribes and by the end of the fifth century, Roman influence over the area had vanished. An age of war and chaos came to the region. The first conquerors of Provence were the Visigoths and the Burgundians. The Visigoths were quickly disposed of when the Burgundians joined forces with the Franks in 507. However, in 508 the Ostrogoths swooped in, defeated the Burgundians and occupied the cities of Arles and Marseille. In 532, the Franks (at the time under the Merovingian dynasty) defeated the Ostrogoths. The Merovingians no longer maintained Roman infrastructure and two kings in this dynasty made Provence their battleground. In addition, an outbreak of the plague swept through the region. As a result, people left the plains again for the safety of hilltop fortresses.

In 732, the Arabs, at the time the new great power in the Mediterranean, reached Provence. It inspired uprisings in 736, 737 and 739 in the cities of Arles and Marseille with the help of the Arabs. Eventually rebellion was brutally supressed, and by the time Charlemagne took over power in 768, trade had seized completely. Provence was one of the poorest regions of France.

Charlemagne brought (relative) peace but after his death in 814 troubles began again. In 838, Marseille was raided and destroyed by Arab pirates, and attacked again in 849 by Byzantine pirates. A band of Normans settled in the Camargue and pillaged the coast and Rhône river towns from there. Quarrelling continued, until finally, in 890, the first king of the independent kingdom of Provence was crowned.

A country of counts

From 890 until 1481, Provence was ruled by counts and was more or less independent. However, it is a confusing period during which rulers over Provence switched multiple times.

Muslim Saracens had established a base near modern-day Saint-Tropez. From here they terrorised Provence, raiding small towns and villages, until, in 973, they were defeated by Count William 1 of Provence. The expulsion of the Saracens became an epic event in the history and legends of Provence and William became known as 'William the Liberator'. His descendants were the recognised leaders of Provence, above the other counts of the region.

During this period of wars and banditry, maritime trade stifled, and little new art or architecture, other than fortification, was created. However, it did see the origin of the Provençal language, closer to Latin than the

HISTORY

> **Papal power problems**
>
> When you think about the Pope nowadays, you think of a religious leader whose job it is to spread the word of God. Looking back in history, this is more the exception than rule. Many popes functioned like kings, governing the Papal States of central Italy as their own fief. Politics played a huge part in the papacy with national interests (particularly of France and Italy) deciding who should or should not be Pope. To counteract the bribery, nepotism and murder, the papal conclave was developed. Via this conclave, popes were elected through secret ballot. This worked out quite well at first, but in 1292, two competing factions of cardinals drew out the voting process from a couple of weeks to two years.
>
> This meant chaos, which ultimately, led to a time known as the Avignon papacy, during which there were two rival popes, both claiming to be the legitimate successor of Saint Peter. One lived in Avignon, the other resided in Rome.
>
> The problems started when, after those two years, Celestine V was finally appointed as the new pope. He resigned already after a period of five months, in which he appointed some confidants of the French king Philip IV to church positions. His successor was Boniface VIII, whose first act as pope was to imprison Celestine V on charges of heresy. He then sacked the people appointed by his predecessor.
>
> This did not sit well with the king Philip and the two quarrelled for several years. This eventually led to Philip assassinating Boniface VIII and moving the papacy to Avignon, where it remained for 68 years (the beautiful papal palace is still the highlight of the city).
>
> In 1377, the papacy was reinstalled in Rome, where one year later a new pope (Urban VI) came into power. His first move was to lock up all of his opponents, leading to a predictable outrage. A large part of the cardinals moved back to Avignon again, where they elected Clement VII as their new pope. After a long time with two popes accusing each other of heresy, cardinals of both sides met to solve the matter, which they did by electing a third pope. Now there were three popes accusing each other of heresy.
>
> In 1418, the council of Constance finally brought peace by making all three popes resign, electing a new pope and reinstalling the papacy in Rome where it has remained ever since.

French spoken in northern France. In the 11th century Provençal terms began to appear in documents.

In 1112, the Count of Barcelona married the Countess of Provence. Provence suddenly found itself under Catalan rule. It was during this dynasty that, following the crusades, naval trade surged again, bringing considerable wealth back to Marseille. During Catalan rule, many new cathedrals and abbeys were constructed.

The demise of the Kingdom of Provence was sheer bad luck. The neighbouring county of Languedoc was in a religious quarrel with France and Germany, which decided to the teach the heretics a lesson. However, instead of sending troops to Languedoc, they were sent to 'the south of France'. So overnight, Provence was at war yet again. Initially, the joint forces of Languedoc and Provence managed to keep French forces out which eventually led to a peace treaty. But when in 1245 the Count of Provence died, he left no heir. Control over the region went to the youngest son of the French king, who had married the daughter of the Count of Provence. In 1480, the final Count of Provence died and in 1486, the region was legally incorporated into the French empire.

French Provence

Not long after Provence became part of France, it was dragged into a conflict that had a profound effect on the history of the country – the prolonged religious wars between the Roman Catholics and Calvinist protestants (or Huguenots). The latter group was fiercely persecuted. Large Huguenot communities were present in the Vaucluse. During the Reformation the Roman Catholics seized control and in 1545, the Parliament of Aix-en-Provence ordered the destruction of the Huguenot villages of Lourmarin, Mérindol and Cabrières-d'Avignon, an event known as the Massacre of Mérindol.

The war raged on until at the end of the 16th century, when power was consolidated by the House of Bourbon. Order was finally restored and by the mid-17th century, trade began to flourish again. This lasted until the end of the 18th century, when Marseille even became the third city in France.

The French revolution

During the French revolution, Provence remained largely royalist. The biggest driver of the revolution in Paris was the poverty of the people. However, in Provence the inequality was not as acute as in the capital. Wealth came through trade and taxes weren't as high as in some other places. However, Marseille was an exception to such Royalist sentiments so on April 30, 1790, a revolutionary mob stormed the city's principal fortress, Fort Saint-Nicolas, killing many of the soldiers. A year later a massacre of royalists and religious figures took place in the prison of the Palace of the Popes in Avignon. This in turn was bloodily balanced in 1794 by a massacre of Jacobins (revolutionaries) in Fort Saint-Nicolas.

When the revolutionaries seized power in Paris, it led to a full-on counter revolution in Marseille, Avignon and Toulon. Marseille was quickly

HISTORY

> **The Marseillaise, a song for everyone**
> Although the French national anthem is called after Marseille, the song is actually from Strasbourg. It was written by Claude Joseph Rouget de Lisle in 1792, right after the declaration of war by France against Austria. It was originally titled *Chant de guerre pour l'Armée du Rhin* (War Song for the Rhine Army) and was commissioned by the mayor of Strasbourg.
> Apart from lifting morale during the war, ironically, the song became the rallying call for the French revolutionaries, who, killed the mayor of Strasbourg the very next year. So much for a thank you...
> Although the song was first sung by volunteers from Marseille, it was quickly adopted by the National Guard of Marseille. They brought it to Paris when they joined the revolutionaries' fight in the capitol on 30 July 1792. Since then it was known as the song from Marseille, the *Marseillaise*. The French National Convention adopted it as the Republic's anthem in 1795.

captured by the revolutionaries, but in Toulon the counter-revolutionaries handed over the city to the English and the Spanish. And this is where a young commander named Napoleon Bonaparte first made his mark by taking the city from Spanish and British forces.

The French Empire

Napoleon became emperor in 1804, and so France became an empire. In the next ten years the French Empire ruled the larger part of Europe. But Napoleon's days were numbered. He was defeated in 1814 and exiled to Elba. However, he escaped in 1815 and attempted to stage a comeback. With a new army of about 1200 man he landed at Golfe-Juan on 1 March 1815. He marched northwards, passing through Cannes, Grasse, Castellane, Digne-les-Bains and Sisteron to his triumphal return to Paris on 20 May. His route through Provence is now a popular hiking trail. Napoleon himself met his Waterloo just after ruling again for merely hundred days. This time he was banished to St Helena where he died in 1821.

The final decades of the 19th century became known as the 'Belle Époque'. During this period, Provence saw the revival of all things 'Provençal', including the language, a movement spearheaded by the poet Frédéric Mistral, who won the Nobel prize for literature in 1904. Secondly, there was rapid economic growth. Nice (now part of France again having been a part of Savoy) became Europe's fastest-growing city thanks to its booming tourism. The city was particularly popular with the English aristocracy, who followed their Queen Victoria's example of wintering on the Riviera's shores. European royalty followed soon after.

HISTORY

It was during this time that the first naturalists discovered Provence. Exploring nature was nowhere as popular in Europe as it was in Britain and nowhere was nature as exciting or accessible as it was in Provence. Infrastructure improved, with a train line reaching Toulon in 1856, followed by one to Nice in 1864. The same year, work started on a coastal road from Nice to Monaco. Arts flourished with art nouveau architecture, a whole array of artistic 'isms', such as impressionism. Wealthy French, English, American and Russian tourists and tuberculosis sufferers (for whom the only available treatment was sunlight and sea air) discovered the Côte d'Azur.

Provence after 1900

During WWI, no blood was shed on Provence territory. However, just like everywhere else in France, young men were conscripted and the losses were terrible. It is estimated that two out of every ten men between 20 and 45 died. However, with its tourist-based economy, Provence recovered relatively quickly from the financial crises that followed the war. In the twenties, Provence became a centre for the avant-garde. More railways were established and in 1922, the first train, quickly dubbed 'the train to paradise' left from Calais in the far north of France to the Côte d'Azur. With the arrival of paid holidays for all French workers in 1936, tourism grew even more.

The Second World War abruptly halted this development, but not for long. During WWII, as part of Vichy France, the conflict's impact was relatively mild in Provence. This helped its speedy recovery after the war (when Western Europe prospered) to become one of the continent's major tourist destinations.

In 1869, the Rhône river arms were encased by dikes, which enabled the cultivation of the northern Camargue.

Like everywhere in Europe, the second half of the 20th century brought many changes to the landscape. Well into the 20th century, traditional agriculture continued as a mixture of vineyards, olives, wheat, sunflowers, hay meadows and lots of grazing land. The high plateaux, particularly, were all virtually treeless summer pastures. The sheep grazed the dry or saline pastures on the coast

LANDSCAPE

NATURE CONSERVATION

Gordes is considered one of the most beautiful villages of France and was discovered in the first wave of tourism in the early 20th century. Today it is popular among the jet set.

in winter and moved up to the mountains in summer. The poljes and dolines were used for hay-making or growing wheat. The forests on the slopes were hunting grounds and used to collect timber and fuel wood. The riches of Provence's natural history were (and still are) very much tied to these land uses that have established since Roman times, or earlier. This general pattern, albeit a ghost of the past, is still visible today.

Things have changed drastically. The combination of immense technological advances, a globalising world and the free market has launched new agricultural era: the better soils have become mega-productive, while the marginal soils are increasingly abandoned. In both cases, the natural world has changed, with many species of open areas and small-scale agriculture the victims. Vineyards, olive groves, meadows, wheat and lavender fields are losing their natural inhabitants as fertilizers, herbicides and pesticides leave no room for them. Flowery and butterfly-rich grazing lands become overgrown with bushes and trees as the sheep disappeared. Nature conservation in Provence is largely directed towards preserving the finer examples of these small-scale landscapes.

Nature conservation

Various organisations are responsible for preserving Provence's wildlife. This is a tough job, as the biodiversity of Provence is very rich, but many of vulnerable species occur very locally. There are many areas that harbour rarities that justify their conservation. They are united in Europe's

NATURE CONSERVATION

Natura 2000 areas – a coherent network of protected areas. Natura 2000 preserves the lion's share of Europe's biodiversity and is at the same time large and robust enough to give room for new populations to establish and to absorb the adverse effects of climate change.

An uncomfortable liaison with farmers

Many Natura 2000 sites are in private hands and/or owe their natural value to traditional land uses. La Crau is a reserve that benefits from shepherds and their grazing sheep. The same goes for the summer pastures of Canjuers (now a military area), Calern and the Vaucluse and Verdon plateaux, much of which is now under some form of protection. The lavender fields of Valensole are private and used commercially, but sport a special birdlife with some rarities of arid plains (e.g. Little Bustard, Montagu's Harrier, Spectacled Warbler). The roadsides, small fields, open patches in woods or abandoned pastures are where in terms of wildflowers and butterflies, much of the action takes place – yet they are not managed as reserves. The Camargue itself consists of a National Reserve and a good many 'satellite' sites, some of which are in private hands. The same goes for the rice paddies, where many birds find their food.

Preserving the wildlife of these places means working closely together with landowners, who sometimes have a different take on nature conservation. Some landowners view nature conservationist organisations as a threat to their liberty or lifestyle, whilst others happily work closely together with NGO's (non-governmental organisations), or work the land in such a way that it preserves or even restores biodiversity. They join organic farming collectives ('le bio' is the official logo) and / or sell their produce on the local markets. As a visitor, buying your food from local organic farmers is one way of contributing to local nature conservation (see page 226).

The intensification of farming in the previous century led to an extreme use of herbicides and pesticides, decimating the wildlife in the agricultural plains (bottom). Many bird species have declined rapidly. The Lesser Grey Shrike (top) is probably the first one to go extinct as a result. Fortunately, an increasing number of farmers change to organic farming – buy their products if wildlife is dear to you.

LANDSCAPE

NATURE CONSERVATION

Camargue Rice – a local product, though often not yet organically grown.

The areas in Provence protected under Natura 2000 (in green).

Tourism – friend and foe

This brings us to another important stakeholder, a group to which you belong: tourists and the tourist industry. Tourism is both a threat and opportunity for nature conservation. Some areas are so popular among visitors that tourism affects or even directly threatens the natural environment. Île Port-Cros is overrun in summer and careful regulation is needed to avoid damage to the fragile submarine ecosystem. Similarly, the peak of Mont Ventoux, where some very rare species occur in a very small area, is easily disturbed. Forest fire is a major hazard in dry areas with coniferous trees, particularly in summer when thousands of visitors also want to use the campsite barbecue. Locally there are issues with visiting naturalists (photographers in particular) who disturb birds, in their desire to get that perfect shot. Damaging in a different way is ignoring private property signs, especially in places where nature conservation relies on maintaining good relations with the owner.

On a more positive note, the many visitors that come to admire the spectacular Verdon canyon, the many reserves of the Camargue, les Calanques or Port-Cros, are testimony to the value of Provence nature. On the one hand, these visitors are a sign of how important nature is, both for its own sake and for our enjoyment and well-being. On the other hand, it brings in the euros, to put it bluntly. Provence's economy depends on tourism, which in turn relies in no small part on the natural treasures and scenery. Even if one strips down Provence's natural world to bare economic resources, it still makes all the sense in the world to preserve it. Because it makes money.

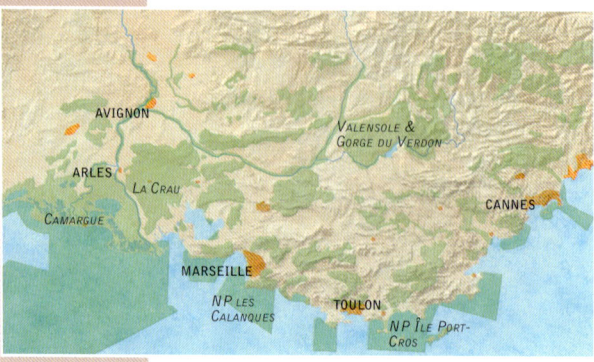

NATURE CONSERVATION

Not all losers – the return of emblematic wildlife

Due to changing land use, the flora and fauna associated with traditional farmland is under pressure in Provence. The decline in insects, wildflowers and birds may not be as great as it is in northern France and in many other parts of temperate Europe, but it is still painfully visible to anyone who has seen the countryside change in the last decades. However, there are winners too and like elsewhere in Europe, these are often spectacular and emblematic species: Purple Gallinules, Glossy Ibises, vultures, wolves and lynxes.

For most of these species, the abandonment of the countryside – the same reason many species are having a hard time – is the reason for their return. Iconic in this respect is the return of the Wolf in the eastern part of the area. Centuries of heavy persecution extirpated the Wolf, but as people are leaving the countryside, Wolves are no longer hunted and slowly return to the mountains (see page 89).

The better preservation of marshlands, combined with decreased hunting and perhaps climate change, has caused some marsh birds to return. Most spectacular is the population explosion of the Glossy Ibis; from being absent a few decades ago from the Camargue (and nearly extinct in the entire Western Mediterranean), it has now become a common sight. The reintroduction of the great vultures is another conservation success story. Griffon and Black Vultures are now well established in the Grand Canyon du Verdon where they are sometimes joined by Bearded Vulture from the nearby Alps (where it was reintroduced as well). Once they were heavily persecuted, now they are valued and well protected. A success story not only for nature conservationists, but local farmers and tourists too. Let's hope similar successes can be achieved with the ailing biodiversity of the fields and small-scale farmlands.

Reintroduced in the mountains of the Grand Canyon du Verdon: the Black Vulture. Many of the large mammals and charismatic birds are returning to Provence, either introduced or on their own, or in a reintroduction program.

LANDSCAPE

FLORA AND FAUNA

Provence and the Camargue form without exaggeration one of Europe's richest regions in terms of biodiversity. Whether you look at the birds (245 species of breeding birds), butterflies (160 species occurring) or wildflowers (including many orchids), the region is top notch.
The "why?" behind this richness is not that hard to understand. Within a relatively small area, there is a wide variety of soils, climates and habitats, and, in spite of the conservation issues discussed on page 70, many of them are well preserved. Dunes and saltmarsh abound in the Camargue with reedbeds and freshwater marshes found along the rivers. Dry, rocky hillsides with Mediterranean scrub and forest cover large areas and are present in both limestone (called *garrigue*) and acidic forms (*maquis*). Furthermore, there are steppe-like plateaux, both at sea level (La Crau) and in the mountains. There are cliffs and gorges, wind-swept peaks, beech woods, scree fields and many more. Each of these habitats contributes to the overall richness of the flora and fauna, which includes Alpine species (e.g. Chamois, Apollo and Glacier Crowfoot), species of temperate, central Europe (e.g. Liverleaf, Banded Darter and Black Woodpecker) and, of course, Mediterranean species (e.g. Greater Flamingo, Spanish Festoon and Three-toed Skink).
The Mediterranean biome is one of the most biodiverse in the world. Only in the tropical rainforests will you find a larger diversity in a given area. Many of these Mediterranean species are rather local. Scrublands in Spain and Portugal for example, are composed of different plants than those of Greece. These western and eastern ranges often overlap in Provence, which is another factor that makes this region so blessed with wildlife. You can find eastern Mediterranean fauna like Lesser Grey Shrike and Southern Swallowtail, alongside western ones such as Spanish Psammodromus and Provençal Fritillary.
But, in fairness, it also means that many such species are scarce or occur in just one or a few spots, as these sites alone suit their needs. Within the area described in this book, only Mont Ventoux is high enough to accommodate Citril Finch and White-winged Snowfinch (the latter only in winter). Pallid Swift has but a few scattered colonies in the warmest ranges on the coast. For the vultures, you need to head to the Gorge du Verdon, while Great Spotted Cuckoo, Little Bustard and Pin-tailed Sandgrouse are (nearly) exclusive to La Crau. And this pattern isn't limited to birds.

Sunset in the Camargue. Flamingos are the hallmark of the region's exotic wildlife.

INTRODUCTION

Reptiles, butterflies and wildflowers all show a similar patchy pattern of distribution. In some cases, this patchiness is natural, but the recent changes in agriculture make the effect more pronounced. Species that depend on small scale, flower and insect-rich farmland are having a hard time.

This following chapter describes, by group, the flora and fauna of Provence and Camargue, with special emphasis on those species you can find yourself.

Main biogeographical regions in Provence

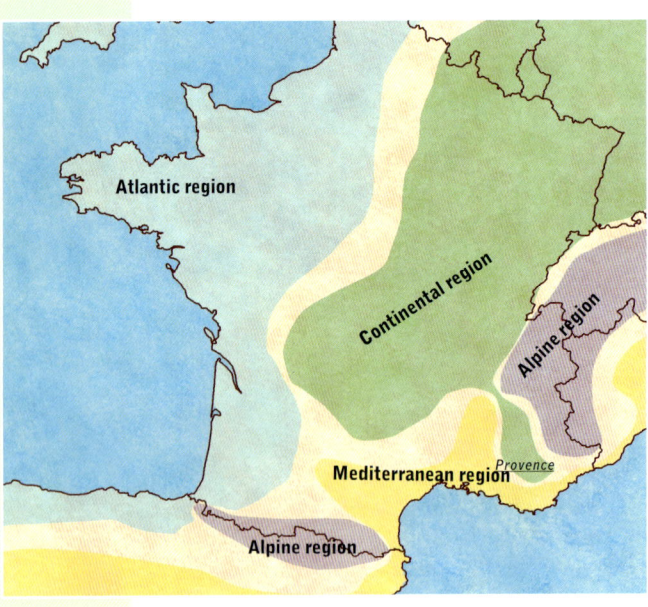

East-Mediterranean region
e.g. Lesser Grey Shrike
(*Lanius minor*)

Continental region
e.g. Liverleaf
(*Hepatica nobilis*)

Alpine region
e.g. Chamois
(*Rupicapra rupicapra*)

West-Mediterranean region
e.g. Provençal Fritillary
(*Mellicta dejone*)

Flora

> The best wildflower routes of the coast are routes 5, 7 and 11. Route 7 has some attractive wildflowers of the wet Crau, while route 8 shows you the species of the dry Crau. The flora of lowland dry limestone scrub is present on routes 10, 15 and sites B, C and D on pages 180-182. For some spectacular flora of the limestone grasslands, try routes 18, 22 and 23, and sites E on page 182, sites A, B and C on page 201-202 and site A on page 217. Great woodland flora features on routes 16, 19 and 20, while the flora of Mont Ventoux is found along route 24.

Flora of the Camargue and the Crau

It seems to be a rule of thumb: where birds thrive, plant biodiversity is low. Whilst the Provençal flora in general is splendid, that of the Camargue marshes is comparatively poor. One of the most eye-catching plants here is the French Tamarisk. It is one of the few trees (if you can call it that) that can survive in the brackish conditions. It fringes the waterways and paints a savanna-like image of the drier *pelouses*.

But there is more to discover than just the tamarisk. The tidal *sansouires* are dominated by glassworts, which are able to cope with extreme conditions – salt, high temperatures and extreme drought. There are three glasswort species: Common, Perennial and Bushy Glasswort* (*Sarcocornia fruticosa*). They are amongst the most salt tolerant plants in the world, capable of storing salt without killing the cells. Instead of 'sweating out' salt, like most plants do, they keep it in their cells, thereby 'sucking in' water through osmosis. Glassworts grow together with Annual and Shrubby Sea-blite, Opposite-leaved Saltwort and various species of sea-lavender, which are the only plants here to bear colourful flowers.

Slightly less saline are the *pelouses* or brackish meadows. The flora here is of a different kind, and generally much more diverse as the salt does not put such a heavy burden on the vegetation. Floristically speaking, the pelouses are often divided in two different types, that mostly diverge based on the salt concentration.

The French Tamarisk is the typical bush in the Camargue (top). Although the Camargue's flora is poor compared to most of Provence, its *pelouse* support a large number of wildflowers, such as these Common Centauries (bottom).

FLORA

La Crau is home to warmth-loving, drought-adapted wildflowers, such as this Iberian Jerusalem-sage (top). It looks a bit like thyme, but this pretty pink dune flower is Coris, member of the primrose family (bottom).

The saltier ones are characterised by sea-lavenders (although different ones from those of the sansouires), such as *Limonium echioides, duriusculum* and *virgatum*. The less saline *haute pelouses* are traditionally rich in wildflowers, such as Round-leaved Birthwort, Sea Iris, Round-headed Leek, Rampion Bellflower, Giant and Western Spider Orchid* (*Ophrys exaltata*). Unfortunately, the latter type of meadow is threatened as the grazing has stopped and they are gradually overgrown with tamarisks. Remnants of these *haute pelouses* are still found along the tracks and roads, which are frequently the best places to find wildflowers in the Camargue.

The narrow belt of dunes forms another interesting area for flora. Here wind and sand are the main challenges. Not only is being sandblasted far from ideal, the risk of being buried is an even more deadly reality for plants in the dunes. One of the most spectacular species that has mastered the art of survival in the dunes is the Sea Daffodil, which flowers from August to October. Other noteworthy species include Coris, Curry Plant, Rosy Garlic and Mediterranean Lineseed.

When moving from the Camargue towards the Crau, you will encounter an interesting zone around the Marais du Vigueirat (route 9), where ground water flowing down from the higher Crau reaches the surface. This seepage water is calcareous, which encourages orchids. In spring the fields turn purple with Loose-flowered Orchids and the much rarer Meadow Orchid* (*Anacamptis palustris*).

The Crau presents a completely different flora from that of the Camargue. The main stresses that plants must adapt to, are the extreme drought and the grazing of sheep. Many plants developed poison or spines. Field Eryngo, Illyrian, Golden and Mediterranean Thistles are the most common spiny plants. Hollow-stemmed Asphodel and Iberian Jerusalem-sage* (*Phlomis lychnitis*) are examples of poisonous plants.

FLORA

> **Wildflowers of the Camargue and Crau**
> **Dunes** Coris (*Coris monspeliensis*), Sea Daffodil (*Pancratium maritimum*), Three-horned Stock (*Matthiola tricuspidata*), Sad Stock (*Matthiola fruticulosa*), Round-headed Leek (*Allium sphaerocephalon*), Curry Plant (*Helichrysum stoechas*), Rosy Garlic (*Allium roseum*), Mediterranean Lineseed (*Bellardia trixago*), Giant Orchid (*Himantoglossum robertianum*)
> **Pelouses** European Sea-lavender (*Limonium duriusculum*), the sea-lavenders *Limonium virgatum* and *Limonium echioides*, Rampion Bellflower (*Campanula rapunculus*), Woolly Clover (*Trifolium tomentosum*), Starry Clover (*Trifolium stellatum*)
> **Sansouires** Common Glasswort (*Salicornia europaea*), *Salicornia ramosissima*, Perennial Glasswort (*Sarcocornia perennis*), Bushy Glasswort* (*Sarcocornia fruticosa*), Annual Sea-blite (*Suaeda maritima*), Shrubby Sea-blite (*Suaeda vera*), Opposite-leaved Saltwort (*Salsola soda*)
> **Wet Meadows** Great Fen-sedge (*Cladium mariscus*), Loose-flowered Orchid (*Anacamptis laxiflora*), Meadow Orchid* (*Anacamptis palustris*), Blue Iris (*Iris (spuria) maritima*)
> **Crau** Cypress Spurge (*Euphorbium cyparissias*), Seguier's Spurge (*Euphorbia seguieriana*), Mossy Stonecrop (*Crassula tillaea*), French Flax (*Linum trigynum*), Upright Flax (*Linum strictum*), Field Eryngo (*Eryngium campestre*), Simplebeak Ironwort (*Sideritis romana*), Iberian Jerusalem-sage* (*Phlomis lychnitis*), Italian Viper's-bugloss (*Echium italicum*), Dwarf Evax* (*Evax pygmaea*), Narrow-leaved Cudweed (*Logfia gallica*), Mediterranean Thistle (*Galactites tomentosus*), Hollow-stemmed Asphodel (*Asphodelus fistulosus*)

Flora of Mediterranean scrubland

Whilst botanists may enjoy some interesting finds in the Crau and the Camargue, they will be thrilled by the floral richness of the Mediterranean scrublands in hilly and rocky terrain from sea level up to roughly 500 metres.

These are home to a dazzling plant diversity. You need to develop an eye for this though. Looking at the scrublands from a distance only reveal a seemingly monotonous landscape populated by a few species of small trees and bushes. Only on closer inspection do these scrublands show their true riches. Well-hidden within the scrub you can find many wildflowers. Each step may reveal a new species, as there are many different micro-habitats found here. The depth of the soil, rocky crevices, shade (or lack of it), dampness or nutrients may change from one metre to the next and can have a profound effect on the species composition. However, the real 'game changer' is whether the soil is acidic or calcareous.

FLORA

Acidic scrublands – *maquis*

The acidic scrublands are limited to the triangle between Toulon, Draguignan and Cannes (see geology section). Compared to the thin bone-dry calcareous scrublands, the first thing to notice is that the acidic ones are lusher. As the acidic soils are less porous, they retain more water. The scrublands have a mosaic of flowery grasslands with small bushes like Sage-leaved Cistus, French Lavender and Mediterranean Mezereon, alternated with taller shrubs like Tree Heath and Strawberry Tree and even woodland, consisting of Cork and Downy Oak.

The flora of the acidic scrubland really shines in some of the more open places. Swathes of Broad-leaved Anemones, Wild Tulips, Jersey Buttercups, St. Bernard's Lilies and the large rockrose *Tuberaria lignosa* put on a spectacular show. You can also find two species of birthwort: Spanish (with wrinkled leaves) and Round-leaved Birthwort or Smearwort (with smooth leaves). They form the larval food plants for the two species of festoon butterflies in Provence.

In April and May, the acidic Plaine des Maures is a feast of wildflowers. Sage-leaved Cistus and French Lavender are dominant (top) but in grassy patches, there are many wildflowers to be found, such as Broad-leaved Anemones (bottom).

There is a score of wild orchids as well, including many different varieties of spider orchid, tongue-orchids and Champagne orchid. Tongue-orchids occur in drifts of thousands, belonging to various species (and their hybrids – see page 88).

As a result of the water retaining capabilities of the acidic rock, shallow, temporary streams and pools form in winter. In the muddy places where the water has evaporated, species like Yellow Centaury and Small Adder's-tongue can be encountered. You will have to search for them though, as they are only a couple of centimetres high.

Calcareous scrubland – *garrigue*

The dominant limestone soils are calcareous. Rainwater directly flows away through the cracks in the rock, making coping with drought a prime challenge. This is why in the driest parts (especially on south-facing slopes), shrubs are dominant and grasses and herbs are uncommon. Common bushes are Kermes Oak, Holm Oak, Grey-leaved Cistus, Shrubby

FLORA

Globularia, Prickly Juniper and Wild Rosemary. Between the rocks, there is a limited number of wildflowers, including Yellow Leek, Swallow-wort, Beautiful Flax, Broad-leaved Snapdragon* (*Antirrhinum latifolium*), Common Jonquil (Rush Daffodil), Red Valerian and a few orchids, all of which grow mainly in spots, often around scrub, where the vegetation is a little richer and the soil a bit deeper. Another curious plant here is the Large Joint-pine. This plant has been used for thousands of years in medicine (first certain use dating back around 5000 years in China). It consists only of compound branches, like the horsetails.

In slightly damper or shadier sites, or where the soil is a bit deeper, the flora is much richer. Such areas are where in early spring, you may find masses of orchids, including various varieties of Sombre Bee and Spider Ochids, Woodcock, Giant and Southern Early-purple Orchids. A common wildflower here is the Blue Aphyllanthes, which looks like a rush when not in flower, but has beautiful blue lily flowers in spring.

In search of wildflowers in the limestone garrigue on the slopes of the Mont Sainte-Victoire (bottom). In late winter, you'll find many Shrubby Globularias here (top).

Flora of limestone cliffs and plateaux

Where the slopes are higher (over 500 metres), the scrublands slowly give way to the grassier vegetation of the plateaux. This transition is very gradual, and there are many in-between habitats, all of which have their own special plant species. Combined, this is the 'fine-fleur' of the Provence flora – the wildflowers are spectacular, in number, diversity and showiness.

In spring, these sites are full of orchids (e.g. Lady, Man, Early-purple, Burnt, Elder-flowered, Green-winged), drifts of Common Grape Hyacinths, Chalk Milkwort, White and Hoary Rockroses and patches of Crimean Iris and the large bells of Provence Snake's-head* (*Fritillaria involucrata*). Elsewhere, you find yourself suddenly amongst swathes of Common Jonquils or meadows full of Pheasant's-eye Daffodil.

FLORA

The calcareous grasslands above, roughly, 600 metres are among the most attractive habitats for wildflowers. Apart from many orchids, there are White Rockroses, Common Globularias and Montpellier Milk-vetches (top). These are also the places to find the Provence Snake's-head* (*Fritillaria involucrata*).

Higher up grow Meadow Saxifrage, the ground-hugging Creeping Globularia, the pink Tuberous Valerian and the large, stemless Acanthus-leaved Carline Thistle.

Rocky edges of dolines or gorges support yet another set of plants. One of the most spectacular ones here is the bright red Turban Lily. This rare plant can be found on the cliffs of the Gorge du Verdon, where it flowers during early summer. Other notable species include Red Valerian, Jenny's Stonecrop and Beautiful Flax.

You'll find limestone plateaux from Sainte-Baume in the south, on the northern slopes of the Mont Sainte-Victoire, in the Luberon, Vaucluse, the plateaux of the Gran Canyon du Verdon and the Plaine de Calern. All of these support different species, which in each site differ as the season progresses from spring to summer. What they all share though, is that they are rich wildflower haunts and frequently turn up interesting rarities. If wildflowers are what you enjoy, these are the places to reserve serious amounts of time for.

Flora of the woodlands

The forests of Provence come in many different shapes and sizes. In the lowlands, most of them are, from a botanical perspective, quite similar to the scrublands. The trees are widely spaced, and between them there are many shrubs of the garrigue, although here they grow much taller. The wildflowers of the scrubland grow here as well, but those species that prefer a bit more shelter from drought and sun, have the advantage. Besides the aforementioned Blue Aphyllanthes and Chalk Milkwort, you may find forest species like Bastard Balm, Common Cowslip and Spanish Greenweed. They are also good places to look for orchids, with Provence Orchid, Lady Orchid and various helleborines being the most interesting species (see orchid section).

On acidic soils, Cork Oak is the default forest species, but the Chestnut groves are botanically better sites. The chestnut leaves fertilise the soil

Conspicuous wildflowers of scrublands, pastures and cliffs
Calcareous scrubland Large Joint-pine (*Ephedra major*), Sea Grape (*Ephedra distachya*), Prickly Juniper (*Juniperus oxycedrus*), Phoenician Juniper (*Juniperus phoenicea*), Kermes Oak (*Quercus coccifera*), Sweet-William Catchfly (*Silene armeria*), Virgin's-bower (*Clematis flammula*), Evergreen Honeysuckle (*Lonicera implexa*), Buckler Mustard (*Biscutella laevigata*), Field Madder (*Sherardia arvensis*), Helianthemum marifolium, Pale Stonecrop (*Sedum sediforme*), Crown Vetch (*Coronilla minima*), Grey-leaved Cistus (*Cistus albidus*), Tuberous Valerian (*Valeriana tuberosa*), Common Thyme (*Thymus vulgaris*), Broad-leaved Snapdragon* (*Antirrhinum latifolium*), Felty Germander (*Teucrium polium*), Rosemary (*Rosmarinus officinalis*), Wall Germander (*Teucrium chamaedrys*), Ground-pine (*Ajuga chamaepitys*), Shrubby Globularia (*Globularia alypum*), Maral Root (*Rhaponticum coniferum*), Spiny Starwort (*Pallenis spinosa*), False Lavender (*Staehelina dubia*), Rosy Garlic (*Allium roseum*), Blue Aphyllanthes (*Aphyllantes monspeliensis*), Common Jonquil (*Narcissus jonquilla*), Yellow Leek (*Allium flavum*)
Acidic scrubland Cork Oak (*Quercus suber*), Broad-leaved Anemone (*Anemone hortensis*), Spanish Birthwort (*Aristolochia pistolochia*), Smearwort (*Aritolochia rotunda*), Small-flowered Catchfly (*Silene gallica*), Judas tree (*Cercis siliquastrum*), Manna Ash (*Fraxinus ornus*), Strawberry Tree (*Arbutus unedo*), Tree Heath (*Erica arborea*), Sage-leaved Cistus (*Cistus salviifolius*), Spotted Rockrose (*Tuberaria guttata*), *Tuberaria lignosa*, French Lavender (*Lavandula stoechas*), Summer Asphodel (*Asphodelus aestivus*), Wild Tulip (*Tulipa sylvestris*), Yellow Centaury (*Cicendia filiformis*), St. Bernard's Lily (*Anthericum liliago*), Scarce Tongue-orchid (*Serapias neglecta*), Heart-flowered Tongue-orchid (*Serapias cordigera*), Provence Tongue-orchid (*Serapias olbia*)
Limestone cliffs Rustyback Fern (*Asplenium ceterach*), Reflexed Stonecrop (*Sedum rupestre*), Mediterranean Spurge (*Euphorbia characias*), Red Valerian (*Centranthus ruber*), Beautiful Flax (*Linum narbonense*), Blue Lettuce (*Lactuca perennis*), Shrubby Globularia (*Globularia alypum*), Turban Lily (*Lilium pomponium*)
Limestone plateaux Common Peony (*Paeonia officinalis*), Box (*Buxus sempervirens*), Meadow Saxifrage (*Saxifraga granulata*), Cypress Spurge (*Euphorbium cyparissias*), White Rockrose (*Helianthemum apenninum*), Chalk Milkwort (*Polygala calcarea*), Swallow-wort (*Vincetoxicum hirundinaria*), Montpelier Milk-vetch (*Astragalus monspessulanus*), *Linum campanulatum*, Tuberous Valerian (*Valeriana tuberosa*), Yellow-wort (*Blackstonia perfoliata*), Heart-leaved Globularia (*Globularia cordifolia*), Acanthus-leaved Carline-thistle (*Carlina acanthifolia*), Cupidone Blue (*Catananche caerulea*), Crimean Iris (*Iris lutescens*), Grape Hyacinth (*Muscari neglectum*), Provence Snake's-head* (*Fritillaria involucrata*), Blue Aphyllanthes (*Aphyllantes monspeliensis*)

FLORA

and the forest floor is frequently cleared, creating good conditions for bulbous flowers and orchids in particular. Typical species to be found in such places are Provence and Champagne Orchids, Violet Bird's-nest and Narrow-leaved and Small-leaved Helleborines.

Beech forest can be found at high altitudes, often but not exclusively on north slopes. The beech is a species typical of temperate regions, and as you would expect, the flora is different from any other area of Provence. Most plants here are typical of temperate Europe and reach their southern limit here, on the edge of the Mediterranean. In spring you can encounter interesting species such as Angular Solomon's seal, Liverleaf, Martagon Lily, Bird's-nest Orchid and Baneberry.

Open woodlands on Montagne Sainte-Baume, with swathes of Common Milkwort (top). In the woodlands grows Bastard Balm (bottom).

Conspicuous wildflowers of deciduous forests
Downy Oak forest Wild Strawberry (*Fragaria vesca*), Spanish Greenweed (*Genista hispanica*), Cowslip (*Primula veris*), Tuberous Comfrey (*Symphytum tuberosum*), Purple Gromwell (*Lithospermum purpurocaeruleum*), Small Yellow Foxglove (*Digitalis lutea*), Bastard Balm (*Melittis melissophyllum*), Box (*Buxus sempervirens*), Bloody Crane's-bill (*Geranium sanguineum*), Common Milkwort (*Polygala vulgaris*), Butcher's-broom (*Ruscus aculeatus*), Elder-flowered Orchid (*Dactylorhiza sambucina*), Provence Orchid (*Orchis provincialis*), Narrow-leaved Helleborine (*Cephalanthera longifolia*), Lady Orchid (*Orchis purpurea*)
Beech forests Liverleaf (*Anemone hepatica*), Bird-in-a-bush (*Corydalis solida*), Green Hellebore (*Helleborus viridis*), Baneberry (*Actaea spicata*), Sanicle (*Sanicula europaea*), Wood Spurge (*Euphorbia amygdaloides*), Spurge-laurel (*Daphne laureola*), Mezereon (*Daphne mezereum*), Dog's Mercury (*Mercurialis perennis*), Yellow Bird's-nest (*Monotropa hypopitys*), Purple Lettuce (*Prenanthes purpurea*), Angular Solomon's-seal (*Polygonatum odoratum*), Herb-paris (*Paris quadrifolia*), Martagon Lily (*Lilium martagon*), Bird's-nest Orchid (*Neottia nidus-avis*)

An interesting twist in these forests is that there are still some Mediterranean species as well, such as Spurge-Laurel.

Mont Ventoux

The highest part of Provence has a flora of its own. The peak of Mont Ventoux is twice as high as the plateaux described on page 61 and the climatic conditions are subsequently much more severe. Here you'll find several Alpine plants that must withstand the cold that comes with the altitude, but also have to cope with the very dry conditions in the short summer growing season. Between the cracks of bare rock or in scant patches of grass, there is a unique flora to be found. Among the more eye-catching plants are the tall Silver Eryngo and the colourful Rhaetian Poppy, Alpine Toadflax and Narcissus-flowered Leek, all flowering in summer. Spring visitors will enjoy Golden Primula and Purple Saxifrage.

Conspicuous wildflowers of the Mont Ventoux
Alpine Meadow-rue (*Thalictrum alpinum*), Lesser Meadow-rue (*Thalictrum minus*), Rhaetian Poppy (*Papaver alpinum ssp. rhaeticum*), Seguier's Crowfoot (*Ranunculus seguieri*), Minuartia capillacea, Saxifrage Catchfly (*Silene saxifraga*), Purple Saxifrage (*Saxifraga oppositifolia*), Alpine Rock-jasmine (*Androsace alpina*), Golden Primula (*Vitaliana primuliflora*), Silver Eryngo (*Eryngium spinalba*), Yellow Germander (*Teucrium flavum*), Lesser Cat-mint (*Nepeta nepetella*), Campanula alpestris, Creeping Globularia (*Globularia repens*), Narcissus-Flowered leek (*Allium narcissiflorum*)

The top of the Mont Ventoux is an exposed, stony cold 'island' in a 'sea' of lower, warmer hills and lowlands. Its flora supports many species you won't find elsewhere in the area, such as the Rhaetian Poppy, a subspecies of the Alpine Poppy that grows in the highest reaches of the Alps.

Orchids

Good news for orchidophiles – Provence is one of the best places in Europe to find orchids. There are rare and endemic orchids (see next page), a large diversity of species, many of which grow in large numbers! Many roadsides, woodlands and dry grasslands are full of these fancy wildflowers. Interestingly, roadsides are among the best habitats for orchid spotting. In spring, it takes serious will-power not to stop constantly to look for orchids. The species found here are the same as those growing scattered in

FLORA

Some typical Provence orchids

Scarce Tongue-orchid
(*Serapias neglecta*)
This impressive tongue-orchid can be found on the acidic soils of the Plaine des Maures in May. Its size (a small plant with large flowers) and colour of the tongue (pale pink) distinguish it from other tongue-orchids. It is a local species that only occurs in the Tyrrhenian region, of which Provence is the most northern limit.
Route 14

Provence Tongue-orchid*
(*Serapias olbia*)
Much smaller than its brother, the Provence Tongue-orchid* is a rare species that can also be found on the Plaine des Maures. It is endemic to the south of France. Route 14

Provence Orchid
(*Orchis provincialis*)
This delicate orchid can be found throughout much of the Mediterranean basin, but is never common. It is characterised by its white-yellow colour with orange dots on the lip.
Routes 13, 16

FLORA

Giant Orchid
(*Himantoglossum robertianum*)
Very common and very impressive. The Giant Orchid is massive in every aspect, with large stalks with large flowers, that tower above the rest of the vegetation. They flower in late winter.
Routes 2, 6, 10, 11

Drome Orchid (*Ophrys drumana*)
Another species that is endemic to the south of France is the Drome Orchid. A spectacular member of the *Ophrys* genus, with pink petals and a dark lip and a shiny 'mirror' in the middle. It is quite rare and mostly found in Vaucluse. A closely related species is *Ophrys saratoi*, which grows in the low mountains in the east of the region.
Route 23

Champagne Orchid
(*Anacamptis champagneuxii*) and
Southern Early-purple Orchid
(*Orchis olbiensis*; on photo)
Two purple orchids that grow, apart from Provence, only in Spain and Portugal. Champagne Orchid is typical of grassy patches in Cork Oak forest on acidic soil; Southern Early-purple is typical of bushes and open woods on dry, warm limestone.
Routes 13, 14, 15

FLORA AND FAUNA

FLORA

Provence is home to a confusing array of spider orchids. Evolution is in full swing within this group of plants, because the flowers are only pollinated by a specific group of solitary bees. Various groups of plants follow different evolutionary paths, dictated by the bees' preferences. Many different subspecies and varieties are the result. This is one of the commoner forms in Provence – the Black Spider Orchid.

garrigue, grasslands and open forests, only in much greater densities. Roadsides are so suited for orchids because of their management; they are not grazed, but mown. The mowing creates the open environment required for the rather frail plants, which recover much faster from the mowing machine than from the jaws of sheep and goats.

Frequently, various species grow together. Looking out for the flashier ones (Lady Orchid, Giant Orchid, Pyramidal Orchid, Champagne Orchid) is a good way to find the more cryptic species. Among the latter is a bewildering variety of the bee orchid family (*Ophrys*). Particularly hard to identify are the spider orchids (those closely related to *Ophrys sphegodes*). Common are *Ophrys passionis, atrata, sphegodes, splendida, provincialis, exaltata, araneola* and *arachnitiformis* – all forming the similar-looking, beautiful complex of spider orchids. In the hotter and drier parts of Provence (mostly in the south) they grow together with Sombre Bee Orchid (the subspecies *lupercalis*), Woodcock Orchid and, very locally, Yellow Bee Orchid. Further north, you'll encounter Drome Orchid, *Ophrys pseudoscolopax* (looking like a cross between Late Spider Orchid and Woodcock Orchid, both of which also occur) mixed with species of warm-temperate regions, such as Green-winged, Early-purple, Elder-flowered, Burnt, Pyramidal, Lizard and Fly Orchids.

Orchid lovers often head for the limestone areas, as these are generally richest in orchid species. In Provence, there is a big difference in orchid richness between the grassier (often high) plateaux and the very dry, rocky lowlands. The latter are unexpectedly poor in orchids, probably because most spots are just too dry. The orchid flora on the higher slopes varies from a thin scatter to large numbers, and it is not always clear where the higher numbers occur.

In Provence acidic soils can have an unexpected diversity of orchids. Notably the Plaine des Maures is very rich. Here it is first and foremost the tongue-orchids that impress. Besides Common Tongue-orchid (fairly scarce), there are Heart-flowered Tongue-orchids (frequent), Provence Tongue-orchid (scarce) and Scarce Tongue-orchid (common). The latter two have very small distribution ranges (see box on previous page). They grow together with various species of *Ophrys*, Champagne Orchid, Violet Bird's-nest and Narrow-leaved Helleborine.

Mammals

To find mammals, you need luck. Many species are nocturnal and encountered on country roads by chance. Chamois can be found on routes 19, 21 and 24. Coypu are common everywhere in the Camargue, while Beaver is frequent in the Marais du Vigueirat (route 9). For whales and dolphins a boat trip on the Mediterranean is highly recommend (see page 229).

The precipitous ranges and steep, forested mountain slopes of Provence are wild places and form a perfect retreat for wildlife. Like many places in Europe, people are moving out of these areas that are challenging to farm. The once formidable herds of cattle and sheep are disappearing, leaving behind the pastures that become overgrown with scrub and eventually woodland. This quietude and shelter is perfect for wildlife.
Wild Boar and Roe Deer are numerous in all scrub and woodland areas in Provence. Red Deer by contrast is largely restricted to the forests in Vaucluse and Haute Provence. Chamois, typical of Alpine areas, is present in Provence as well, and in good numbers too. Again, the northern mountains bordering the Alps have the highest numbers, but it occurs in the Mediterranean ranges including Mont Ventoux and the Massif de Sainte-Baume (routes 24 and 16 respectively).
The Mouflon is the wild ancestor of sheep and has Sardinian roots. It has been introduced in Provence as a game animal and dwells in open areas and forests of Mont Ventoux between 1,000 and 1,600 metres altitude. In 1961 a group of 21 individuals was introduced here and the population is currently estimated at around 400 animals.

Predators

The Wolf gains most from the human abandonment of the mountains. This fiercely persecuted animal disappeared from most of western Europe before the modern era, as more and more people settled in the mountains and cut down the forest. As the mountains in Provence become wilder and more natural, the Wolf is reclaiming its territory. The Wolf is protected by law and an increasing number of people love Wolves and even see their return as a hopeful sign of restoring wildness to a world that has been disturbed and exploited by people for so long. Local farmers and hunters take a different view and see the Wolf's presence as a danger to their way of living. People may have wildly different attitudes towards Wolves, but from Wolves' point of view, the feelings

MAMMALS

are unambiguous: wolves fear people. This carnivore is therefore rarely seen and remains rare.

Following in the Wolf's wake comes another formerly extinct top predator, the European Lynx. This majestic cat had been extinct in France for almost a century when in the 1970s it returned after a successful reintroduction program in Switzerland. The Swiss animals extended their range into the Jura and Alps and moved further south from there. Since 2011, a small population of the Lynx has established itself in the Plan de Canjuers and in 2018, it was found in the Monts d'Azur.

Smaller predators like Foxes, Beech and Pine Martens, Weasels and Badgers are common. The European Wildcat is hard to identify as some domestic cats closely resemble it and they can interbreed. However, this carnivore lives in dense forests and avoids all contact with people. Its diet consists mainly of voles, shrews and rabbits. Another cat, the arboreal Genet, is more widespread, but still very rarely seen. It has populations in the Massif de Sainte-Baume, around Marseille, Vaucluse, the central mountains and the Massif des Maures.

Aquatic mammals

One mammal you are almost certain to find, at least in the Camargue, is the Coypu. It is a big rat-like aquatic rodent, almost the size of a Beaver but without the flat tail. The Coypu is distinguished by its pale face and white moustache. In contrast to the Beaver, which also occurs in the Rhône and Durance rivers, most of the Coypu's back is exposed above the water when it swims. The Coypu is an invasive species and a strict vegetarian.

The carnivorous Otter is much rarer and found mostly in the Rhône, the Camargue and western Vaucluse.

Coypus are very common in the Camargue. These aquatic rodents are strict vegetarians.

Bats and mice

Provence is home to no less than 25 of France's 34 species of bat. Among them are some species of interest, because they are rare or absent elsewhere in France, such as Geoffroy's Bat. Without a bat detector and specialist guide, most visitors won't be able to tell the different species apart. But it is not all about species. Observing the erratic flight of bats when they hunt is itself a feast for the eye.

MAMMALS

The Camargue horse: fact and fiction

It's such a romantic sight: in early spring, a beautiful white horse slowly breaks the palissade of quietly waving yellow reeds and emerges like Pegasus out of Medusa's head.

The Camargue horses certainly are beautiful. In their settings of marshlands, lagoons and reedbeds they fire the imagination, offering inspiring images of strength, grace and freedom, images that sell very well. Therefore, the myth around the Camargue horses is carefully nurtured and thoroughly commercialised. The truth is stretched a little for the benefit of both tourist and postcard seller: Europe's last wild horse!

The Camargue horse is not a separate species but a breed of the typical farm horse. Nevertheless, the Camargue breed is one of the oldest in the world and unique to the region. Camargue horses are a little shorter than average and readily distinguishable from other breeds as mature adults appear white (white hairs over grey skin). The foals are born with black or dark brown hair.

The Camargue horse is not a wild horse. All herds are managed by *gardians* (Camargue cowboys) and the horses are used to having people on their backs. However, the horses are left to roam freely over large areas of land and salt marsh. The poor nourishment of the salty soil has a lot to do with this. The horses need large areas to get their daily supply of calories. (The same goes for the black Camargue bulls).

Therefore, the horses are not tended more than necessary and have been able to establish a near-wild lifestyle. They go around in self-established herds of one stallion, a few mares and their offspring. Young males and females leave the group when reaching puberty. The young stallions are usually thrown out by the dominant male (their father) and the young mares choose to go themselves, which avoids inbreeding.

It is not just people that ride the Camargue horses.

The unique half-wild lifestyle of the Camargue breed offers a great research opportunity. Numerous studies have been done on Camargue horses and have provided science with a wealth of information on the social behaviour of horses in natural conditions.

FLORA AND FAUNA

BIRDS

It is equally hard to get a glimpse of the many mice, dormice and voles that inhabit Provence. Some exciting species are present though, like Mediterranean Pine Vole and Algerian Mouse. The native and widespread Edible Dormouse is a well-known but unwelcome species in France. After seven months of sleep, these fluffy and cute animals wake up in spring and keep farmers and sometimes campers awake as they chase each other around the attics of houses, barns, mobile homes or abandoned buildings in the countryside. Much shyer are its relatives the Hazel Dormouse and Garden Dormouse, which also occur in Provence.

Whales and dolphins

The eastern coastline of Provence borders the so called *Pelagos Sanctuary* – a marine area of 87,500 sq. km. Italy, Monaco and France agreed on protection of all the marine mammals in this area. The best time of the year to observe them is in summer, when 'gentle giants' like Fin Whale and Sperm Whale visit these waters, together with the smaller Risso's Dolphin, Pilot Whale and Cuvier Beaked Whale. Most abundant and jolly are Striped and Common Dolphins, sometimes accompanied by Bottlenose Dolphins.

Birds

> In the Camargue, any of the routes will yield great observations. Route 2 and 9 are best for the birds of agricultural land, routes 2, 4 and site C for freshwater marshes, and routes 6, 7 and 11 for saltmarsh. Bird photographers, consider a visit to Pont de Gau (site A on page 151). The birdlife of La Crau is best seen on route 8, 9 and site B on page 151. Your best chance of spotting seabirds are route 11 and site C on page 181. Raptors and birds of cliffs are found on routes 10, 22 and especially route 19. The Mediterranean birds of scrublands and forests are found along routes 10, 11, 15, 17 and 18, plus sites A, B and C on pages 180-181.

With more than 500 species recorded in the region, it is not surprising that Provence (and especially the Camargue) was one of the first places in southern Europe to become a popular birdwatching destination. Before air travel became available to the masses, the Camargue was one of the few locations that was within reach and harboured a large number of new birds for northern observers. The quantity and variety of birds, together with the famous flamingos, made the region a must-visit for any birdwatcher.

BIRDS

To this day, the diversity remains impressive. However, as flights have become cheaper, the Camargue is now often replaced by destinations further south. This is a pity, as, especially when taking Provence as a whole into account, the birdlife is very rich, with a unique mix between Mediterranean, montane and northern European species.
Typical of the birdlife of Provence is that it differs strongly from region to region. Birds of the Camargue are in marked contrast to those of the Crau, which in turn are different to those of the coastal mountains and islands, the high plateaux and the montane forests.

Birds of the lowlands, marshes, rivers and deltas

The Camargue is the largest and most well-known area to search for wetland birds, but not the only one. The lower Durance, several marshes in the Crau and the Saltpans of Giens and the Étangs de Villepey also harbour important wetlands, packed with birds.
In our description of the birdlife of wetlands, we obviously must start with the one bird that is the icon for the entire exotic birdlife of the region – the Greater Flamingo. Flamingos are exclusively found in the brackish to saline lagoons, with highest concentrations in the salt pans (see box on page 95). They share their habitat with a huge variety of other birds. The lagoons closest to the sea typically harbour Shelduck, Slender-billed Gulls, Gull-billed Tern, Little Tern, Sandwich Tern, Black-winged Stilt, Avocet, Oystercatcher, Ringed and Kentish Plovers and a large variety of other birds on passage (mostly waders). The rare Collared Pratincole breeds in small colonies in grazed saltmarsh on the edge of the Étang de Vaccarès and in the fields of the northern Camargue (route 2).
The glasswort flats or *sansouires* is where many marsh birds breed. Tucked away deep into the strictly protected Petit Camargue and Camargue

Bee-eaters are just one of the tropical looking species of Provence and Camargue.

BIRDS

Several small colonies of Collared Pratincole are scattered in the grazed sansouires around the Étang de Vaccarès.

reserves, ducks, waders, gulls and terns breed in colonies, safe from Foxes and other predators.
The bushier parts of the sansouires attract their own birdlife. One of the places to see them is along 'la Digue' (route 6), where you can find the rare Spectacled Warbler, among the more numerous Yellow Wagtails and Skylarks. On passage, you can find all sorts of songbirds here.
Away from the coast, in the brackish meadows, the vegetation is more diverse. As a result, insect life increases, which does not go unnoticed by the birds. This is where you'll find colourful birds like Hoopoe, Roller and Bee-eater, as well as a number of other song birds, such as Iberian Grey Shrike, Zitting Cisticola, Short-toed Lark, Skylark and Corn Bunting. The tamarisks here and along the many channels host large numbers of Sardinian and Cetti's Warblers (plus many migrants at the right time of year).
The freshwater marshes lie a little further inland. Reedbeds and swamp woodlands are the most important habitats here. The shelter of the reedbed and large amount of food (insects, fish, crayfish) make it a birds' heaven. The number and diversity of birds here is dazzling and the species are very different from those found in the salt marshes. Night and Purple Herons, Marsh Harrier, White Stork, Garganey, Little Bittern, Water Rail, Bearded Tit and Common and Great Reed Warblers are all well represented. Less numerous are Purple Gallinule (a recent colonist which has its only colony in France in the Étang de Scamandre; route 4), Bittern (which has its largest population in France in the Rhône delta) plus Savi's and Moustached Warblers (in France the latter is only found here and the adjacent Languedoc).
Most of the herons breed in large heronries on reedy islands, riverine forest and in tamarisk thickets. Although the species composition differs from one heronry to another, Little and Cattle Egrets are overall the commonest species. They are often joined by Grey and Purple Herons. Scarcer breeders of the heronries are Great White Egret, Night and Squacco Herons.
Another exciting and now common inhabitant of these colonies is the Glossy Ibis. After a long period of sporadic breeding, in 2006 this exotic-looking bird finally established itself as a breeding bird. At first there were only 14 pairs (although they fledged 45 young), but in the next ten years the

BIRDS

Flamingos – Camargue's pink pride

The Camargue is mostly known for two features: it's pink salines and the inhabitants of these, 'Les Flamants Roses' or Greater Flamingos. The Camargue is the only place in France where Flamingos breed, and one of the few in Europe. In the Camargue, they vast majority breeds in a single colony in the Étang de Fangassier (route 7). To feed however, they fly great distances and often stay in other places for quite some time. The flamingos in the salt pans of Hyères (route 11) also come from the Camargue.

With their exotic and bizarre appearance, it is not hard to imagine why the Camargue adopted this bird as its symbol. Apart from looking both graceful and clumsy at the same time (especially in flight with strong wind), its coloration is wildly fascinating. When the first Flamingos were kept in captivity, people were surprised to find that their pink colour faded. As it turns out, the pink salt pans themselves are the explanation. Their colour is the result of an incredible high concentration of salt loving bacteria that produce an organic pigment known as a carotenoid. These same bacteria are also present in the saline basins where shrimps and algae live, that take up the pigments the bacteria produce. These are in turn the main diet of Flamingos, which store the pigment in their feathers, turning them in an intense pink. This also explains why it is often thought that pinker Flamingos are healthier: they were able to eat more.

Glossy Ibis took the Camargue by storm. By 2017 there were over 2,000 pairs spread over ten colonies.
The rice paddies are only inundated during part of the year, from spring to autumn. During this period they attract a specific group of birds. Glossy Ibis very much appreciates this man-made habitat, as do flocks of Mediterranean Gulls and Gull-billed Terns, plus Little Egret, Cattle

BIRDS

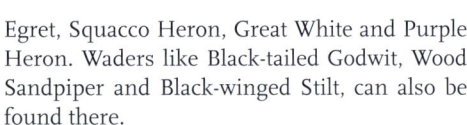

For feeding, both Squacco Heron (top right) as Glossy Ibis (bottom) prefer the open freshwater marsh and its artificial counterpart, the rice paddies.
Like the Glossy Ibis, the Purple Gallinule (top left) established recently in the area, following a huge increase of the population in Spain. Purple Gallinule is currently still restricted to the Étang du Scamandre.

Egret, Squacco Heron, Great White and Purple Heron. Waders like Black-tailed Godwit, Wood Sandpiper and Black-winged Stilt, can also be found there.

Finally, there are the lowland streams and rivers. The Durance is one of the biggest, with large areas of near-natural riverside habitat. Although these are not nearly such a prime spot for birds as the coastal marshes, they still harbour some interesting species. Kingfishers, Sand Martins and Bee-eaters breed in the steep river banks whilst Little Egrets, Little Ringed Plovers and Grey Wagtails favour its gravel shorelines. Some of the herons and egrets of the Camargue breed along the rivers as well, albeit in lower numbers. Stone bridges over the rivers are the breeding spots of Red-rumped Swallows, primarily in the valley of the Argens west of Fréjus. The tall stands of poplars and willows form another bird habitat, supporting Black Kite, Green and Lesser Spotted Woodpeckers, Hobby, Golden Oriole, Turtle Dove, Cetti's and Melodious Warblers. Many of these you'll find in hedges and woodland patches in the plains as well.

Birds of plains and agricultural lands

In the plains you can find 'goodies' like Roller, Golden Oriole, Hoopoe, Woodchat Shrike and Little Bustard, next to a score of more familiar and widespread species.
It must be said though, that while the diversity of birds may be high, the numbers of the more sought-after species are rather low. On the one hand this is a natural phenomenon as Provence is right on the edge of both the Mediterranean and temperate regions, and therefore towards the margin of the distribution ranges of many species. On the other hand, the intensification of agriculture and change in land use causes many birds to decline or even bring them to the brink of local extinction – the same sad old story that applies to so many rural areas in Europe.

Most plains (e.g. Vaucluse, around les Alpilles, north of Hyères) have an attractive, small-scale landscape with fields, vineyards, meadows and in some places lavender, speckled with woodlands, hedges, farms, small streams and limestone pastures. Lots of songbirds prefer this varied environment. Greenfinch, Goldfinch, Serin, Cirl Bunting, Nightingale and Cuckoo are widespread and often abundant. In more open, drier places, Linnet, Hoopoe, Little and Barn Owl, Woodchat Shrike and Corn Bunting are frequent, while the damp woodlands support Turtle Dove (in decline, like in many parts of Europe), Bee-eater, Marsh Tit, and Green Woodpecker.

Two colourful birds of fields and farmland – the Hoopoe (top) and Roller (bottom). Both feed primarily on large insects and are under pressure due to intensification of agriculture.

The larger, open plains have more attractions. Cereal and alfalfa fields are especially important for the Little Bustard. This bird is in sharp decline throughout Europe but still has a healthy population in and around La Crau. This was also one of the few strongholds of Lesser Grey Shrike in France, but which failed to breed in the country for the first time in 2019. It is likely to be the first bird in the 21st century to go extinct in the country.

Other birds of these fields are Quail, Bee-eater and Roller – all three being particularly numerous in the Camargue-Crau area but also present in the plains of Vaucluse.

The dry plains of La Crau are famous for their birdlife, which includes many species that are typical of steppes and semi-deserts. For example, the area is home to the only population of the elusive Pin-tailed Sandgrouse in France (in Europe it is otherwise restricted to Spain). Its plumage so perfectly disguises it on the stony plains that it is hard to census and so there is debate over its population trend in France. Most ornithologists think it is in decline. La Crau is also one of the very few places in Provence to see Tawny Pipit, Calandra Lark and Short-toed Lark, Stone Curlew and Bonelli's Eagle (coming from the nearby Alpilles). Finally, it is also one of the few places in France where Lesser Kestrel breeds.

The gorges of Provence are the preferred habitat of the Alpine Swift. With its white belly and its size (twice as large as a Common Swift) it is easy to recognise. Be aware though that during the middle of the day, Alpine Swifts often fly very high and are therefore easily missed.

Birds of the scrubland, rocky slopes and cliffs

Whilst the Camargue offers easy birding, you'll need to work a whole lot harder to find the mostly elusive and often scarce birds of the Provence scrublands. Spring is by far the best time to do this, as for a short period, the birds are singing and displaying, which makes them easier to locate. After they have built their nests, they disappear into the dense vegetation, skulking around to find food for their young. Many of these birds are warblers belonging to the *Sylvia* genus. Most species in this group of songbirds favour scrublands and have a rather hidden lifestyle. Many of them are found exclusively in the Mediterranean basin. In Provence, five species are typically found in scrublands: Sardinian, Orphean, Dartford and (Western) Subalpine Warblers, with the latter having a particular liking for the Box bushes on the higher plateaux.

The cliffs of the low ranges are home to various raptors. Here, they breed in safety and use the air currents that rise up from the cliffs to fly. Three sought after species that breed here are Bonelli's Eagle, Egyptian Vulture and Eagle Owl. All of them prefer the hotter, lower ranges, such as the Alpilles, Mont Sainte-Victoire, the Luberon and the Gorge de la Nesque.

The cliffs and forests of the Gorge du Verdon is home to yet another group of raptors. Here you can find Griffon and Black Vultures and the majestic Golden Eagle and Short-toed Eagle. All are formidably large, broad-winged birds. The Black Vulture has a wingspan of almost three metres, the largest of the European raptors.
Among the songbirds there are some attractive cliff and rock slope breeders too. Alpine Swift and Crag Martin are numerous in many places, just like House Martin, which breed in villages as well as on cliffs. Peregrine and Red-billed Chough are present in the Gorge du Verdon, while Rock Bunting, Rock Thrush (summer only) and less commonly, Blue Rock Thrush may be observed.
The rocky slopes and cliffs close to the Mediterranean Sea (e.g. Les Calanques, Les Alpilles) harbour a surprisingly different birdlife than the inland mountains. The Blue Rock Thrush serves as an example – rare or absent on slopes inland, but present and locally even common on the dry cliffs close to the coast. Black-eared Wheatear and Pallid Swift, two other widespread Mediterranean species, are in Provence most common near the coast. Several pairs of Peregrine and some large colonies of Alpine Swift breed on coastal cliffs as well.

The small, adorable Scops Owl is common in forests, small woodlands and gardens in the lowlands. In spring and well into summer, you can hear it every evening.

Seabirds

Although the diversity of the seabirds in the region is not especially great, the species that do occur are worth searching for. Yelkouan and Cory's Shearwaters (the latter now often referred to as Scopoli's Shearwater) are two Mediterranean specialties that breed on the cliffs of the islets off the coast of Les Calanques (mostly Cory's) and Île Port-Cros (mostly Yelkouan). Both populations are unfortunately in decline. Although the cliffs offer relative safe breeding, there are problems with rats eating the young.
Two other species that breed here in low numbers are the Mediterranean subspecies of the European Shag and the European Storm-petrel. Furthermore, Sandwich Terns, Gannets, skuas, gulls, grebes and divers frequent the coastline in winter. Yellow-legged Gull and various species of terns breed on the coast (see page 93) and are frequent in spring and summer.

BIRDS

Birds of the forests, the high plateaux and the Mont Ventoux

Visitors from northern Europe would consider most birds that occur in the forests quite normal. Nevertheless, they greatly add to the bird diversity of the region, not to mention that they help to boost your bird list. Amongst them are Tawny Owl, Chafffinch, Firecrest, Nuthatch, a variety of tits, thrushes, Great Spotted Woodpecker, Short-toed Treecreeper, Common Redstart, Bonelli's Warbler and Robin. Goshawk is also one to look out for.

Many of these birds do not seem to have a preference for a certain type of forest, but others do, including some species that do make the birder's heart race faster. One of them is the Citril Finch – a green, canary-like bird, endemic to the mountains of south-western Europe. It can be found in the coniferous forests of Mont Ventoux at around 1500m and above. In similar places, Bullfinch, Crossbill, Siskin (scarce), Goldcrest, Crested Tit and Coal Tit can be found. In the beech forests lower down the slopes, Black Woodpeckers breed, whereas Wryneck can be found in oak forests above 500m altitude. At night in lowland forests, you can hear Nightjars as well as the typical, one syllable submarine sonar-like beep of the Scops Owl. This small owl reaches its highest densities in the lowland woods, particularly on the island of Île Port-Cros, but can be heard near villages in the lowlands too. Seeing the bird is another matter though...

Although most of the truly Alpine bird species fall (just) outside the area covered in this book, the high plateaux and in particular the Mont Ventoux harbour an interesting birdlife with some species that are uncommon, rare or absent elsewhere in the area. One of them is the Rock Thrush, of which the males add a splash of colour in an otherwise barren landscape. Other species found in this zone, especially on the Mont Ventoux, are Northern Wheatear, Dunnock, Black Redstart and Rock Bunting. The latter often sings conspicuously from the top of a small tree or a large rock.

The plateaux of Canjuers, Verdon, Valensole and Caussols are different

In the last centuries, the Camargue has become a major hub on the Crane migration route. An increasing number stay here during the winter.

BIRDS

again. Their appearance is open with steppe grasslands and scant boxscrub, alternated with mostly open woodland with Austrian Pines or Downy Oaks. The typical birds here include Cirl and Ortolan Buntings, Rock Thrush, Subalpine, Orphean and Bonelli's Warblers, Black-eared Wheatear, Mistle Thrush, Little Owl, Woodlark and Nightjar. They are also used as hunting grounds by Short-toed Eagle and Honey Buzzard.

Some of these plains have a very open character. The Valensole, with its lavender and wheat fields, harbours a birdlife with a particular steppe-like character. Testimony of this is the occurrence of Little Bustards and Stone Curlew. A few Calandra and Short-toed Larks can be found here too, but they are very rare. Keep your eyes open for Spectacled Warblers that breed in the lavender fields, as well as for Rock Sparrows that breed in sheds and old walls. Finally, the Valensole Plain is the best spot in the region to see Montagu's Harriers.

Migratory birds

The Rhône valley and the Camargue are particularly important areas for migratory birds. The river functions as a north-south highway, while the Camargue (and surrounding area) forms an important stopover site. Many birds use the Camargue as a final resting place to regain some strength before going down the coast and crossing the Mediterranean Sea. On their way back north in spring, Provence is the first landfall birds encounter after the tiring flight over the Mediterranean Sea. They gratefully plunge into the very first bush they encounter.

The list of species that pass through the area is huge, and encompasses nearly every bird that migrates between both western and northern Europe, and western Africa. Highly visible are the waders such as Wood Sandpiper, Curlew Sandpiper, Little Stint, Dunlin and Black-tailed Godwit with occasional Marsh Sandpiper. In the Camargue, Whiskered and Black Terns are numerous and Black Stork, Osprey, Spotted and Little Crakes are regular. Red-footed Falcon and even Eleanora's Falcon are regularly recorded in lowland Provence. In addition, check every bush that you can find in open areas and there is a good possibility that you might encounter flycatchers (notably Pied Flycatcher pass through in large numbers), pipits, warblers or even a Wryneck. Also keep an eye on the sky for the passage of Common Cranes and White Storks.

Wintering birds

Winter is a great time to watch birds in Provence and Camargue. The saline lagoons seldom freeze over and as such they are a popular wintering spot

BIRDS

The surroundings of Les-Baux-de-Provence are considered to be one of the easiest places to find Wallcreepers between November and March. However, they winter everywhere in the region where there are tall, exposed cliffs.

for many ducks and waders. Add to that the number of 'altitudinal migrants' in the hills and mountains (birds coming down from the icy heights of the Alps), plus the resident birds and you get a highly attractive mix of species. Fields draw groups of wintering Yellowhammers, Cirl Buntings, Skylarks and many pipits. Sparrowhawks and Buzzards are more abundant as birds from the north join the local breeding populations. They are also joined by other raptors as Merlin and White-tailed Eagle. Perhaps the highlight of winter birding is the presence of several Greater Spotted Eagles (a Russian breeding bird) in the Camargue.

Lots of wetland species can be found throughout the Camargue and marshes further east. Some are found exclusively in winter (e.g. Bluethroat and Penduline Tit), while resident species have their populations augmented by thousands of visiting birds from the north. An example of the latter is the Spoonbill, which is much more common during winter. Ducks are also much more common in the colder months. Among thousands of Teal, Shoveler, Wigeon, Gadwall and Pochard, there is also a scattering of the rare Ferruginous Duck. Out at sea, Red-breasted Merganser is frequent, occasionally joined by rarities like Long-tailed Duck and Velvet Scoter.

La Crau of course has its own set of wintering birds. Among the many pipits, there are sometimes rarities like Richard's Pipit. Red Kites winter in good numbers, as do Lapwings, Golden Plovers and Dotterel.

In the mountain foothills, some of the hard to find mountain birds show themselves much more easily than they do in their remote breeding quarters during summer. One of them is the much sought-after Wallcreeper, that visits cliffs from Verdon (route 19) to the Alpilles (route 10). In Les Baux (which is more interesting to visit in winter, as it is not overrun by tourists), Wallcreeper and Alpine Accentors can be found with relative ease. On Mont Ventoux, White-winged Snow Finches are often seen, while Red-billed Choughs and Citril Finches come down to Montagne Sainte-Baume and Sainte-Victoire.

All that in a mild winter sun (if the mistral doesn't spoil it for you) – What else could you wish for?

CROSSBILL GUIDES • PROVENCE

Reptiles and amphibians

Stripeless Tree Frog is common in the Camargue (routes 1, 2, 3, 4, 5, 9). Your best chances on finding snakes are in ruins and 'messy' agricultural land (e.g. routes 2, 9, 12 13, 14, 15, 17 22, 23). Areas with tall grass are best for finding Western Three-toed Skink (e.g. route 17). Look for geckos on walls of villages close to the coast (route 12, sites A and C on page 180-181). European Pond Terrapin is best seen in the Camargue (route 5). Hermann's Tortoise is one of the specialties of Provence, found on routes 13, 14, 17.

Amphibians

The list of frogs, toads, newts and salamanders is quite large. It includes between 15 to 20 species, depending on where exactly you draw the border of Provence. The Fire Salamander is among the more impressive animals on that list. It leads a hidden life near small, forested streams and pools (in which the tadpoles live), but comes out during and after rainy spells, generally at night. Still more secretive is the Strinati's Cave Salamander, which lives in old moist walls in the *Préalpes* north of Nice. Provence has only two widespread newts, the Palmate and Alpine Newts. Both prefer still waters with lots of water plants.

The huge toad you sometimes encounter in the evening, even in dry places, is the Spiny Toad. It is a close relative of (and only recently taxonomically separated from) the familiar Common Toad. The Midwife Toad prefers small ponds or very slow-flowing water, such as little rivulets and shallow pools. It is the sound, a single-pitched soft whistle, which gives its presence away (although be aware that Scops Owl sound very similar). Natterjack Toads can be found in all sorts of sites. We even found one in the car park of a Supermarché. However, they have a preference for open habitats with sand or other material into which they can dig. The secretive Western Spadefoot is limited to the Iberian Peninsula and the west and south coast of France. It is found in shallow coastal slacks with sandy fringes, such as in the Camargue, but is scarce.

Stripeless Treefrogs are very common in the Camargue and other marshy areas in Provence. They can be very hard to find or impossible to miss, depending on the weather conditions. Damp, warm spring days and evenings are the best.

REPTILES AND AMPHIBIANS

The harsh croaking nocturnal chorus of the Stripeless Tree Frogs is about as typical of the region as Flamingos and cicadas. These handsome little frogs are particularly abundant in the Camargue. Their loud calls are accompanied by the abrupt melancholic hoots of Scops Owl and the exuberant extended song of Nightingale – a wonderful night-time concert. On damp days they occur just about anywhere in the lowlands and climb up outdoor terrace furniture or hide behind the window shutters.

The situation with 'the green frog', is rather complicated. There are plenty of green frogs belonging to various, similar-looking species. To confuse matters further, they readily hybridise. The Iberian Water Frog, the Marsh Frog and their hybrid, the Graf's Hybrid Frog, all occur in the area (plus a very small population of Pool Frog). The Parsley Frog is another rather widespread but very secretive species that few people get to see. It prefers shallow, well vegetated waters and is active at night. The Common Frog, so familiar in most parts of northern Europe, is rather rare and generally only found in the north-east of the region (e.g. Gorge du Verdon). In the Massif des Maures (and eastwards to roughly Nice) a similar-looking species can be found, the Agile Frog. Finally, there is the Tyrrhenian Painted Frog, an animal from Corsica and Sardinia, and the islands of Giens, Porquerolles and Port-Cros.

Reptiles

There are 10 species of snakes in Provence, some of which are common and widespread. Nevertheless, you don't see snakes easily. They have an uncanny ability to crawl away into cracks, under bushes, leaf litter, rocks and logs. Since snakes detect vibrations in the ground, such as those from footsteps, they are usually gone before you arrive.

Most snakes are under a metre in length, but of some can grow up to be impressive beasts of 1.5, or in rare cases even 2 metres. The longest are Western Whip Snake, Aesculapian Snake, Ladder Snake and Montpellier Snake. Of these, the Aesculapian, known from the universal sign for medicine, prefers damp, tall woodlands. It is rather dull-coloured (brown, olive or grey) with a blunt head (see page 37). Much more colourful is the Western Whip Snake, with its bold green-yellow markings. It is widespread in open woodland, but also occurs near farmsteads, old sheds and wild gardens. Both Aesculapian and Western Whip Snake are good climbers and frequently ascend into shrubs and trees. By contrast, the Ladder Snake is strictly terrestrial. Adult Ladder Snakes sport two dark dorsal stripes; the juveniles have dark bars on their backs (see photo). Tha Ladder snake occurs in warm scrublands and evergreen forest. The Montpellier Snake is again plain-coloured, but

REPTILES AND AMPHIBIANS

easily identified by its large eyes and stern stare. Its attack (it can be quite aggressive when cornered) is like that of cobra – head raised and with fast bites; very intimidating. This clearly is a snake you don't want to mess with, although its attack is not dangerous.

Provence has two species of vipers. The Asp Viper is widespread in semi-open, bushy areas, particularly in the mountains. It has a potent venom and is potentially dangerous. The short, squat posture and 'zigzag' stripe on the back makes it a distinctive snake, only to be confused with the rare and even smaller Meadow Viper (or possibly the Viperine Snake – see below). The latter occurs only on karst plateaux, such as on the Mont Ventoux and Calern. Its venom is weak and its prey consists mostly of large invertebrates such as bush-crickets. Another small snake and one that is not poisonous, is the Southern Smooth Snake. It prefers dry stony areas and lives a hidden life. Its core area within Provence is centred on La Crau. The most frequently encountered snakes are the two water snakes: the familiar Grass Snake and the Viperine Snake of south-western Europe. Both are harmless. The latter is not related to the vipers, but got its name from the viper-like zigzag pattern on its back. Both occur widely in Provence.

Provence's 'default lizard' is the Wall Lizard. It is by far the most numerous and found in pretty much any part of the region. It is very common in old walls, rocky areas and in most villages.

Three of the more common snakes of Provence: Montpellier (top), Western Whip (centre) and Ladder Snake (bottom).

REPTILES AND AMPHIBIANS

The males of the Western Green Lizard have a smashing blue throat in the spring breeding season.

In the dunes and dry calcareous lowlands of the south-west you may also find the Spanish Psammodromus, a small ground dweller of hot, open terrain. The colourful Western Green Lizard is much bigger and prefers open woodlands. In spring, the males have a bright blue throat. Bigger still is the impressive Ocellated Lizard, which is largely confined to the warm, open plains of the Crau, Alpilles and the southern Var Province. It is quite scarce and rapidly declining. In tall grassland you may also encounter the Western Three-toed Skink, which is slim and shiny like a Slow Worm (which also occurs in the region) but has tiny residual limbs.

In the evening in the coastal areas, lookout for geckos. The Moorish Gecko is common and widespread and you can easily find them on walls, especially by lights which attract insects. Its relative the Turkish Gecko prefers more humid coastal areas and is quite rare. Very special is the rare European Leaf-toed Gecko, which is largely confined to the Tyrrhenean islands (Corsica and Sardinia) with isolated colonies on nearby coasts in Italy and France. In Provence, it is restricted to the islands, such as Port-Cros, Porquerolles and Calanques and the adjacent coast.

Besides snakes and lizards, Provence hosts a third group of reptiles: the sea turtles, tortoises and terrapins. The Camargue is one of the French strongholds of the European Pond Terrapin, which is common in the freshwater marshes. It also occurs in water bodies from Hyères to Cannes. Locally, they are accompanied by the American Red-eared Slider, the common pet terrapin, now an invasive species.

Very special is the presence of the Hermann's Tortoise. Outside Greece, there are just a few places where it occurs in Europe (where it was perhaps once introduced by the Greeks when they established colonies on the Mediterranean coast). In France, it is only present in the Massif des Maures and surroundings. The rustle of the leaf litter is what gives its presence away. It is not very common though. We found it along the Endre River (route 17). There is a tortoise hospital, the *Village des Tortues* in the village of Gonfaron (**www.villagedestortues.fr**).

Insects and other invertebrates

The best routes for butterflies are routes 13, 14, 15, 16, 17, 18, 20, 22 and 24. Of this 13, 14 and 17 are the haunts for Mediterranean rarities like Chapman's Green Hairstreak and Two-tailed Pasha. Routes 16, 19 and 22, plus site E on page 182 and A and C on pages 201-202 have a diverse butterfly fauna of the dry limestone grasslands.
The best dragonfly routes are routes 5, 8, 9 14 and 17, plus site E on page 153 and E on page 219. For other insects and invertebrates, explore the dry grasslands such as those on routes 8, 9, 10, 14, 18, 21, 22 and 23.

Butterflies

From the Mediterranean coast to the *Préalpes*, Provence is one of France's hotspots for butterflies. Nearly 65% of the approximately 250 butterfly species of France are found in this region! Even on a European scale, Provence is one of Europe's butterfly hotspots.
To get a rough and ready grasp of this diversity, the A8-motorway forms a neat tool. It divides the butterfly world of the lower, truly Mediterranean Provence (with its large swathes of garrigue, maquis and evergreen woodland) from the higher parts of the region. The latter harbours Alpine and Central European species.
Visiting the south is most productive in April and May, and again in autumn, in September and October. Any abandoned or lightly grazed grassy slope with sufficient wildflowers will have a good number of butterflies. These include Knapweed, Spotted, Queen of Spain and Glanville Fritillaries, Adonis and Mazarine Blues and Red Underwing Skipper. In woodlands and damp places, Large Tortoiseshell, Camberwell Beauty and Southern White Admiral are common and attractive butterflies.
Conspicuous Mediterranean spring beauties are the Spanish and Southern Festoons, respectively a western and an eastern Mediterranean species that overlap in distribution in southern Provence. The Provence Hairstreak is scarce and flies from March to April in abandoned fields, such as near Draguignan and Cuers. A rare relative of

In Mediterranean woodlands the Southern White Admiral is a common butterfly.

INSECTS AND OTHER INVERTEBRATES

this species is the Chapman's Green Hairstreak. This look-alike of the familiar Green Hairstreak (which is much more common in Provence) has a red instead of white ring around the eyes. Its caterpillar feeds on the Strawberry Tree. Another butterfly whose caterpillars feed on Strawberry Trees, is the Two-tailed Pasha. This is one of the largest and most spectacular butterflies of Europe. Over hot limestone hillsides in spring you can find the Provence Orange-tip, which has yellow where the familiar Orange-tip is white. Other conspicuous or notable species which prefer the hot southern hills are Yellow-banded, Sage and Tufted Skippers, Spanish Purple and False Ilex Hairstreaks, Nettle-tree Butterfly and Southern and Spanish Gatekeeper.

North of the A8-motorway there are plenty of woodlands, flowery meadows and karstic plateaux. May to August are the most productive months for butterfly watching here. Particular species to look for are Sooty and Scarce Coppers, Large, Amanda's, Furry, Ripart's Anomalous and Meleager's Blues, Hermit, Lesser Purple Emperor, Duke of Burgundy, Pearly and Dusky Heaths and various large graylings.

One of the more sought-after spring species is the Southern Swallowtail. At the base of the Mont Ventoux and near Digne-les-Bains you can find them in the fields but also in the villages visiting Red Valerian in the gardens and old walls. Usually amongst Common and Scarce Swallowtails. Many other spring species can be mentioned, but here we limit ourselves to two other Provence specialties. First is the Chequered Blue which is one of the most elegant small blues of Europe. It flies in the rocky parts of limestone grasslands where stonecrops grow (the larval food plants). Baton Blue, another smashing and rather similar little butterfly, is often found in such places too.

The second species to be mentioned is the Iolas Blue. It is very rare in Europe and has a small population in Provence. As they are very inconspicuous,

Two sought-after butterflies that within France are found only in the far south: the Spanish Festoon, which flies in spring (top) and the Southern Swallowtail, flying mostly in June (bottom).

INSECTS AND OTHER INVERTEBRATES

it is hard to find them, but keep your eyes out near Bladder-senna, on the seed pods of which the larvae live.
From June onwards, it is time for browns, ringlets and graylings (in short, the Satyridae). Most of them rely on grasses to lay their eggs and feed their caterpillars. Each grassland type has its own set of species. In the rocky habitats, look for Dusky Meadow Brown, Hermit, Striped and Tree Grayling, Black and Great Sooty Satyrs and various wall browns. Great Banded and False Graylings dwell in more grassy areas, where they are accompanied by Common Heath, Meadow Brown, and various Marbled Whites.
Summertime yields a different set of blues. Some are simply the second generation of 'spring species', such as Adonis, Chapman's and Common Blues. A true summer species is Meleager's Blue – easy to recognise by the jagged edge of the hindwing. The females, in particular, have strongly contrasting markings and very distinct 'teeth' on the hindwing. Escher's, Furry, Damon, Large, Amanda's and Turquoise Blues are other summer species. Summer also brings out the skippers and larger fritillaries including the beautiful Cardinal. The high slopes of the Mont Ventoux and the *Préalpes de Côte d'Azur* are different again. Beside the impressive Apollo, Eros Blue, the ringlets (*Erebia*)

The Provence Hairstreak is a rarity of the southern Provence. It flies very early in the year (basically April) and prefers sheltered, small fields and patches of maquis.

The Provence five
The richness of Provence's butterfly fauna is evidenced by the butterfly names. There are several species that carry Provence in their name: Provence Hairstreak, Provence Chalk-hill Blue, Provence Orange-tip, Provençal Short-tailed Blue and Provençal Fritillary.
Interestingly, none of these species are unique to Provence. Rather they have a generally Mediterranean distribution. The vernacular name does not point towards a unique area in which the butterflies occur, nor towards a specific trait of Provence. Rather it points to the people who gave them their names: the British. English names often refer to the first place a species is found. Just like a Kentish Plover is not very typical of Kent nor Dartford Warbler typical of the town in the same county, the Provence five simply received their vernacular name from British lepidopterists (butterfly experts) visiting Provence. Apparently, these people found in Provence a very attractive area to hunt for butterflies. And in that, they were quite right!

INSECTS AND OTHER INVERTEBRATES

form the most distinctly Alpine group of butterflies here. The highest diversity of them is found on the high slopes outside the area of this guide, but there are some that can be regarded as specialties of the Provence' mountains. Scotch Argus (a ringlet!) plus Arran, Larche and Piedmont Ringlets are fairly widespread. Spring Ringlet is, like the name suggest, early on the wing and has a small distribution range in Europe. It has a doppelganger that is on the wing after summer – the Autumn Ringlet. Both are restricted to Mont Ventoux and the high plateau of the Gorge du Verdon National Park.

Dragonflies and damselflies

Provence is an exciting region to watch dragonflies and damselflies (odonates in short). Several species are exclusive to (a small area of) the Mediterranean basin and as such a great draw to dragonfly lovers of northern Europe.

Most damselflies frequent still waters. Among the bluets, the Azure and Variable Bluets are most numerous. The Mediterranean Bluet is the least common but can be found along the Durance and in La Crau – two areas that stand out as hotspots for odonates. Other bluets are Mercury, Dainty and Common Bluets, Common and Small Bluetails, Blue-eye and Small Red-eye. In addition, there are six species of spreadwings. Common and Robust Spreadwing can be found in still waters in the highlands, whereas Migrant and Dark Spreadwings are more frequent along the coastline. The latter is a beautiful and rather rare, nomadic species that prefers the brackish waters of the Camargue. Small

Small, somewhat shaded streams (top) are the places to look for the graceful Western Demoiselle (bottom).

CROSSBILL GUIDES • PROVENCE

and Western Willow Spreadwings are more generally distributed as are Winter, Large Red and Small Red Damselflies.
The beautiful and fairylike demoiselles are a frequent sight in both slow and fast-flowing brooks and rivers. Like butterflies they flutter over the water, a single greenish female often followed by a stream of metallic blue males. The Beautiful Demoiselle, the male of which has all-dark wings, is most conspicuous. It flies over shaded streams. In more open terrain, look for Banded and Western Demoiselles, the latter of which has a dark wingtip and a transparent wing base. In the channels of La Crau, a fourth species, the Copper Demoiselle, flies in massive numbers.

Among the damselflies, the featherlegs are frequent along small streams. Of the three species that occur, Blue, White and Orange Featherleg, the latter is the least common. We found it along the Endre River (route 17). The brooks and rivers in the mountains have oxygen-rich and fast flowing water with sections of shade and sunshine. Such habitats are the place to find Small Pincertails, often in large numbers. Take care though as in some places, it is accompanied by the very similar Large Pincertail. Interestingly, the smallest water courses are the breeding sites of some of the largest dragonflies of Provence – the Common and Sombre Goldenrings. The dragonflies themselves often hunt over tracks, trails and rivers. With some luck you may see them resting on a branch.

The Violet Dropwing with its unmistakable purple colour is a newcomer among the Provence dragonflies. This southern species is colonising ponds, lakes and slow-flowing rivers in the lowlands. Its expansion in Europe is probably the result of the warming climate.

Further downstream, where the rivers are wide but still oxygen-rich, you enter the realm of the clubtails. Three species occur in Provence: Western Clubtail is fairly common and occurs scattered all over Provence. Common Clubtail is, in spite of its name, scarce and restricted to the north. In the south it is replaced by the Yellow Clubtail.

The Durance and Rhône rivers are good spots not only for clubtails, but also for finding Blue-eyed Hawker and Downy Emerald. In the shadier parts, they share the territory with Orange-spotted Emerald and the mysterious Western Spectre – a species that hunts at dusk and in the shadows, resting under bridges and amongst vegetation.

INSECTS AND OTHER INVERTEBRATES

The large marshes of the Camargue are the haunt of yet another group of species, the Emperors. Both Blue and Lesser Emperor are typical here. The Vagrant Emperor, as the name implies, has a rather irregular occurrence. In some years it is frequent, with most sightings coming from La Crau. The marshes are also the place to see large numbers of darters. Amongst which are Southern and Red-veined Darters. In late summer, look out for the conspicuous Banded Darter, with its dark wing patches. It is a locally occurring species, mostly seen in the Wet Crau and the lower sections of the Durance. Damp woodlands and riverine forests (e.g. Marais de Vigueirat; route 9) are the places to find Green-eyed and Hairy Hawkers and various species of chasers and skimmers. Among the former is the Blue Chaser and amongst the latter is the White-tailed Skimmer which both fly in the Camargue (e.g. route 5). The Violet Dropwing, which arrived from Africa in the 1990s, has increasing populations in the south.

A final habitat with attractive dragonflies is that of the temporary pools and groundwater-fed marshes and ditches. Typical species are Southern and Spotted Darters, which breed in pools that frequently dry out – a tough place to survive, but one where they can escape predators. Last, but not least is the Balkan Emerald, which has its only west European population in the area of the Plaine des Maures and Estérel.

Other insects

Anyone who has visited Provence will know the flowery, aromatic grasslands, lavender fields and scrublands. The sound that comes with that

---

Dragonfly specialities of Provence

Copper Demoiselle endemic to the western Mediterranean; impressive numbers in La Crau.
Dark Spreadwing extremely rare, only found in Camargue; nomadic.
Orange Featherleg limited to the south; rare.
Mediterranean Bluet rare in Europe, large population on La Crau.
Vagrant Emperor vagrant, best chance in this part of Europe on La Crau.
Yellow Clubtail largely replaces Common Clubtail in the area; scarce in Europe.
Sombre Goldenring very rare in France.
Orange-spotted Emerald rare and rather elusive.
White-tailed Skimmer within our region, limited to the Camargue.
Spotted Darter elusive species that occurs in the south.
Southern Darter vagrant species that can be very abundant.
Banded Darter conspicuous; coastal marshes and the River Rhône.

INSECTS AND OTHER INVERTEBRATES

landscape is that of a thousand buzzing insects. Each type of habitat, whether rocky grasslands, woodlands, Alpine meadows, saline marshes or riversides, have their own specific insect fauna. There are too many to name them all but these are some of the most remarkable species. Summer tourists can't escape the sound of the most typical insect of Provence: *Cicada orni* – a big singing cicada that dwells in dry woodlands. It is a large, rather plump, fly-like insect that most people wouldn't consider elegant, yet it is without doubt the most famous insect of the region. Cicada means 'buzzer' in Latin. This is a deceptive euphemism for one

Cicadas are extremely noisy, yet so well camouflaged that they are hard to find.

La Cigale, the mascot of Provence

Let's be frank – it is unpleasantly loud and has an unappealing physique. Yet *Le Cigale*, the cicada, is close to the heart of the Provençois. In its ceramic form it is for sale in every tourist shop (you are supposed to hang it on the wall of your home).

Why, with all the pink prettiness of the Flamingo and the imperial purple of lavender, did *le cigale* become emblematic of the region?

Well, naturally, it all started with an entomologist, Jean Henri Fabre. Farbe, who was also poet, formed a literary society aiming to preserve the Provençal language and customs. This ensemble created a poem around the phrase, *Lou soulei mi fa canta*, Provençal for 'the sun makes me sing'. The poem was illustrated with a cicada. It was precisely what, in 1895, the local potter Louis Sicard was looking for. Sicard was approached by the wealthy manufacturers of *les Tuileries de Marseille* to design a promotional gift that symbolized Provence. What better than a sun that makes me sing, with the cicada the obvious heat-loving singer. Sicard created the famous ceramic cigale sitting on an olive branch signed with Mistral's lyric *Lou soulei mi fa canta*. It was spot-on. The cigale rapidly became Provence's mascot with Sicard earning himself the nickname 'father of the cicadas'. It didn't end with ceramics though. If you walk into a gift shop today, you are treated to cigale linen, cigale towels and even cigale-shaped hand soaps. The one thing we couldn't find though, is a pair of nice soft, cicada earplugs!

INSECTS AND OTHER INVERTEBRATES

of nature's most obtrusive, piercing sounds. The volume of a single male (only the males sing) at a pitch of 7kHz, can be heard from up to one kilometre away in a dense forest. It doesn't stop with one cicada, though. If one starts, the others chip in and soon an entire choir produces a deafening sound in the hot still afternoon. In contrast to the crickets, the sound is not produced by the rasping of the wings, but by vibrating a thick membrane in the abdomen. The buzzing is thereafter amplified by special air sacks in the tracheal system that echoes the sound.

From cicadas, it is but a short step to beetles. At the end of June, Stag Beetles are active and with some luck you will find one on an old oak trunk or branch. They attract most attention by their evening flights when they produce a deep buzz that matches their size. Together with the Stag Beetle, the European Rhinoceros Beetle is among Europe's largest beetles. It can be found all over southern Provence. The large distinctive horn on the head is used by males to fight one another to impress the females. The fights are as impressive as those of the Stag Beetle.

One of the most amusing beetles is the scarab beetle *Onthophagus vacca*.

This small but strong animal is active in spring and early summer, when it collects dung in open pastures to mould into a ball. The beetle rolls it towards its burrow by running backwards on four legs, pushing the ball with its two hind legs. In the burrow, the beetle makes multiple nests of dung, in each of which its lays a single egg.

The brightly-coloured little leaf beetles such as *Chrysolina* are beautiful and gather together on the screen-shaped flowers of the umbellifers. Impressive in a different way are Fireflies. The males of this tiny beetle (they are not flies!) have their nuptial flights after dark in June when they emit a weak flashing light. Females have no wings and attract males by their glow. In humid areas the twinkling lights illuminate the dark. The adults live for only two weeks so you need to get the timing right for this unforgettable night time show...

INSECTS AND OTHER INVERTEBRATES

With almost one hundred species of crickets and grasshoppers, Provence is also a great place to study this group of insects. Some species are so impressive that they appeal to the casual observer as much as to the specialist. Bush-crickets are most impressive because they are big and frequently colourful. The Provence Saddleback Bush-cricket and the Southern Saw-tailed Bush-cricket are frequently seen. The giant amongst these giants is the Predatory Bush-cricket; better known by its scientific name *Saga pedo*. It is a carnivorous species (feeding on other grasshoppers), and at 12 cms, impressively large. It is considered as Europe's largest insect. Interestingly, all specimens are females, as *Saga pedo* only reproduces through a process called parthenogenesis – offspring comes from unfertilised eggs.

The best time for grasshoppers and locusts is in summer and autumn when adults are common. In rocky areas there are various species of blue-winged and red-winged grasshoppers to be found. The specialist's heart beats faster on the Mont Ventoux where the very colourful endemic Ventoux Mountain Grasshopper (*Podisma amedegnatoae*) occurs. The wingless endemic Crau Grasshopper lives, as the name this time accurately suggests, only in La Crau and is critically endangered by the loss of habitat.

The number of wasp and bee species is immense. One of them is unmistakable and very common in the region – the large, dark Violet Carpenter Bee. It visits flowers, but you can also see it near wooden poles, fences or electricity masts scraping wood for a its nest. This, Europe's largest bee, is a solitary species. Despite its rather fearsome looks, it is a gentle animal. Another giant is the Mammoth Wasp. It feeds on nectar, but lays its eggs inside the larvae of the Rhinoceros Beetle. A case of one beast killing another.

Another attractive group of insects is that of the mantids. In Provence several species of mantids occur including Praying Mantis, Mediterranean Mantis and European Dwarf Mantis, as does another public favourite – the French Stick Insect. All of these are masters of disguise – not rare but hard to find. This is not the case for the owlflies or ascalaphids, which are fast and flashy. If you see a pale yellow flying beast dashing by that makes you wonder if you just saw a dragonfly or a butterfly, you probably encountered an owlfly. Four species are present in Provence including *L. coccajus*, *L. longicornis*, *L. lacteus* and the less colourful *L. ictericus*. Owlflies are related to antlions, of which again several species can be found. The Giant Antlion is a true beauty, which we found plentiful in La Crau in summer.

Opposite page: Provence has an amazing array of six-legged critters. Owlflies (top) you'll see frequently in spring and summer, as they fly fast and low over the flowery grasslands. The spectacular Predatory Bush-cricket (bottom) is one of Europe's largest insects. It is one of the few carnivorous locusts, feeding on other grasshoppers and bush-crickets.

PRACTICAL PART

The following section contains detailed routes and site descriptions in Provence and the Camargue. We've selected the routes carefully, in order to showcase the region's different habitats and landscapes and give you the best chances to find the the birds, wildlife, reptiles, butterflies, dragonflies and flora – in other words, the basis for a fine wildlife holiday. You'll find that some of these routes take you to little visited places, whilst others are hotspots for tourists or locals. Although tranquillity is a factor in choosing the itineraries we propose, it is the wildlife, the scenery and quality of habitats that predominantly guided our selection. At the start of each route, small symbols and a brief qualification indicate why that particular route is worth exploring.

The routes form a mix of walks and car routes 'with stops-and-strolls'. The walks vary in strenuousness and length, offering something for all, regardless of your physical condition.

Provence and Camargue are far too large to cover from a single base. In order to see it all, you need to travel around, staying a couple of days in each area. For each of these areas, we've grouped the routes and sites together with the full route descriptions first and the site descriptions later.

The first region described is the Camargue and adjacent Crau and Alpilles. These ten routes are shown on page 118 to page 150 and the sites on pages 151 to 153. The next region is the Côte d'Azur (routes 11 to 17 on pages 154-179 and the sites on pages 180-183). Then follows the Haute Provence (routes 18 to 21 on pages 184 to 200 and the sites on pages 201-202). Finally, the Vaucluse and Mont Ventoux form an area (routes 22 to 24 on pages 203 to 216 and the sites on pages 217-219).

On these routes, wonderful encounters with wildlife are almost guaranteed and we wholeheartedly recommend to explore each and every one of them. That doesn't imply however, that the trails and country roads we don't describe are devoid of interest. One of the great things about Provence is that there are so many options to explore. In fact, some of the routes in this very book were 'discovered' simply by following the unmarked path because it looked attractive. So, to rephrase an old Japanese saying: "those who stick to the routes described in this book will meet with great things. Those who don't stick to them, will discover wonderful things too." Either way, enjoy!

In Provence, nature starts right where the tarmac ends. Many roadsides are full of butterflies and wildflowers, such as here on a back road near Saint-Paul-en-Forêt, where Lizard and Man Orchid grace the roadside.

CAMARGUE, CRAU AND ALPILLES

Camargue, Crau and Alpilles

The Camargue is a jewel in the crown of European wetlands. It ranks among the largest and most important estuaries of the continent, famous for its birdlife, flamingos in particular, and for its 'wild white horses' (see page 91). The Camargue is not a single reserve. It consists of a main 'Réserve National' and a large number of other nature reserves, such as Étang de Scamandre, La Capelière, Tour du Valat and Domaine de la Palissade, which are all part of the Camargue in the broader sense. The Petit Camargue, which lies west of the Petit Rhône, is ecologically part of the area and splendid and wild, but completely private and inaccessible.

The huge area has countless fresh and saline marshes, plus rice paddies, meadows and agricultural land. Its position on the Mediterranean Sea ensures a large variety of Mediterranean birds, including exotic ones like Bee-eater, Roller, all European heron species, Glossy Ibis and Purple Gallinule. For much the same climatic reasons, the Camargue is hugely important for wintering waterfowl. Routes 1-7 and site A on page 151 explore the Camargue.

In a wonderful twist of fate, the Camargue has two other splendid natural areas as neighbours which are entirely different in character: the low but wild limestone mountains of the Alpilles and the steppe plateau of La Crau. The latter boasts a habitat that is unique within France: stony lowland steppes. Again, it is the birdlife that stands out with species that are not or hardly found elsewhere in France, like Lesser Kestrel, Little Bustard, Pin-tailed Sandgrouse and Calandra Lark. Much less known is that La Crau also boasts extensive marshes and wet meadows, which merge into the wetlands of Marais du Vigueirat. Unlike the Camargue, the wet Crau and Marais are fed by groundwater and have a rare type of flora, plus large numbers of wetland birds. Routes 8 and 9, plus sites B and C on page 151-152 explore La Crau.

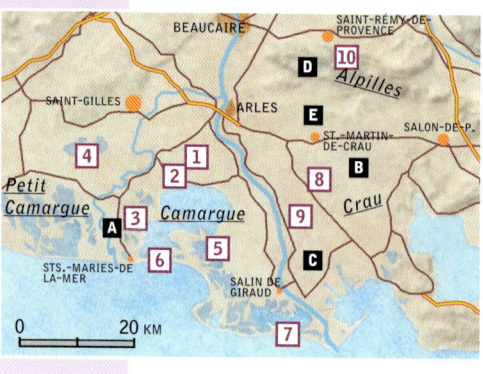

The rugged limestone range of the Alpilles borders on the northern edge of La Crau. The Alpilles are an isolated, low forerunner of the great Alpine massif, but are different from any other mountain range in Provence because of their dry, hot and rocky slopes. Route 10 and sites D and E on pages 152-153 explore the Alpilles.

CROSSBILL GUIDES • PROVENCE

Route 1: Mas du Pont de Rousty

2-3 HOURS, 5.2 KM
EASY

Perfect introduction to the landscapes of the Camargue.

Habitats salt marsh, rice paddies, brackish meadow, reedbed, freshwater lagoon
Selected species Bearded Tit, Great White Egret, Spoonbill, Melodious Warbler, Giant Orchid, Common Birthwort, Smearwort, Stripeless Tree Frog

The vistors' centre of Mas du Pont de Rousty in the heart of the northern Camargue is the logical first stop on your visit to the Camargue. Apart from being the nature park's headquarters, it has a museum on the Camargue's history and a nature trail that leads you through some of the most important habitats of the region. It is also an excellent route for birdwatching, in particular the far end of the trail.

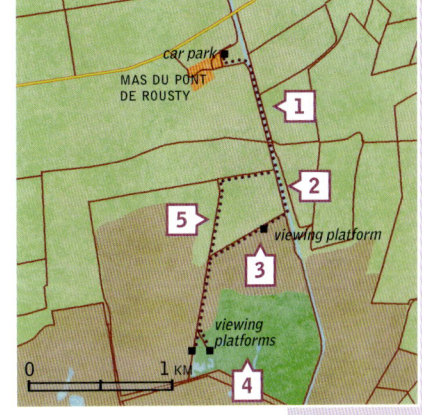

Starting point Musée du Parc at Mas du Pont de Rousty (GPS 43.624663, 4.529145). From the car park, follow the indicated route.

1 The first stretch of this trail leads to some paddies. Signs (in French) introduce you to the history of rice production in the Camargue, which is one of the major economic activities in the delta. The benign climate, the fertile soil of the delta and the permanent access to fresh water, makes the northern delta ideal for rice production. In spring, the dry paddies are levelled and the rice is planted. Then, via an intricate system of channels, the paddies are flooded and the rice grows until harvested in autumn.

2 The trail passes through some shrubs with Dogwood and Elm. The trees were planted as wind breaks – something best appreciated when doing this walk in fierce Mistral (see page 24). The birds and

ROUTE 1: MAS DU PONT DE ROUSTY

wildlife of this spot are best discovered when it is not too windy. They include Melodious, Cetti's and Sardinian Warblers and Nightingale. During migration periods, many Pied Flycatchers can be found here, especially in autumn.

3 The track bends to the right. Ahead, you will find some viewpoints that overlook a brackish meadow. One of the attractive features of the Camargue is the constant changing of fresh, brackish and saline environments that produces a patchwork of habitats, even on a short walk as this one. In the open meadows, you can find Cattle Egret and Zitting Cisticola in the meadows, while Cuckoo, Great Spotted Cuckoo (rare), Glossy Ibis and various herons fly by. Closer by, note the two species of birthwort that flower in spring: Common Birthwort and Smearwort.

The well-maintained nature trail is lined with trees and bushes (bottom). From the platform at point 4, you watch over a reedbed where Bearded Tits are frequent (top).

4 The track forks with the right branch leading back to the visitors centre and the left one leading to reedbeds and a freshwater lagoon. The Camargue harbours some of the most extensive reedbeds in the whole of France. They are home to Bearded Tit, Reed Bunting, Reed Warbler and Great Reed Warblers. On and around the lagoon you can find Great White Egret and Purple Heron. In winter, it shelters many ducks and also Spoonbill can be found.

5 Return to the junction and follow the left trail back to the museum. The road leads through some salt marshes. The flora is characterised by Saltwort, a succulent scrub which is able to cope with high salt concentrations. You can also find the sea-lavender *Limonium narbonense*, Sea Purslanes and Annual See-blites.

Route 2: The northern Camargue

5-6 HOURS, 53 KM

Great route for birds of freshwater marshes, fields and rice paddies.

Habitats rice paddies, brackish meadow, reedbed, fields, riverine forest
Selected species Mediterranean Gull, Glossy Ibis, Great Spotted Cuckoo, Stone Curlew, Whiskered Tern, Squacco Heron, Wood Sandpiper, Stripeless Treefrog, Roller, Glanville Fritillary

A flat land of fields, rice paddies and small hamlets, tucked away behind windbreaking avenues of trees – that is the landscape of the northern Camargue. This part of the delta is still far enough away from the sea not yet to be strongly influenced by salt water, although there are already some zones with brackish and even saline meadows.
This route brings you through the diverse landscape of the northern Camargue. It is an excellent route for birdwatchers. In addition to a good range of waders, herons and ibises, several of the scarce birds of the Camargue may be in the cards for you, like Stone Curlew, Great Spotted Cuckoo, Collared Pratincole or Roller.

Starting Point Mas du Pont de Rousty (GPS 43.624663, 4.529145).

ROUTE 2: THE NORTHERN CAMARGUE

From the Musée, follow the D570 in the direction of Saintes-Maries-de-la-Mer. Take the first left (D37) to Salin de Giraud.

1 You can stop at several places along this road to scan the brackish marshland. Here you can find Camargue horses with Cattle Egrets – a great, wild and romantic sight that in the right light conditions is perfect for photography. The wildness of these horses is debatable (see page 91). In wet patches you can find waders and several heron species.

On many points of the route you can see the white Camargue Horses grazing in the saltmarsh. Usually there are some Cattle Egrets among them, which feed on the insects that fly up when the horse moves.

2 After 7.4 kms you arrive at a viewpoint at the right side of the road. Park here and overlook the reedbeds across the road from the platform. Herons and Marsh Harriers fly over regularly. On the south side view is limited by Tamarisks, which shelter migrating songbirds in spring and autumn.

Turn left towards Mas D'agon directly after the viewpoint (first left).

3 This narrow country road passes through reedbeds which are part of the big *Marais de la Grand Mar*. Stop in the side of the road to look for Reed and Great Reed Warblers, Purple Heron, Squacco Heron, Bearded Tit, Whiskered Tern and Moustached Warbler.

4 The marshes give way to fields and brackish meadows. This is one of the best areas for finding Great Spotted Cuckoo and Roller. Keep an eye out for Stone Curlew and Collared Pratincole as well. None of them are common or easy to spot, but all do occur here regularly.

Continue. Ignore the first turn to the right and at the next crossing, take the road to the right, signposted *Gageron*. Follow this road to a T-junction, where

ROUTE 2: THE NORTHERN CAMARGUE

you turn left to Arles (note all the lanes and hedges here, planted to break the fierce mistral winds; see page 24). The road brings you to the D570. Turn right and almost directly (300 m) left again, on the narrow C150 road called *Route de la Dougue de Gimeaux*. Proceed to and through the hamlet of Gimeaux and then go left onto the C113 signposted *de Palunlongue*.

5 The road passes through open fields. Check the bushes, tree tops, wires and fences for Roller, Bee-eater, Hoopoe and Great Spotted Cuckoo. Stone Curlew and Collared Pratincole are sometimes seen on the open fields, but, like at the previous point, they are scarce and hard to spot. Collared Pratincole, here at the very northern limit of its range, is not present every year. It is easy to recognise by its graceful and swift flight, like an oversized swallow. Also keep an eye out for raptors flying over like Black Kite and Short-toed Eagle. A little further on you can park the car in the side of the road and walk through some saltmarshes along a hedge of shrubs. Expect more songbirds here, like Cetti's, Melodious and Sardinian Warbler and Nightingale. The shrubs are full of Stripeless Tree Frogs.

The northern Camargue is the best place in the area to see the rare Great Spotted Cuckoo.

6 Further along the road you will find the first rice paddies, which will be the theme for much of the remainder of the trip. Here you can find the Glossy Ibis and lots of Mediterranean and Black-headed Gulls. Other species that can be found here include Black-winged Stilt, Cattle and Little Egret (resident), Wood Sandpiper, Whiskered Tern, Greenshank and other waders (passage) and Purple and Squacco Heron and Gull-billed Terns (summer). During migration, check the Whiskered Terns carefully, as Black and (less commonly) White-winged Tern might be among them.

At the D37 turn right until you arrive at the large D572N. Cross the road and follow the dead-end street to the river.

7 Take a stroll over the dam and enjoy the massive trees that grow alongside the Petit Rhône. There are Elms, Oaks, Sycamores, Aspen,

PRACTICAL PART

ROUTE 2: THE NORTHERN CAMARGUE

Two common birds on this route: the Mediterranean Gull with its all-white wings (top) and the Glossy Ibis (centre).

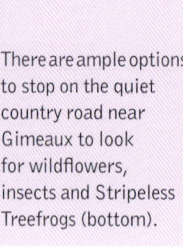

Trembling Black and White Poplars growing alongside one another. In particular the White Poplars can grow to impressive trees. It is not easy to catch a glimpse of the birdlife here, but Melodious Warbler, Green Woodpecker, Turtle Dove and Golden Oriole are the typical inhabitants of these forests.

Return to the D572N and turn right. After 400 metres, turn left.

8 You pass along the *Marais de Saliers*, a large freshwater marsh that has been converted into rice paddies. There are still many small patches of reed left. All the birds that could be found along earlier rice paddies can be found here.

The road ends at the D37. Turn right here, pass through Albaron (Tree Sparrow breeds here) until you reach the D570. Turn left to return to the starting point.

There are ample options to stop on the quiet country road near Gimeaux to look for wildflowers, insects and Stripeless Treefrogs (bottom).

CROSSBILL GUIDES • PROVENCE

Route 3: Around Saintes-Maries-de-la-Mer

6 HOURS, 36 KM

Great birdwatching route on the western side of the Étang de Vaccarès. Many flamingos and a visit to Saintes-Maries-de-la-Mer.

Habitats salt and freshwater marsh, freshwater and saline and fresh lagoons, fields
Selected species Greater Flamingo, Avocet, Squacco Heron, Purple Heron, White-Whiskered Tern, Red-Crested Pochard, Glossy Ibis, Bee-eater, Slender-billed Gull, Violet Dropwing, Banded Darter

Saintes-Maries-de-la-Mer is Camargue's famous village. Its gypsy background, the Spanish-looking white-washed houses, the bull-fighting, horse riding macho culture and the deep Catholic history of the Black Madonna give the town a unique atmosphere. This, plus the many tourists that flock to Saintes-Maries, all add up to the odd mixture of authenticity and charade.
The marshes on the border of the village are superb, with saline and freshwater areas, rural backwaters and small country roads. In this fine landscape, it is the birdlife of the salt marshes that stands out – waders, gulls, terns and flamingos. This is a great route to cover by bike as it runs largely over quiet, flat backroads, but it can just as easily be explored by car.

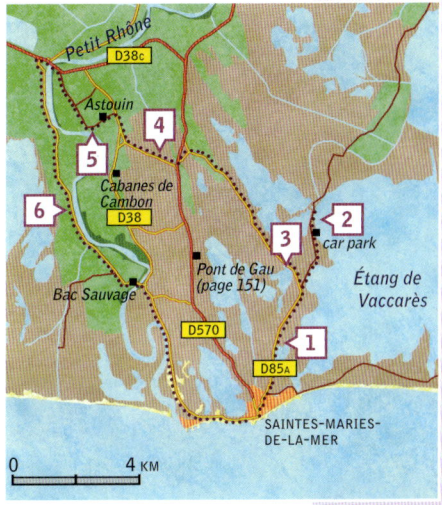

Starting Point Saintes-Maries-de-la-Mer (GPS 43.452184, 4.428952) Leave the village following the direction *Arles par Cacharel* on the D85a.

1 The road takes you through an empty landscape of open salt marshes with the enormous Étang de Vaccarès behind it. You'll probably see your first Flamingos of this trip right outside the village. They are joined

PRACTICAL PART

by Black-winged Stilt, Kentish Plover, Little Egret and Avocet, with a score of other waders outside the breeding season, such as Grey Plover, Dunlin and Curlew Sandpiper (Sept to March). On the Glasswort bushes you can find Whinchat and Yellow Wagtail (migration periods). Keep an eye out for Slender-billed Gull as well.

3.5 kms after leaving Saintes-Maries, just after the road bends to the left, a broad rough track continues straight on. Follow it.

2 For the next 1.5 kms this bumpy road takes you through excellent habitat. On the left lies a freshwater lake with extensive reedbeds and on the right salt marsh with the Étang de Vaccarès in the distance. Both are excellent for birds with on the freshwater side Purple Heron, Reed Warbler, Great Reed Warbler, Bearded Tit, Red-crested Pochard, Marsh Harrier and in winter ducks on the lake. On the saline side, similar birds can be found as at the previous point. Look out for Collared Pratincole too, which has small colonies in

The Banded Darter has unmistakable dark marks on its wings (top).
Yellow Iris flowers massively in May in several of the marshes on the route (bottom).

ROUTE 3: AROUND SAINTES-MARIES-DE-LA-MER

the grazed *sansouires* here and further north. This is a good area for dragonflies too. Look for White-tailed Skimmer, Spotted Darter and Violet Dropwing.

Continue for 1.5 kms until you find a small carpark on the right where a track brings you to the edge of the Étang. This is a good end point for this little detour, but it is possible to drive all the way to the Domaine the Méjanes.

Back on the D85e continue the route. A little further, on the left, you will encounter a large lake.

3 Scan from the road to find Avocet, Spoonbill and Red-Crested Pochard. During migration periods you can find Whiskered Tern and waders like Greenshank and Spotted Redshank.

The road continues through a pleasant rural landscape with some fields and several pools. Places to stop are frequent along the road. Once you reach the large D570 turn left and take the first right again onto the D38b direction *Cabanes de Cambon*.

The Red-crested Pochard breeds in the reedy marshes north of Saintes-Maries-de-la-Mer (top). On the lagoons and rice paddies in spring, the Whiskered Tern is a common visitor (bottom).

4 On your right you pass a large marsh, which in April and May gleams gold because of the enormous numbers of Yellow Irises. Note that the saltwater has been replaced by fresh or perhaps just slightly brackish water. This place is well worth a photo stop and as good as any spot on the route for waders, terns, raptors and egrets.

The road continues and reaches the D38. Turn right and directly after turn left onto a minor road (signposted *Astouin*).

PRACTICAL PART

ROUTE 3: AROUND SAINTES-MARIES-DE-LA-MER

5 The road turns right and runs through some rice paddies edged by reeds. Glossy Ibis is common here, next to Gull-billed Tern and Whiskered Tern (during migration). The reeds offer excellent shelter for Purple and Squacco Herons. In the turn the road meets with the dike behind which the Petit Rhône flows. You can park here and walk towards the left over the dike. Note the sign stating that it is not allowed to follow the dike by car. After several metres, you will have a viewpoint over the Little Rhône on your right. Between late spring and early autumn, this is also a good site for dragonflies. From August onwards, look for the beautiful Banded Darter.

All European heron species breed in the Camargue. The Purple Heron is one of the more common ones in the reed marsh.

Where the road meets with the D38c turn left. You will cross a bridge over the Petit Rhône. Directly after the bridge turn left, following a sign with *Bac Sauvage*.

6 The road passes through fields, paddies, reedbeds and salt marshes. Look here for the same birds as mentioned earlier on. Also check the wires for Bee-eater and look for Squacco Heron – the latter is a fairly scarce species that seems to be a little more common around these parts. This is another interesting area for dragonflies too, such as Orange-spotted Emerald and Blue Chaser.

The road leads you south towards a ferry that takes you over the Petit Rhône (free of charge). While waiting for the ferry to arrive, check tamarisks for migrating birds (there can be large numbers of Pied Flycatchers here) and enjoy the view over the Petit Rhône. With luck, you may see a Kingfisher racing by.

Once across, the road will meet with the D38. Turn right to return to Saintes-Maries-de-la-Mer.

CROSSBILL GUIDES • PROVENCE

Route 4: Étang de Scamandre

2-3 HOURS, 4.5 KM
EASY

Beautiful freshwater marshes with the largest reedbeds of the country. Best route to see reedbed birds.

Habitats reedbeds, freshwater lagoons
Selected species Purple Gallinule, Bearded Tit, Moustached Warbler, Melodious Warbler, Night Heron, Purple Heron, Great Bittern, Little Bittern, Glossy Ibis, European Pond Terrapin

The Étang de Scamandre (with surrounding lakes) is the largest reedbed area in France. It is also the most accessible one in the Camargue. This route promises a relaxing stroll through the reeds and along freshwater marshes, where birds are the key attraction. Étang de Scamandre hosts a large egretry, which is one of the few places where Glossy Ibis breeds (in large numbers). It is also the main place in France with breeding Purple Gallinules. So plenty of reasons to visit this nature reserve. Access is free.

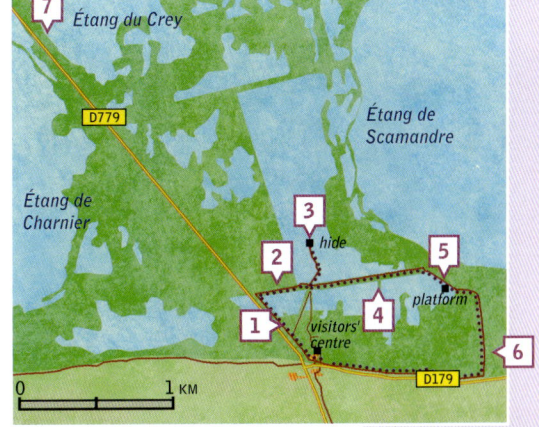

There are two options: a long route around the area and a short route over boardwalks through the marsh. We describe the longer one because it is the most attractive for birds, but the short route does offer some beautiful scenery. Choose, if possible, a wind-free day, as the birds show themselves much better.

Starting point Visitors centre' Étang de Scamandre on the D179 at the crossing with the D779. (GPS 43.605663, 4.337490)

1 Follow the trail past the visitors' centre to the left from the parking place. On your right are several large ditches with European Pond Terrapin and Little Grebe.

PRACTICAL PART

ROUTE 4: ÉTANG DE SCAMANDRE

2 The trail turns right and follows the edge of a large reedbed. Tall reeds block the view over much of this stretch, but there are places where you can peek into the reedbeds. Use every opportunity to do so, as this is where Purple Gallinule breeds, plus other species like Bearded Tit, Moustached Warbler, Reed and Great Reed Warblers and Purple Heron. On the other side of the trail there is a lagoon on which you can find Red-crested Pochard and sometimes Ferruginous Duck. Also keep an eye out for Night Heron. The best spot to look for Purple Gallinule is found at the end of the reedbed where the vegetation is lowest and a small sluice offers a good viewpoint.

Turn left at the crossing.

3 This path runs over a boardwalk between some lagoons to a hide. This is a very good spot to look for wildfowl. Also Coypus can be found here.

Return to the crossing and turn left.

4 In the tamarisks to your right you can overlook a heronry with Grey Heron, Little and Cattle Egret and Glossy Ibis. With telescope, you have excellent views on the nests.

The marshes of the Étang du Crey (point 7; top). The reedbeds around the Étang du Scamandre host a healthy population of Little Bitterns (bottom).

5 Continue the route to another viewpoint. From here you can overlook the tamarisk marsh and the Étang de Scamandre and its reedbeds.

6 The road loops back to the visitors' centre, passing through damp woodland and some fields. You can find Melodious Warbler, Hoopoe, Nightingale and Cetti's Warbler here.

7 If your hunger for marshbirds isn't satisfied, follow the D779 in northern direction, which passes between Étang du Charnier and Étang du Crey and their extensive reedbeds.

CROSSBILL GUIDES • PROVENCE

Route 5: The Eastern Camargue

6 HOURS, 40 KM
ONE WAY

One of the most bird rich areas of the Camargue, with views of the flamingo colony.

Habitats brackish meadow, salt marsh, saltpans, woodlands, reedbeds, lagoons
Selected species Greater Flamingo, Kentish Plover, Slender-billed Gull, Greater Spotted Eagle (scarce, winter), Spectacled Warbler, Curlew Sandpiper, Giant Orchid, Lizard Orchid, European Pond Terrapin, Western Green Lizard, White-tailed Skimmer, Blue Chaser

This route leads you to from verdant riverine forest to the wind-beaten and sun-scorched salt steppes of the Camargue, all the way down to, eventually, the sea. Along the route, which leads over a quiet backroad with little traffic besides birdwatchers, you pass reedbeds, woodlands, *sansouires* and *pelouses*. It goes without saying that such a large stretch with such a varied landscape hosts a diverse flora and fauna. As everywhere in the Camargue, birds are key, but in this case, reptiles and wildflowers are of interest too.
This route is equally attractive for cyclist as for car drivers. The first should realise that the winds can be (very) fierce and that there is no shade on the last stretch.

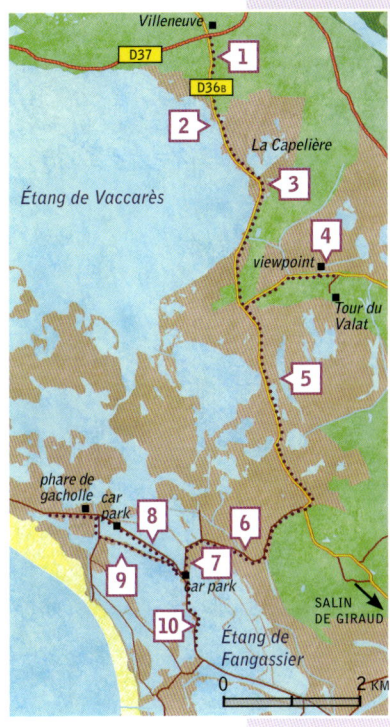

Starting point Villeneuve on the junction of the D36b and D37 (GPS: 43.573761, 4.623604).

Getting there From the Musée du Parc follow the D570 towards Saintes-Maries-de-la-Mer. After Albaron, turn left on the D37 towards Salin de Giraud. Turn right at Villeneuve onto the D36b.

ROUTE 5: THE EASTERN CAMARGUE

1 The first few hundred metres, the road passes through some lush woodland. It is interesting to take this landscape in for a second, as it could not be more at odds with the open salt steppes at the end of this route.

2 Further along, the road edges the Étang de Vaccarès with reedbeds and tamarisks on either side of the road. This large central lagoon of the Camargue has an interesting biology: the water on its northern end is fresh. Salinity gradually increases as you proceed further towards the coast. Hence, it is reedbeds (which depend on fresh water) that grow on the shores here, while the salt tolerant glassworts dominate further down. This point on the north shore is where most water birds usually are, seeking shelter from the fierce northerly winds. Another interesting feature is that the lagoon is for the larger part very shallow. It is possible to see flamingos standing in the middle of the lake.

There are various places to stop, such as near the conspicuous dead tree on your right, which has a Grey Heron colony. We also found White-tailed Skimmer (a dragonfly) hereabouts.

3 On the left side of the road lies the reserve of La Capelière. It is a private nature reserve (entry € 3) with a 1.5 km trail through damp woodland, meadows and reedbeds and some freshwater lagoons overlooked by hides. It is an attractive walk, not in the least as it brings you into the woodland – a hard-to-explore habitat in the Camargue. The woodland hosts Green Woodpecker, Blackcap, Nightingale, Cetti's Warbler and there is a colony of White Storks. Around the lagoons, Purple Heron and Black-Winged Stilt can be found. This site is best in winter, when lots of ducks take shelter in the tree-lined lagoons. European Pond Terrapin can be found in the ditches along the trail and a Western Green Lizard may slip away in front of you.

The Étang de Vaccarès in winter.

Continue the road and after several kilometres turn left to Tour du Valat.

ROUTE 5: THE EASTERN CAMARGUE

4 This road passes through some Glasswort scrublands with a viewpoint at the left side of the road. From the viewpoint you overlook a lagoon with a chance of herons and many ducks during winter. The lake is distant and a telescope is not a luxury. In the scrubland, look for Corn Bunting, Whinchat, Yellow Wagtail. Check the wires along the road for Bee-eaters.
Continue the road until a track to Tour du Valat branches off to the right. Tour du Valat is a research centre for the conservation of marshlands as well a a natural area of almost 3,000 hectares (only accessible on guided excursions; see **www.tourduvalat.org**). At crossing look for orchids like Giant and Western Spider Orchid* (*Ophrys exaltata*) in March and Lizard and Pyramidal Orchid in May – June.

You can see European Pond Terrapins from the hides in La Capelière.

Return the way you came and continue your way south.

5 The road passes through a scenically attractive stretch of saltmarsh with tamarisks at the side of the road. Along the ditches on the side of the road masses of Yellow Iris grow.

A few kms ahead, the road turns right. Ignore the turn to the left. Instead, go straight, direction *Digue a la Mer*.

6 After a short stretch through a remarkably lush patch of woodland (indicating freshwater), you finally enter the open plains of the salt steppes. From here on, salt rules the ecosystem. The salt steppes are a part of the salt pan system of Salin de Giraud. Some are nearly dry, while others are inundated.

A little further on, the tarmac gives way to a very potholed (but driveable) dirt road. Proceed.

7 The second saltpan on the left is the Étang de Fangassier where the Flamingo colony of the Camargue resides. Check the edges of the saltpans for waders like Kentish Plover and migratory species like Dunlin, Sanderling, Curlew Sandpiper, Little Stint, Ringed Plover, Grey Plover,

ROUTE 5: THE EASTERN CAMARGUE

Spotted Redshank and of course masses of Greater Flamingos. Check the gulls carefully for Slender-billed Gull, which is fairly common in this area. At sunset, this site is a beautiful spot to watch flamingos which, when returning to the colony, fly in front of the setting sun.

8 After 500 metres over this dirt road, you arrive at a car park. From here you can explore the saltpans in three directions. One of these is the path to the Phare de la Gacholle (also explorable by car). Salt flats expand on either side. Look in the glasswort scrub for Yellow Wagtail and Tawny Pipit. All breed, but during passage, their numbers are augmented by migrants. These bushes are also the haunt of Spectacled Warbler, which is largely restricted in France to two areas – the saline Camargue and the Valensole plain (route 21). Check wet patches for waders and look in the tamarisk bushes for migratory birds. Almost anything is possible: Woodchat Shrike, Wood Warbler, Pied Flycatcher, etc. These bushes are the very first shelter birds encounter after crossing the Mediterranean Sea.

At the end of the trail you arrive at the *Phare de la Gacholle*, where some low bushes form an excellent migrant trap. There is a hide that overlooks a lagoon. With a scope you can find massive numbers of waders here like the previous waders but also Bar-tailed Godwit, Redshank, Oystercatcher and Avocet.

Around sunset, the flamingos fly right overhead as they move from their feeding grounds to the colony in Étang du Fangassier. A great photo opportunity.

9 The second trail is like the previous one but follows a sandy, narrow dam with an attractive flora that includes Coris, Rosy Garlic, Curry Plant, Mediterranean Lineseed and Hollow-Stemmed Asphodel. Sometimes birds take shelter against the wind. When we were walking here in early May we discovered several Tawny Pipits, Northern Wheatears and even a Wryneck.

10 The third track is a continuation of the main track which ends at a barrier after around 300 metres. From here you have the best views over the Étang de Fangassier. In the distance, you can see a broad pink band: thousands of Flamingos in their colony. Also, this is an excellent spot for Slender-billed Gull.

Route 6: Along 'La Digue'

**UP TO A FULL DAY
10 KM, ONE WAY**

! Large sections without shade

Splendid tour along the coast.
Large numbers of waders and migrant birds in spring and autumn.

Habitats brackish lagoons, beach and sea, dunes, coastal lagoons
Selected species Greater Flamingo, Grey Plover, Curlew Sandpiper, Oystercatcher, Kentish Plover, Spectacled Warbler, Spanish Psammodromus, Curry Plant, Giant Orchid

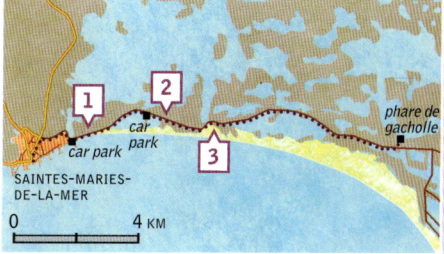

'La digue' shields the Étang de Vaccarès from the Mediterranean Sea. On both sides you are treated to some of the finest salt marshes the Camargue has to offer. This is a wild and open landscape with lots of birds.

The long dam can be covered on foot or by bicycle and you can start either in Saintes-Maries-de-la-Mer or at the car park near Étang de Fangassier (see previous route). To reach the latter it requires a longish drive, hence we describe the route from Saintes-Maries-de-la-Mer. Note that in this open landscape, there is no escape from wind or sun. Check the weather forecast and avoid going out in heavy mistral or when thunderstorms are forecast. The digue is a popular route during the tourist season. At that time, it is advisable to leave early.

Starting point Saintes-Maries-de-la-Mer (GPS: 43.456227, 4.444021). Follow the seaside boulevard in an easterly direction. At the eastern roundabout, go left and the first right again (*Aire Camping-Car Plage Est*). Follow this road to the car park at the end of the road. Park and continue on foot.

1 During migration periods, check the tamarisks near the car park and further on along the digue. They are real 'migrant traps': exhausted migrating birds often drop into them after their big trip over the Mediterranean.

ROUTE 6: ALONG 'LA DIGUE'

2 The small dike and the dunes form the border between the sea and the coastal lagoons, which offer excellent opportunities to watch birds. In winter, Shovelers, Pintails, Wigeons, Pochards and Teals are frequent here. Little Egrets and Flamingos are present all year round. Between August and April, the great attraction is the large number of waders, which typically include Redshank, Grey Plover, Black-tailed and Bar-tailed Godwits, Kentish Plover, Dunlin, Sanderling, Curlew Sandpiper, Avocet, Black-winged Stilt and Oystercatcher. The glasswort bushes attract Yellow Wagtails, Skylarks and quite a few Crested Larks. This is also the most reliable spot for the Spectacled Warbler: a rare and hard-to-find bird.

The dike and dunes are a good place for a tranquil exploration of the flora. Look for Sea Chamomile, Curry Plant and Golden Samphire. In late winter and early spring, you can admire Giant Orchids along the dike. In late summer, Banded Darter (a dragonfly) is sometimes seen here.

The seemingly endless 'digue' crosses equally eternal saltmarshes (bottom). It is an area where you can find many waders, often in big flocks. Dunlin (top) is one of the more common species.

3 About 6 kilometres from the departure point you will cross a bridge and enter the Camargue reserve proper. The landscape ratchets up a notch on the scenery scale with even wider vistas and more extensive salt marshes.

You can walk all the way to the Phare de Gacholle (see point 8 of the previous route). The way back is the same as the way you came.

Route 7: Via La Palissade to the coast

6 HOURS, 24 KM
EASY-MODERATE

!

This is the route for pink salinas and dune flora.
One of the best places to find waders, terns and other salt loving species.

Careful, pickpockets active in the area

Habitats salt marsh, saltpans, saltwater lagoons, dunes, beach
Selected species Slender-billed Gull, Avocet, Little Tern, Sandwich Tern, Curlew Sandpiper, Kentish Plover, Spanish Psammodromus, Blue Iris, Sea Bindweed, Sea Spurge, Sea Daffodil

This route will take you through the most extreme salt habitats of the Camargue. The first stretch leads past the 'salines' of the Camargue where the famous Camargue salt is produced. Along the way towards the coast you will pass through saltwater lagoons which are excellent for waders and 'lagoon birds', like Slender-billed Gull, Avocet and Little Tern.
The route passes the Domaine de la Palissade, a private reserve with hides and boardwalks, and ends on the beach. Here you can explore the dunes on foot.

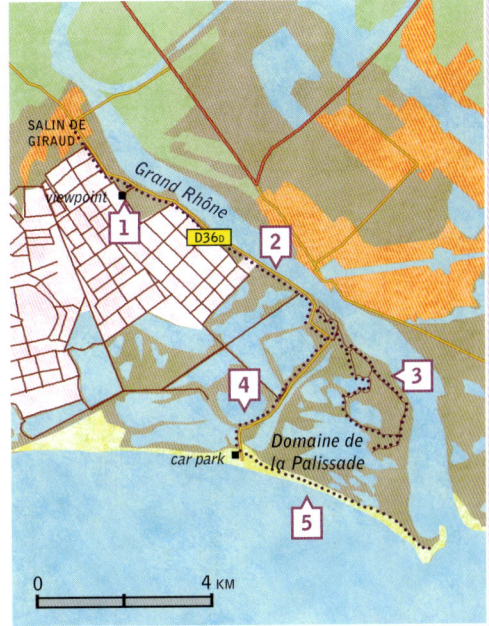

Starting point Salin de Giraud.
(GPS: 43.415808, 4.737539)
Take the D36d southwards.

1 After 1.6 kms, park at the viewpoint on your right and enjoy the otherworldish views of the salinas. The pink basins and salt mountains, divided by linear dikes, forms a strange, industrial landscape that has a peculiar attraction (bring sunglasses!). Salt production started at least as far back as the Romans and has ever since brought prosperity to the area. How important the salt

ROUTE 7: VIA LA PALISSADE TO THE COAST

production and export was, may be best exemplified by the elaborate trading routes that were built, running to the north and to the Italian region of Piedmont, which were all appropriately called *Route du Sel*.

2 The road continues parallel to the Rhône river, a verdant ribbon of trees in a landscape where salt inhibits the growth of trees. The riverine vegetation is once again excellent for migrants which use the trees as steppingstones during their journey north.

Continue your way and on your left you will find the Domaine de la Palissade.

3 The Domaine de la Palissade is one of the private reserves of Camargue (open from Feb. to Nov.). Entry is € 3.-, for which you can explore several trails of in total 8 kms and 2 hides. They lead you along the lagoons, salt marshes and sandy grasslands – the reserve's main habitats. In the grasslands, there is a fine population of spurges and Spurge Hawk-moth. The hides offer views of Flamingos, the typical waders of the Camargue and, in winter, a lot of wildfowl. For opening hours, see **www.palissade.fr**.

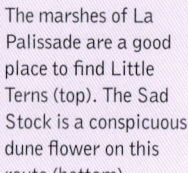

The marshes of La Palissade are a good place to find Little Terns (top). The Sad Stock is a conspicuous dune flower on this route (bottom).

ROUTE 7: VIA LA PALISSADE TO THE COAST

Return to the car and proceed towards the beach.

4 There are saline lagoons on either side of the road, which are excellent for finding Slender-billed Gull, Curlew Sandpiper, Avocet, Little Stint, Dunlin, Red Knot and Kentish, Ringed and Grey Plovers. Keep an eye out for Little Tern that sometimes hunts here.

The road ends at a car park. Walk along the dunes towards the mouth of the Rhône river.

5 This is one of the few places where you can easily reach the dunes of the Camargue. If you are familiar with the dunes of the Atlantic, these are surprisingly low. Whereas the Atlantic transports loads of sediments towards the coast and has a large tidal difference, the Mediterranean Sea is poor in sediments and there is little ebb and flow. The dunes are consequently much lower. They nevertheless support a rich flora with Sea Spurge, Sea Bindweed, Sea Holly, Sad Stock, Sea Medick, Sea Rocket, Sea Daffodil and two species of sea-lavender.
Looking out over the sea, you can find Sandwich Terns and, in winter, Gannet.
You can walk all the way to the mouth of the Rhône River.

The lagoons hold spectacular numbers of Slender-billed Gulls, which are often close to the road and show themselves well.

Return via the way you came.

PRACTICAL PART

ROUTE 8: CRAU – PEAU DE MEAU RESERVE

Route 8: Crau – Peau de Meau reserve

**2-3 HOURS, 4.2 KM
EASY**

!
Permit required, to be obtained in Saint-Martin-de-Crau

The heartland of the steppes of la Crau.
Rich birdlife with chance on seeing Lesser Kestrel, Pin-tailed Sandgrouse and Little Bustards.
Surprisingly rich dragonfly fauna.

Habitats Stony steppes, channel
Selected species Iberian Jerusalem-sage, Black Kite, Stone Curlew, Red-legged Partridge, Calandra Lark, Short-toed Lark, Little Bustard, Pin-tailed Sandgrouse, Ocellated Lizard, Lesser Purple Emperor, Banded Darter, Orange-spotted Emerald, Copper Demoiselle, Predatory Bush-cricket

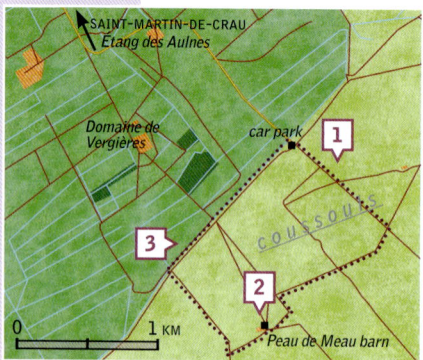

This short walk brings you into the heartland of the dry *coussouls* of the Crau. This is a habitat that has no equivalent anywhere else in France. At first glance this seems a monotonous plain but it harbours one of the most special and sensitive bird and plant communities in France. An additional attraction is a glimpse into the life of the traditional shepherds, who have largely shaped the unique Crau ecosystem. To see the special birdlife, you'd best do this walk very early in the morning, starting just before sunrise. Note that you need a permit to get in the reserve, which you can obtain during office hours in the visitors' centre of Saint-Martin-de-Crau, 10 kms from the start of the walk (so best obtained the day before). This route is the same as the one described on the brochure you get from the visitors' centre and is also recognisable in the field by the information panels along the path. Pick a day without the mistral (if you have the luxury). A telescope may come in handy.

Starting point Maison de la Crau in Saint-Martin-de-Crau (GPS: 43.637129, 4.806231; see map on page 143). The visitors' centre lies on the main road through the town, next to the church. It has a great exhibition on the Crau life.

ROUTE 8: CRAU – PEAU DE MEAU RESERVE

Follow the main road in eastern direction and turn right after 350 metres towards Arles, Mas Thibert and Étang des Aulnes. Cross the N113 road and continue on the D24 past the railway station and the industrial area, all the while following Fos-sur-Mer. Past the industrial area, turn left to Étang des Aulnes (worth a stop for Gull-billed and Caspian Terns, plus butterflies like Lesser Purple Emperor). The road turns left before the *Domaine de Vergières* and then right, through a forested patch until the *coussouls* plain opens up to you. Here is a car park on your right from which the route starts.

Follow the track on foot further onto the plain.

1 This is the dry coussouls, with all its plants, insects and birds. Look carefully for plants (e.g. Iberian Jerusalem-sage, Hollow-stemmed Asphodel, Illyrian Thistle) and for the birds of the steppes. In the hotter months you'll see Blue-winged Grasshoppers, Giant Antlion and, with a little effort, Praying Mantis or the Predatory Bush-cricket, a ferocious-looking locust that preys on other grasshoppers (see page 114). Among the butterflies, Spanish Gatekeeper and Marbled White are present.

Take your time on this walk to appreciate the subtle difference in vegetation on the *coussouls*. From a steppe bird's perspective, the grazing pressure is the most important factor in deciding which piece of land to occupy. The grassy patches attract Little Bustards, while Pin-tailed Sandgrouse fancy the bleaker terrain. Other birds you may find are Crested, Calandra and Short-toed Larks, Red-legged Partridge, Short-toed Eagle, Hoopoe, Tawny and, in autumn, Richard's Pipit and Dotterel.

A striking feature of this landscape is the stone piles, put there by the German

The impressive coussouls steppe of La Crau (bottom) holds one of the healthiest populations of Little Bustards of France (top).

PRACTICAL PART

ROUTE 8: CRAU – PEAU DE MEAU RESERVE

forces in the Second World War in order to make the plain unsuitable for Allied planes to land. Today these piles form the necessary breeding holes for Ocellated Lizards, Little Owls and Lesser Kestrels. Scan them carefully for birds.

After 900 metres, follow the track to the right. It leads through the *coussouls* to the barn of *Peau de Meau*.

2 Peau de Meau is a 150 years old barn oriented such that its full length is exposed to the mistral, creating a luxurious wind shelter. The eastern wall is also of interest as it shows the traditional engravings of all the shepherds who have used the building over its long existence.
Part of the barn is redecorated as a hide from which you can observe steppe birds. Don't expect the avian wealth you see from the average Camargue hide. Watching birds from the Peau de Meau hide takes patience. In summer, this is a good spot to see Little Owls, Jackdaws, Lesser Kestrels, Stone Curlews and Pin-tailed Sandgrouse (the latter mostly as fly-bys in the very early and late hours; you detect them first by their calls).

The Orange-spotted Emerald is one of 49 different species of dragonflies known from the Canal de Vergières.

Continue beyond the barn and turn right onto a track towards the trees and the channel. Just before the channel, there on your left the remains of a Roman sheep barn.
Turn right and follow the path along the *Canal de Vergières*.

3 If you thought this walk is all about the dry coussouls, the Canal de Vergières may come as a surpise. It is fed with ground water and of great interest for its many species of dragonflies and damselflies. With 49 species counted, it tops the list of the most interesting dragonfly spots in France. Look for Copper and Western Demoiselles (which occur in large numbers), Common Goldenring, Orange-spotted Emerald, Spotted and Banded Darters). During the summer months this is also a good spot to search for the Predatory Bush-cricket.

Additional remarks Due to the sensitivity of the area it is forbidden to stray off the indicated circuit.

Route 9: The Wet Crau and Marais de Vigueirat

5-6 HOURS, 35 KM
ONE WAY

A wonderful route from the dry Crau to the wet Marais.
A little visited and exquisite route for fauna, flora and landscape.

Habitats stony steppes, garrigue, meadows, hedgerows, swamp forests, reed-beds and lagoons
Selected species Little Bustard, Stone Curlew, Roller, Great Spotted Cuckoo, Purple Heron, Squacco Heron, Bee-Eater, Beaver, Coypu, Western Green Lizard, European Pond Terrapin, White-tailed Skimmer, Spring Snowflake, Loose-flowered Orchid, Meadow Orchid

The Crau consists of two parts: a dry, stony steppe, which is most well-known, and a wet, boggy zone that is surprisingly unknown. That is remarkable considering what can be found here: Rollers, Savi's Warblers, Little Bustards, Great Spotted Cuckoos, Meadow and Loose-flowered Orchids and many more. Not all of it is easy to find, but nevertheless, you should have a rewarding field trip on the edge of the dry and wet Crau.
This route zigzags from dry to wet Crau and ends at the Marais du Vigueirat, an outlier of the Camargue, yet one of its finer marshes, fed by ground water. The landscape is pleasant and leads over picturesque country roads.

Starting point Saint-Martin-de-Crau (GPS: 43.637129, 4.806231).

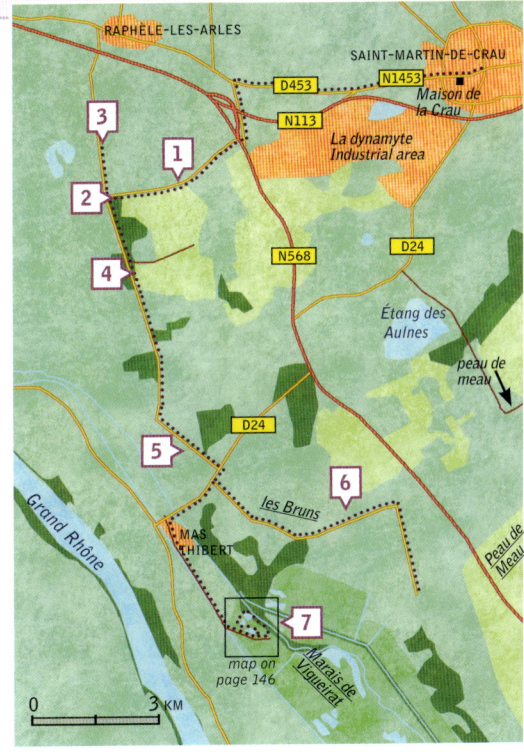

PRACTICAL PART

ROUTE 9: THE WET CRAU AND MARAIS DE VIGUEIRAT

Leave in the direction Arles on the N1453. Before turning onto the N113 motorway, turn right, following signs for Raphèle, onto the D453. After 2.6 km turn left towards Fos-sur-Mer. You'll pass underneath the railway and over the motorway and arrive at an intersection. Follow the direction Arles but instead of turning right onto the N568 toward Arles, cross the road onto a minor road leading into the *Domaine des Chanoines* (note the little sign on the right side of the road).

1 This small road brings you to the northwestern part of the dry Crau. On the left there is a large area of *coussouls* (dry steppe), alternating with alfalfa fields. Look here for Stone Curlew, Little Bustard (which prefers Alfalfa fields in spring), Red-legged Partridge, Corn Bunting and Crested Lark. Raptors include Black Kite (common) and Marsh and Montagu's Harrier (in spring and summer), and Red Kite and Hen Harrier (in winter). Here and for the remainder of the route, be alert for Roller, Great Spotted Cuckoo, Lesser Kestrel and Hobby – all spring and summer birds of the Crau, which, although not common, have a stronghold in this region.

Loose-flowered Orchids grow by the side of the road that crosses the wet Crau (top). You have great views of the colony of Bee-eaters near the entrance of the Marais de Vigueirat. Besides bees and dragonflies, the birds feed on cicadas (bottom).

2 Beyond the fields lies a rocky *garrigue* woodland on your left dominated by Holm and Kermes Oak and lots of Grey-Leaved Cistus. The roadside is full of Western Spider Orchid* (*Ophrys exaltata*) in late winter and early spring.

At the intersection, turn left to follow the route, but before you do, we advise to make a short detour to the right.

ROUTE 9: THE WET CRAU AND MARAIS DE VIGUEIRAT

3 After 1 km, you arrive at the lowest point of the Crau. Park and explore the wet meadows and sedge marshes on either side of the road. You can't enter them, but from the road you can spot (with bins) the stout flowers of the rare Meadow Orchid* (*Anacamptis palustris*) in the fields. Note the 'odd-shaped reeds', which are actually plants of the Great Fen-sedge, indicating calcareous groundwater. Look for Savi's and Great Reed Warblers here, plus the birds mentioned at point 1.

Return to the junction and go straight.

4 The road leads through more *coussouls* landscape and even some *garrigue* on the remains of marine limestone hills that surfaced when the region rose during the Alpine orogenesis (see geology section). The valleys were filled up by sediments from the Durance, but this crest just kept (by centimetres) its head above the surface!
There are various tracks that cross the *garrigue* which you can follow on foot (check carefully that you're not trespassing private property). Look in the roadside and *garrigue* for orchids in early spring. Giant Orchid, Black Spider and Western Spider Orchids occur here.
On the other side (a few hundred metres) you arrive at more *coussouls*, with chances on seeing Stone Curlew and Little Bustard.

5 The road gradually descends and brings you to the wet Crau again, with grassy meadows and hedgerows with Elm, Ash and Poplar trees. Look and listen for Green Woodpecker, Golden Oriole and Turtle Dove. Also check the wires for Roller and Bee-Eater. Just before the junction with the D24 towards Mas Thibert, note the Loose-flowered Orchids on the left side of the road in April and May. It's a typical species of wet meadows.

There are some wonderful swamp forests on the trail through the Marais de Vigueirat.

PRACTICAL PART

ROUTE 9: THE WET CRAU AND MARAIS DE VIGUEIRAT

Turn right towards Mas Thibert and directly left again, into an area called 'les Bruns'.

6 This road leads through area on the transition zone of wet and dry. You can find 'wet Crau species' here like Loose-flowered Orchid (abundant in the side of the road), but also pass through much drier scrublands. The whole area is suitable for Roller and a variety of raptors.

Beavers evidently appreciate the trees in Marais de Vigueirat.

Return to the D24 and turn left to Mas Thibert. In the village turn left following the signs Marais du Vigueirat.

7 The Marais du Vigueirat has swamp forest (with Ash, Elm and Poplar trees), mixed with lagoons, reedbeds and meadows in the north and a huge area of reedbeds in the south. The latter rivals Étang de Scamandre in size, but is not accessible, except with a guide (see page 152).

In the northern section, you can walk a wonderful loop (€ 3,- entry) over boardwalks through swampy terrain that you would otherwise not be able to cross, offering an opportunity to observe birds (e.g. Squacco, Night and Purple Herons, Great White Egret, Whiskered Tern, Hobby, Kingfisher and a variety of ducks in winter). European Pond Terrapin and Coypu are common in the water. On the boardwalk you can find Wall and Western Green Lizards and various dragonflies. Keep an eye out for Montpellier and Viperine snakes. Most attractive is the large colony of Bee-eaters near the entrance of the reserve.

Return via the same way.

Route 10: A walk in Les Alpilles

4-5 HOURS, 11.5 KM
MODERATE

Fine walk along massive chalk-white cliffs, through woodland and garrigue. Rare cliff-breeding birds.

Habitats Mediterranean scrubland and forest, rocks and crevices, karst plateau
Selected species Bonelli's Eagle, Short-toed Eagle, Wallcreeper (winter), Blue Rock Thrush, Rock Thrush, Alpine Swift, Black-eared Wheatear, Subalpine Warbler, Ladder Snake, Giant Orchid, Western Spider Orchid*, Violet Bird's-nest, Bastard Balm, Blue Aphyllanthes

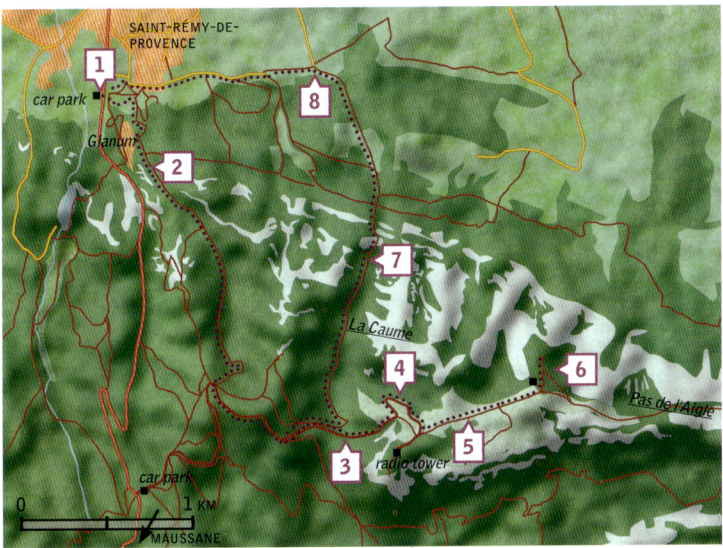

The Alpilles are fascinating – small and low, yet wild and rocky. This grandness on a small scale is probably what gave the range its name: Alpilles – little Alps. The range nevertheless has all the trimmings of true mountains: massive cliffs, steep slopes and karst plateaux. This is one of the driest and hottest mountains in the whole of France and therefore harbour a special flora and fauna.

PRACTICAL PART

ROUTE 10: A WALK IN LES ALPILLES

Opposite page:
There are some great wildflowers to be found on this walk, such as Violet Bird's-nest Orchid (top), Yellow Leek (centre) and Woodcock Orchid (bottom).

This route leads up to the limestone cliffs of La Caume – one of the scenic highlights of the Alpilles. Along the way, you'll be able to see some typical wildflowers of the region, plus a number of mountain birds, all in a setting that is nothing short of spectacular. Pick a clear day for this route and be amazed.

Starting point Saint-Rémy-de-Provence; the car park of the *Glanum* archaeological site (small fee; GPS 43.775906, 4.831171).

1. Before heading out, note the high numbers of Western Spider Orchids* (*Ophrys exaltata*) and Giant Orchids, both flowering in February/March. Look for Cirl Buntings too, which are numerous in these parts. With some luck you will find the first Two-tailed Pasha or Camberwell Beauty too (spring/summer).

As you come closer to the radio tower of la Caume, the views get more impressive with every step you take.

Walk towards the entrance of the archaeological site and follow the small trail to the left that crosses a field and arrives at the main trail. Turn right and walk around the perimeters of the archaeological site. At the Y-junction of trails, take the right branch following the valley behind the Glanum site.

CROSSBILL GUIDES • PROVENCE

ROUTE 10: A WALK IN LES ALPILLES

2 The walk up the mountain leads through a wonderfully shady, mixed forest of Aleppo pines, Downy and Holm Oaks, Atlas Cedars and several other Mediterranean trees. At regular intervals, small signs tell you about the trees and bushes along the route. Chaffinches, Crested Tits, Crossbills, Firecrest and Short-toed Treecreepers represent the birdlife. Along the path you will encounter many Blue Aphyllanthes (looking like an undistinguished rush until it displays its bright blue flowers at the end of April) and Bastard Balm (with its large, white with pink flowers). Keep an eye out for White Helleborine and Woodcock Orchid.

Once on the ridge you'll find a small paved road. Follow it to the left.

3 A little further ahead, the large radio tower of La Caume first appears from behind the trees. It is built on a massive cliff. From the ridge you have a beautiful view that becomes more impressive as you proceed. This is a good place to spot Short-toed and Bonelli's Eagles (although they remain rare), some of the cream of the Alpilles' birdlife. The even luckier sight is of an Egyptian Vulture soaring over. Blue Rock Thrush and Alpine Swift breed on the cliffs, which are in winter the haunt of the Wallcreeper, an Alpine bird that spends the cold months on the vertical rock faces of the Alpilles.

4 On your ascent to the radio tower it is worth checking the scrubland. Four species of *Sylvia* warblers live here: Blackcap, Sardinian Warbler, Dartford Warbler and Subalpine Warbler. Botanically, the Blue Aphyllanthes, Grey-leaved Cistus, Felty Germander, Blue Lettuce, Beautiful Flax, Joint-pine, White and Hoary Rockrose and Montpellier Milk-vetch are the eye-catchers.

Just before you reach the radio tower, take the track to your left.

5 You cross a stony plateau with a low *garrigue* of Box, Grey-leaved Cistus and Phoenician juniper. Of interest here is the Large

PRACTICAL PART

Joint-pine, a woody look-alike of the horsetails (and a natural drug). Woodlarks sing their *lulu*-song over the stony plateau, which is also a very good spot to search for reptiles of rocks and scrublands. Look again for the aforementioned warblers and Black-eared Wheatear. On some days, Alpine and Common Swifts swoop by at close range.

Follow the trail to another, much more modest radio tower. The trail curves around the tower and ends on a rocky outcrop.

6 Of all the splendid views you have been treated to already, this one is the winner. To your right you will see the Alpilles ridge running like a rocky spinal cord towards the east. The same raptors as mentioned before could be present here. If you wish, you can prolong your hike by continuing along the ridge. Follow the trail that splits off just before you reached the radio tower. Remember though that there is no trail leading down from the mountain so you'll have to walk the same way back.

Return. Once back at point 3, turn right onto a trail that descends on the northern slope and that indicates *St. Remy*.

7 The walk down offers a fine mixture of evergreen Mediterranean forest of Holm Oak and Maritime and Aleppo Pine, similar to the forest you traversed on your way up the mountain. A little further down you cross a small rocky gorge. Look here for warblers and Blue Rock Thrush.

At the first junction (*Mas de Seraillet*) go straight and turn left at the junction of tracks, following the GR white red signs which will bring you back to your starting point.

8 Look for orchids at the junction. We found Violet Bird's-nest, Western Spider Orchid* (*Ophrys exaltata*), Giant Orchid, Lady Orchid and White helleborine here.

Additional remarks

An alternative departure point for this route is south of St. Rémy on the road towards Maussane. More or less on the highest point you can park and walk eastwards on the small paved road (barred for cars) towards La Caume. As you start already on the ridge, this route is less demanding.

ADDITIONAL SITES IN THE CAMARGUE-CRAU-ALPILLES AREA

Additional sites in the Camargue-Crau-Alpilles area

A – Parc Ornithologique Pont de Gau

The Parc Ornithologique is an interesting place. It holds the middle between a nature reserve, a zoo with native, local birds, and an animal recovery centre. For naturalists, it is above all, a superb place to see birds from up close, offering excellent opportunities for photography. Pont de Gau is also great for families, as birdwatching is made so easy here.

!

The location of the sites described here is shown on the map on page 118.

Pont de Gau was founded in 1949, originally as a small zoo, but spread out to become a 60 hectares nature reserve, with all types of Camargue habitats. The habitats are carefully landscaped and managed, optimizing them for the birds that live there. There is in total 7 kilometres of trail that lead you through the site, from which you have excellent views of the birds. Many of them are residents of Pont de Gau and are used to people. They were found wounded or abandoned in the wild, and brought to Pont de Gau to recover. They are released back into the wild when they are fit enough. Those that aren't, stay in the reserve. It is the mix of recovering birds and wild ones that are attracted by the prime habitat, that make Pont de Gau such a great spot for birdwatching.

Pont de Gau is on the main D570 road, 4 kms out of Saintes-Maries-de-la-Mer. It is open year-round, and access is € 7.50 (€5.00 for children). For opening times, see **www.parcornithologique.com**.

B – Miscellaneous sites in La Crau

La Crau is a superb natural area, that, unfortunately, is highly fragmented. The unique birdlife includes spectacular species like Little Bustard, Stone Curlew, Pin-tailed Sandgrouse, Lesser Kestrel, Calandra and Short-toed Lark. Scarce breeding birds are Lesser Grey Shrike (perhaps now extinct), Roller and Great Spotted Cuckoo, while on passage, you may see Booted Eagle, Montagu's and Pallid Harriers, Red-footed Falcon, Richard's Pipit, Dotterel, etc. In short – a list that makes the heart of any birder beat faster.

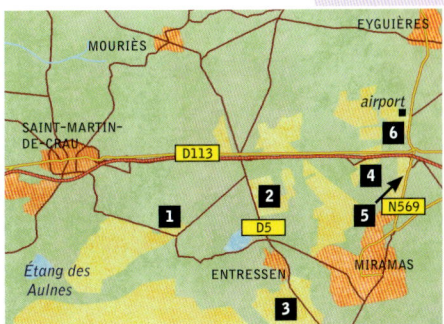

The best areas are described in routes 8 and 9, but here we mention some other spots, from where you can view good bird habitat from the road.

PRACTICAL PART

ADDITIONAL SITES IN THE CAMARGUE-CRAU-ALPILLES AREA

A shepherd with his dogs and herd in one of the many patches of *coussouls* in La Crau.

In order to visit these places, head east from Saint Martin de Crau on the D113 (parallel to the motorway) and then turn right on the D5 towards Entressen. There is a large gas distribution centre on your left. Turn right here (signposted CTBRU). After several kilometres you reach some areas of steppes (point 1 on the map).
Back on the D5, turn right, where you pass two more large areas of steppes (point 2 and 3), before and beyond Entressen village (careful where you park; the D5 is a busy road!). Return to the D113 and just before passing underneath the motorway, turn right onto the parallel road, which after several kms brings you to more steppe areas on your right, just before the entry to the motorway (point 4). At the latter junction, turn right to Istres on the N569, where the first kilometres take you along more *coussouls* (point 5). Heading the opposite direction, you can park at the aerodrome, where the grasslands hold good numbers of birds (point 6).

C – Guided excursion to the reedbeds of Marais du Vigueirat

The Marais du Vigueirat is a nature reserve between La Crau and the Camargue and is, together with Étang de Scamandre, among the largest freshwater marshes in the area. Swamp forests, reedbeds and open water are the main habitats. The Marais is part of route 9, but the large, reedy southern part of the reserve can only be visited on a guided excursion. These are not cheap (€ 18), but well worth the money as they take you to little visited parts of the region and usually offer fine views of the birds (the main attraction of the reserve). The typical Camargue birds can be found here, but also some harder-to-find ones, like Moustached Warbler and Great Bittern. There are guides who speak English and German.
For more information and bookings, visit **www.marais-vigueirat.reserves-naturelles.org** or ask at the reception.

ADDITIONAL SITES IN THE CAMARGUE-CRAU-ALPILLES AREA

D – Les Baux-de-Provence

The small village of Les Baux-de-Provence on the south side of the Alpilles sits beautifully and strategically on a rocky outcrop on the south side of the Alpilles. The young soft limestones are oddly sculpted, contributing to the enchantment of the place. In the middle ages, Les Baux was an important place, where the 'Lords of Les Baux' ruled, from the impressive hilltop fort, over a large part of Provence.
Today, the fort is in ruins, but still very much worth visiting, as are the narrow streets of the village itself. The best time for this is in winter, for one because it is not so busy with tourists, but much more so for the birdlife. Alpine Accentor visits the village and can be seen on the village streets, while several Wallcreepers are present in the area, often sitting on the walls of the fort, the houses or the cliffs around the village. Les Baux is often regarded as the easiest place in Europe to see this much sought-after species.

E – Canal de la Vallee des Baux

One unexpected, but very attractive spot to poke around, is the marsh along the Canal de la Vallee des Baux. It flows on the northern edge of the small limestone range just north of Saint-Martin-de-Crau, where it feeds some reedy marshes on the edge of the mountain. It is a very good site for Roller, Kingfisher, Green Woodpecker, Turtle Dove and Golden Oriole. It is a good spot for dragonflies too. Small Spreadwing, Orange Featherleg, Orange-spotted Emerald and Pronged Clubtail are just some of the attractions listed for this site. Getting to the Canal is easy: From Saint-Martin-de-Crau, follow the D27 to Maussane. Just after crossing the garrigue-clad hill, you cross the canal and directly thereafter you can park. Follow the dam on foot in eastern direction. The marshes are on your right after a few hundred metres.

The path along the Canal de la Vallee des Baux.

PRACTICAL PART

Côte d'Azur

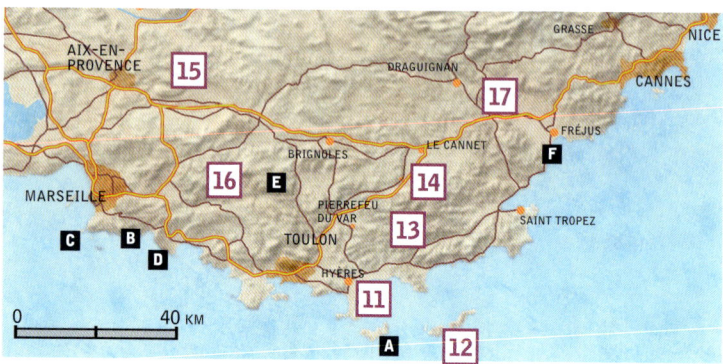

With the high mountains of the *Préalpes* blocking the northern mistral wind, the Côte d'Azur is the warm and sweet flower garden of France. The mild winters and warm summers create a perfect climate, the landscape is gorgeous and the water azure blue. It is no wonder that Europe's jetset has chosen the Côte d'Azur as a favourite hangout. In places, such as near Nice, Cannes and Saint-Tropez, this has resulted in a busy coast, but elsewhere and above all in the hinterland, the southern Provence maintains a wonderful, quiet and provincial atmosphere.

The landscape of the interior consists of low to mid-level mountain ranges, separated by relatively flat lowlands where the villages are situated and grapes and olives are grown. The flora and fauna are mightily rich. Within France, many species of warm Mediterranean climates only occur here (and again in Spain or Italy). This wealth is increased by the fact that there are both limestone (base-rich) and metamorphic (acidic) soils present, each with a different but special flora and fauna.

The following routes and sites will aid you in discovering the southern Provence. The first two (routes 11 and 12), plus the sites A, B, C and D described on pages 180 - 182 explore the coast, which is largely rocky. Route 11 and site F on page 183 are the exceptions – these introduce you to the small coastal marshes of the region. Be aware that the coastal areas are crowded with tourists during the holidays, especially in summer. The inland sites are much quieter. Here, route 13 and 14 explore acidic terrain, while routes 15 and 16 and site E on page 182 visit the limestone mountains. All these routes have a splendid flora and butterfly fauna, which is represented by different species in each of these routes. Route 17 is different as it focusses on riverine habitats.

Route 11: The saltpans of Giens

4-5 HOURS, 15 KM ONE WAY

The 'Little Camargue' – saltpans, waders, flamingos and a rich dune flora

! This site is very busy in summer

Habitats salt marsh, saltpans, dunes
Selected species Three-horned Stock, Sea Daffodil, Jupiter's-beard, Little Tern, Slender-billed Gull, Greater Flamingo, Kentish Plover, Black-winged Stilt

The saltpans of Giens lie between the double tombolo that connect the Presqu'île de Giens to the mainland. *Presqu'île* is literally 'almost island', which is an apt description as it is only two narrow strips of dunes with the saltpans in between, that connect the rocky peninsula of Giens to the mainland. Geologically it is, together with the Île de Porquerolles, Île Port-Cros (route 12) and Île du Levant, an offshore archipelago, which is in turn part of the Massif des Maures. The double tombolo (two parallel sand spits, deposited by the currents) is a geological highlight of its own – one of only two sites in the world where a double tombolo has formed.

The Presqu'île de Giens makes for a great birdwatching trip, especially if the Camargue is not on your agenda. Although no match for the actual Camargue, the good numbers of flamingos and a large variety of waders, terns and gulls make the saltpans of Giens a good alternative. During migration in spring and autumn, many birds that follow the coastline pause here for a moment, making it an exciting birdwatching spot.

This route connects two different areas of salt pans: the old pans near les Salins d'Hyères, and the larger Salins de Pesquiers. Note that the first are closed for visitors on Monday and Tuesday. The Salins de Pesquiers can always be visited, but this area is so crowded in July and August that

PRACTICAL PART

ROUTE 11: THE SALTPANS OF GIENS

we advise against it. The level roads, many of which have separate bicycle lanes, make this a perfect route to cycle.

The old saltpans of Giens with the Massif des Maures in the background.

Starting point Salins d'Hyères (GPS 43.116645, 6.197190)
Park near the stadium just behind the flats on the northwest of town (see map below). From here, a footpath leads into the saltpans and to an LPO-run visitors' centre.

1 These are the old saltpans of Hyères. With the hills of the Maures in the background and away from the built-up areas of the Côte D'Azur, this is quite a scenic place. Along the path, you have good views over the partially overgrown saltpans. In spring and autumn, there are large numbers of migrating waders, such as Wood Sandpiper, Redshank, Greenshank, Dunlin. Black-winged Stilt, Little Egret, Common Shelduck. Lots of Zitting Cisticolas and Sardinian Warblers breed on site. In the bushes look for Sardinian Warbler. Just beyond the little bridge over a canal, look on the right for Giant (Feb-March) and Yellow Bee Orchid (April). The latter is not frequently found in Provence.

2 On the eastern side of the village lies an observation platform that offers more views of the old saltpans.

Follow the D42 road towards Hyères Plage (when cycling, you have a separate lane that offers some good views over the salt marshes). In Hyères-plage, at the roundabout that forms the junction with the D197, take the first right, onto the car park *Arromanches*. Cross the roundabout on foot and overlook the lake on the opposite of the car park from the cycling lane.

3 This lake has brackish water and can be good for Shelducks and egrets, in addition to gulls and Common and Little Terns.

CROSSBILL GUIDES • PROVENCE

ROUTE 11: THE SALTPANS OF GIENS

Continue the D197 down to Presqu'île de Giens. Just beyond the sign of the village of la Capte, turn right onto the terrain of a large salt farm.

4 This area of the salt pans of the Salins de Pesquiers is managed by the *Conservatoire* and you can walk a small circuit over the dikes between the salinas. During migration, this can be excellent again for waders and there are often Flamingos.

Continue and on the roundabout, turn right, signposted *la Madrague* 3,5. Take the first right and find a parking spot somewhere between here and the barrier further ahead. Continue on foot all along the tombolo to the northern end of the Salins.

5 First, you pass two large basins on your right – part of the salt pans that are still in use. These are usually best for gulls (Yellow-legged, Slender-billed) and terns (Common, Little and Sandwich). The northern part is reserved for the older, partially overgrown basins, where waders and large numbers of Greater Flamingos can be seen.

You now walk over one of the two tombolos or sand spits that connect the Presqu'île de Giens with the mainland. The sandy strip has a great dune flora, with Sea Holly, Cottonweed, Sea Rocket, Sea Medick, the pretty pink Three-horned Stock (its only site in France) and the Jupiter's-beard (related to the vetches, but a bush growing 2 metres tall!), while the beautiful Sea Daffodil (flowering August – early October) reaches enormous densities.
To protect it against the masses of visitors, the dunes are shielded with fences, with regular paths from the salt pan side to the sea side of the tombolo.

A spring day on the seaside of the tombolo. The big, dark-leaved plants are Sea Daffodils that flower in summer (bottom). The Three-horned Stock has its only population in mainland France in these dunes (top).

PRACTICAL PART

Route 12: Île Port-Cros

FULL DAY, 12.1 KM
EASY-MODERATE

An island with stunning landscapes and uniquely intact Mediterranean vegetation.
Special flora and fauna – One of the few places in France to find 'Tyrrhenian' species.

Habitats Mediterranean woodland, Open sea, Shores, Seagrass beds
Selected species Yelkouan Shearwater, Cory's Shearwater, Pallid Swift, Alpine Swift, Blue Rock Thrush, Leaf-toed Gecko, Tyrrhenian Painted Frog, Tree Spurge, Jupiter's-beard, Neptune Grass

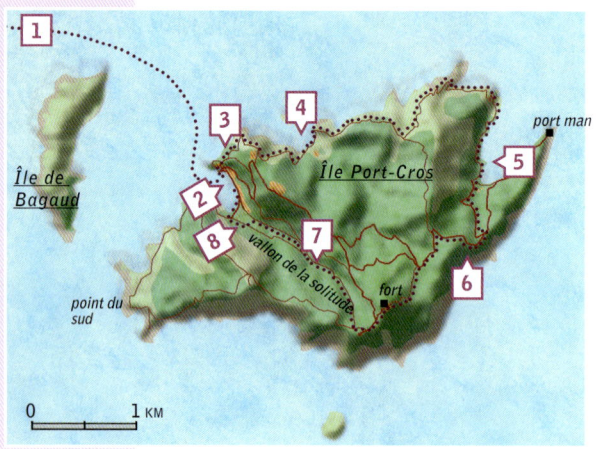

Île Port-Cros is one of the four islands of the Îles de Hyères. It harbours intact Mediterranean woodlands and a rich flora and fauna, which includes species that you also can find in Corsica, but (almost) nowhere else in mainland France, like Leaf-toed Gecko, Tyrrhenian Painted Frog, Jupiter's-beard and Tree Spurge. On the boat trip towards the island you have a good chance to see the endangered Yelkouan Shearwater. Around 90% of the French population breeds on these islands.

There are no roads on Île Port-Cros, but there is a network of trails. Here we describe a longish route with several options for short-cuts. Be sure to be in time for the return trip, as the boat will not wait!

Note that the marine part of the National Park is, with its intact Neptune Grass beds, at least as interesting. There is an underwater trail set out for snorkelers in the northern part of the island – an approximately 45 minute walk from the harbour (see point 4 on the map).

ROUTE 12: ÎLE PORT-CROS

Starting point boat trips can be booked from Port d'Hyères (**www.tlv-tvm.com**), La Londe-de-Maures (**www.bateliersdelacotedazur.com**) and Le Lavandou (**www.vedettesilesdor.fr**).
Boat trips cost between the €20-30 and leave in the morning, with the return trip in the late afternoon. Make sure not to miss your return trip!

1 The ferry stops at the island of Porquerolles first, which is similar to Port-Cros but inhabited and more touristy. During the trip, you're treated to wild cliffs and capes, which you will pass again once the ferry sets sail towards Île Port-Cros. Just west of Port-Cros lies the small Île de Bagaud, a strict reserve where only the National Park staff are allowed. Behind it lies the bay and harbour of Port-Cros.
During the trip you should be able to see Yelkouan Shearwaters and with luck you might even see its bigger brother, the Cory's Shearwater. In winter, there are Cormorants, Sandwich Terns and Gannets.

The Cory's Sheerwater is the rarer of the two shearwater species that can be seen from the boat to Île Port-Cros.

2 Port-Cros harbour consists of a tourist information centre, a post office, a hotel and four bars. In total no more than 40 people live on the island. At the information centre, you can buy a map of the island (€ 3) and several pamphlets (free). The helpful staff will also be able to provide you other information (in French).
In the harbour, examine the crystal-clear water and find sea cucumbers and many fish. Carefully check the swifts above you. All three species of France (Common, Pallid and Alpine Swift) breed on this small island! In the village and on rocky outcrops, you may find Blue Rock Thrush and Peregrine is also frequently seen.

From the village, take the trail up past the post office and towards a fort. Follow the signs for Port Man.

3 Now your trip through the Mediterranean forest begins! The trail runs over the northern slope where vegetation is dense and consists of Holm and Cork Oaks, Strawberry Tree and Aleppo Pine. In shrubby

PRACTICAL PART

ROUTE 12: ÎLE PORT-CROS

places look for Tree Spurge and Jupiter's-beard, which only occurs on these islands and the mainland coast opposite.

The old forest of Île Port-Cros is something special. It takes centuries to form such a mature woodland, because the rough Mediterranean climate does not allow fast growth, in particular on such a small, dry and wind-beaten island.

Along the way you will have multiple viewpoints over the sea. Crevices in rock formations and holes in trees are places to look for the elusive Leaf-toed Gecko. Note that Moorish and Turkish Gecko also occur on the island. In the underbrush, you may find Hermann's Tortoise and Ladder Snake.

The harbour of Port-Cros (top).
The trails over the island all lead through thick Mediterranean forest, alternated with *maquis* (bottom). Such undisturbed, original woodland is a rarity in the Mediterranean region.

4 You pass a small beach, covered in the washed up Neptune grass. This is the only part on the island where snorkelling is allowed. Wall Lizards are common on the beach.

Continue your way.

5 The next stop of note is a second, smaller beach. From here you can have a taste of the amazing sea life that can be found around the isle. From the rocks you can see the dark seagrass patches, which filter the water. All around it you can see different kinds of seaweeds and sea anemones.

ROUTE 12: ÎLE PORT-CROS

The area around the Island is a strictly protected marine reserve, the first in Europe. In 1999 it became part of the large International Sanctuary of Marine Mammals, which protects sea life, cetaceans in particular, between the French and Italian coast all the way to and beyond Corsica.

Continue your way. Once you arrive at a bigger track, turn right. A few metres further on, take a short trail to the left, to a viewpoint over the sea.

6 You arrive at the south side of the island. From here you look out over the Mediterranean Sea. Less than 2 km out at sea, the sea floor drops dramatically. An enormous submarine cliff runs from south of Marseille eastwards to the French-Italian border. It is on average 2km deep, but in places even a dazzling 5km. The edge of this cliff is where nutrient-rich water wells up from the deep, which is why whales and dolphins often feed here. Chances of seeing them at this distance are not that great, but Bottlenose and Striped Dolphin, Sperm Whale and Fin Whale have all been seen from the island.

Return towards the track and continue your way. Just after a curve to the right and once you arrive at a house, turn left onto a steep, small track. Follow it all the way up until you reach an old military fort. From here continue along the coast, ignoring the track to the right signposted *village* and turn right at the second track signposted to *Les Crêtes* marked by purple and green route markers. At the next sign, signposted for *Vallon de la Solitude*, turn right.

A jellyfish in one of the sheltered coves along the route.

7 The road makes a steep descent following a (partly dry) stream. Search here for the rare Tyrrhenian Painted Frog. The sheltered position of the valley allows for a very lush growth of trees.

Continue your way to the village.

8 The trees and the fields near the village are a true migrant trap where in spring and autumn, there can be massive falls of passerines. Also keep an eye out for Eleonora's Falcon in spring – it is sometimes seen hunting over the island. Closer by, note the Japanese Honeysuckle – not native, but nevertheless beautiful and with a very pleasant scent.

PRACTICAL PART

ROUTE 13: MASSIF DES MAURES

Route 13: Massif des Maures

6 HOURS, 72 KM

Scenic car route with short walks through forested hills.
Rich flora and fauna of crystalline hills – very different
from that of the other ranges.

Habitats cork oak woodland, maquis, stream, chestnut plantation
Selected species Strawberry Tree, Cork Oak, Narrow-leaved Helleborine,
Small-leaved Helleborine, Champagne Orchid, Narrow-leaved Cistus, Western
Spider Orchid*, Wild Tulip, Bonelli's Warbler, Firecrest, Common Redstart,
Hermann's Tortoise, Ladder Snake, Two-tailed Pasha, Chapman's Green
Hairstreak, Cleopatra, Small Pincertail, Copper Demoiselle

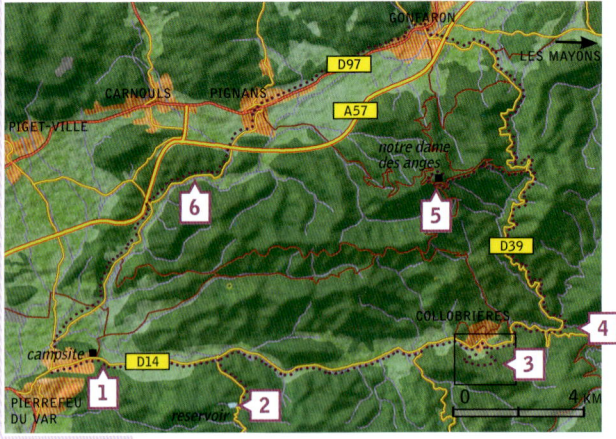

This beautiful car route is the perfect introduction to one of the most scenic parts of Provence – the Massif des Maures. This range is much more thickly forested than the other mountains in the region. The Cork Oak is the characteristic tree, although locally stands of Downy Oak and pine occur, while Strawberry Tree and Laurustinus are common in the undergrowth. Numerous small rivers lace the mountains and add to its lush character.
The best way to explore the Massif des Maures is by walking the trails in the area. The tourist office of Collobrières is a good starting point. The route we describe here is meant as a first orientation of the area, helping you to choose your walk, or as a 'best of', if you have only a day to spend. It combines various short walks along one of the prettiest roads of the region.

Starting point Pierrefeu du Var (GPS: 43.227679, 6.143222)

CROSSBILL GUIDES • PROVENCE

ROUTE 13: MASSIF DES MAURES

Leave town on the D14 in direction Collobrières. Just beyond the campsite, a small road, the *chemin de Maraval* turns left, direction *hameau de Tuilere* and a number of other *hameaus*. Park at this junction under the big cork oak tree and explore the woodland and roadside on the south side of the D14 road.

1 In March and early April, this is an excellent site for wildflowers, with many Broad-leaved Anemones and early orchid species, most notably *Ophrys arachnitiformis* (flowering March to early April), Champagne Orchid (endemic to the Iberian Peninsula and Provence), Giant and Dense-flowered Orchids.

Continue along the road to Colobrieres over the scenic road through vineyards and hills dominated by Cork Oaks.

Roughly 4 kms after the previous point, turn right onto a small road indicated La Londe. Follow it for 2 kms and park in the hairpin near the small reservoir.

2 The area around the reservoir (as well as the road leading up to it) is great to explore. The Cork Oak woods are lovely in spring, with Cirl Bunting, Bonelli's Warbler and Golden Oriole. There are also plenty of Black Kites, attracted to a concealed but nearby garbage dump. Look for wildflowers as well. There are plenty of Champagne Orchids below the dam and scattered in the forest, where you will also find good numbers of Violet Bird's-nest and a few Dense-flowered Orchids. Around the dam, Small-flowered Catchfly and the large, yellow-flowered rockrose *Tuberaria lignosa* put on a great show. Check the stream for Viperine Snake and the surrounding scrub for Western Green Lizard. The grassy area around the reservoirs is the preferred habitat of Three-toed Skink and the general site is as good as any for snakes and Hermann's Tortoise, which has its only population in France in and around the Massif des Maures.

Much of this route leads through beautiful Cork Oak forests (top). In grassy patches the rockrose *Tuberaria lignosa* is a common spring flower (bottom).

PRACTICAL PART

ROUTE 13: MASSIF DES MAURES

Return to the D14 and turn right towards Collobrières.

3 From this lovely village (which is ideal for a coffee stop), there is a great, 3 kms walk, the *Sentier Botanique*. It starts from the tourist office, which is on the main road, just after the second bridge that crosses the stream. From the tourist office, walk back to the bridge, and turn left through the narrow *Rue Gambetta* and find your way to the large church ruin on the eastern edge of the village. Here you pick up the signs of the *sentier botanique*.

The Massif des Maures is one of the few places in France where the Hermann's Tortoise lives. If you're lucky you stumble upon one.

On this walk you get a good view of the different environments of Massif des Maures. Four types of tree dominate here: the Cork Oak and Sweet Chestnut favour the shadier and damper parts of the slope. Both are used at least for a thousand years, as a source of food for both the people and their livestock. On the trail, you see many old chestnut groves, which were so important in bygone days.

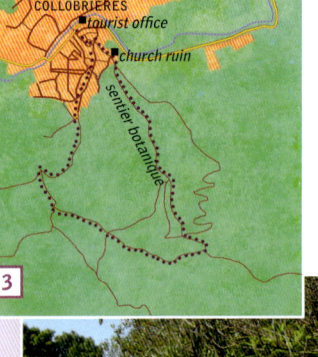

On the shallow, rocky soils, the Maritime Pine prevails, while in intermediate environments it is the Downy Oak that dominates the forest. The forest also has a diverse mix of shrubs and small trees, which thrive in the years after a forest fire or clearcut and persist for many years in the mature forest. Among them is the Strawberry Tree, larval food plant of two special, Mediterranean butterflies – Chapman's Green Hairstreak and Two-tailed Pasha. Another is the Manna Ash, which is mostly found in the East-Mediterranean region.

Continue by car further into the Massif des Maures. Some 2.5 kms beyond Collobrieres, turn left onto the D39 towards Gonfaron.

4 Just after the turn, you can stop at the river and walk the dirt road towards *Rascas* – not more than 200 metres. Here you have good views over the river, where you can look for Viperine Snakes. There are also some of Narrow-leaved Helleborines and Wild Tulips.

Continue for another 8.5 kms along the D39 towards the pass. At the crossing (with a cork oak in the middle), go left. Here you can either drive or park and walk the potholed tarmac track to the monastery of *Notre Dame des Anges* (5 km one way).

5 The first part of the road leads through a beautiful, shady Cork Oak and Sweet Chestnut wood, with occasional views over the forested Massif des Maures. In the undergrowth, there are many Strawberry Trees, so look again for the Chapman Green Hairstreak and Two-tailed Pasha.

From the Notre Dame des Anges chapel you have superb views down to the coast. On clear days, you can see with the Presque-île de Giens (route 11) and Île de Porquerolles (site A on page 180). Crag Martin, Green Woodpecker, Firecrest and both Common and Black Redstart are frequent around the chapel.

The river that flows through Collobrières (top). Wild Tulips grow in clumps along the river (bottom).

Return to the junction and turn left in the direction Gonfaron. On either side of the road there are tracks and small forest roads that you can explore on foot. The woodland here on the north-facing slope is denser and shadier, and there are countless rivulets that flow downhill.

Just before arriving at Gonfaron, you come to a T-junction. Turning right would take you to Les Mayons (6 kms), which is part of route 14 over the Plaine des Maures. This route, though, turns left into Gonfaron.

In the village, go left onto the D97 in the direction of Toulon. Follow this road until the next village, Pignans. Go straight at the roundabout with the supermarket and turn the first left, pass underneath the railroad and turn the first right, signposted *Pierrefeu du Var*.

6 This road first winds through some uninspiring outskirts of Pignans before passing underneath the motorway. The next and final section of this route leads through highly attractive woodlands again, with some areas of cistus scrub and small fields and vineyards.

Route 14: Plaine des Maures

5-6 HOURS, 33 KM
EASY

Lowlands with maquis and Umbrella pinewoods.
Temporary streams and puddles with a flora and fauna unlike any other in Provence.
Masses of tongue-orchids in spring.

Habitats garrigue, stream, lake
Selected species Wild Tulip, Loose-flowered Orchid, Heart-flowered, Provence and Scarce Tongue-orchids, Dartford Warbler, Subalpine Warbler, Short-toed Eagle, Golden Eagle, Hoopoe, Ocellated Lizard, Natterjack Toad, Southern Festoon, Two-tailed Pasha, Chapman Green Hairstreak

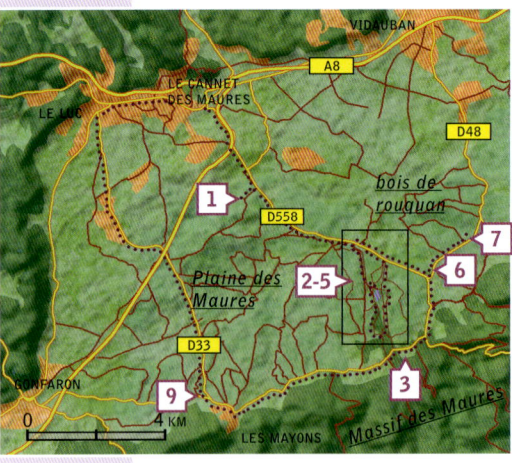

The Plaine des Maures is one of those highlights of Provence that is only known to a select group of naturalists. Come here in spring and of the few people that you meet, many will carry a camera and binoculars.
The rolling Plaine des Maures lies between the A8 motorway and the Massif the Maures, between Le Luc and Vidauban and consists of sandstone, which is unusual in Provence. The landscape is one of scattered Umbrella Pines, Strawberry Trees and Cork Oaks over low scrub of cistus and French Lavender. There is a remarkable number of shallow, temporary streams and pools, dry in summer, but wet in winter and spring. They harbour a special flora (with thousands of tongue-orchids), plus numerous reptiles, amphibians, birds and a few attractive butterflies.
This route combines an easy, 3-hour walk with a short car route on the nearby minor roads, which combined, gives you a good taste of the area.

ROUTE 14: PLAINE DES MAURES

Starting point Le Cannet de Maures (GPS: 43.391917, 6.343375)
From the village, follow the D558 to La Garde-Freinet. Turn the 2nd road right after the sign *Plaine des Maures* (3 km after leaving the village). There is a sign *D 155 Le Balacan* at the entrance of the road.

1 After 500 metres, where the road turns left, you look out over a large rubbish dump. Not the prettiest of sites, but an excellent one to watch raptors. Black Kites, Raven and Yellow-legged Gulls are common and often pass by at close range. With a little more luck, you may spot Red Kite (winter) or Golden Eagle.
The scrubland on either side of the road already has the shrubs (French Lavender, Sage-leaved Cistus, Strawberry Tree) that are so typical of the sandstone of the Plaine des Maures. More attractive examples will follow further en route. This is already the home of the rare Hermann's Tortoise, so keep an eye out for them in the scrub. They have an uncanny resemblance to an ordinary rock!

Return to the main road and turn right. Just before the large wine house of Chateau Bertrand on your left, turn right on a track. Park here and walk the trail *Le Vallon des Escarcets west* that brings you, after 1.5 kms, to a small reservoir (see map on next page).

2 The area around the reservoir dam is very attractive. Look for orchids here in April-May, when Heart-flowered Tongue-orchid, Scarce Tongue-orchid and Provence Tongue-orchid* (*Serapias olbiensis*) are in flower. The latter two species occur only in Provence and an adjacent small area in Italy. They grow all over the plaine, so keep looking for them throughout the walk. Champagne and Painted Orchid* (*Anacamptis picta*) are two other orchid species frequently encountered here, next to Crimean Iris, French Lavender, Saint Bernard's Lily, Narrow-leaved

The Escarcets reservoir with the Massif des Maures in the back.

PRACTICAL PART

ROUTE 14: PLAINE DES MAURES

and Sage-leaved Cistus, Spotted Rockrose, the stout yellow rockrose *Tuberaria lignosa* and Seaside Centaury* (*Centaurium maritumum*). On damper spots, there are good numbers of Wild Tulips and Bloody Crane's-bill.

The lake may hold some marshland birds. Sometimes, Alpine Swifts hunt over the water. Scan skies for raptors – Black Kite, Common Buzzard, Short-toed Eagle and even Golden Eagle pass by regularly.

Follow the trail that borders the reservoir.

3 The path guides you along reedy banks into a shady riparian woodland with Cork Oak, Alder and pine, harbouring Firecrest, Golden Oriole and Grey Wagtail on the stream. This is a pretty area, very different from the surrounding dry *maquis*.

At the first opportunity, go left and cross the stream. On the other side, turn left again and follow the eastern bank of the reservoir until you reach an abandoned farm house.

4 The ruins form a good spot to look for reptiles, butterflies and dragonflies. Among the butterflies, Southern White Admiral, both Southern and Spanish Festoons, Common and Chapman's Green Hairstreak and Two-tailed Pasha all occur (in the appropriate season of course). Among the dragonflies, Blue Chaser, Western Clubtail, Blue and Orange Featherleg are present.

Provence Tongue-orchids* (*Serapias olbiensis*) grow around the reservoir, together with Scarce, Heart-lipped and Common Tongue-orchids.

Follow the track to the right (away from the lake). At the T-junction, go left and at the next junction left again.

5 You now cross another section of open *maquis*. This is a good area for Dartford Warbler, but Subalpine occurs too and Sardinian is common. Woodlark, Corn Bunting and the occasional Woodchat Shrike – they are all possible here and the remainder of the trail. The low bushes with scattered pine and Strawberry Trees form the perfect habitat for Nightjar, which you can hear in the evenings. Look for reptiles here as well. The plaine des Maures harbours a sizeable population of the scarce Ocellated Lizard – Europe's largest lizard species.

Just before you reach the road, follow the trail to the left that crosses the valley and continues parallel to the road. It brings you back to the starting point.
Take the car and continue further down the road in the direction of La Garde-Freinet. Take the first junction left onto the D48 to Vidauban.

6 The first kilometres of road cut through a superb open pinewood, known as the *Bois de Rouquan*. On both sides of the road there are gullies with seasonal pools and tiny streams that only carry water in winter and spring.

Much of the Plaine des Maures is covered in a wild vegetation of rocky grasslands, *maquis* and scattered trees (bottom). In temporary pools, such as those on point 7 of this route, there is a rare vegetation of dwarf plants. Here you may find, if you search carefully the tiny Yellow Centaury, a relative of the gentians.

There is a small car park some 1.5 kms from the junction on the left side of the road underneath the pines. Park there and walk further along the road through the gully that runs parallel to it.

7 After some 50 metres, the gully carries some water in wet springs. We found 9 species of orchids here (including Scarce Tongue and Loose-flowered Orchid), Crimean Iris, Wild Tulip,

ROUTE 14: PLAINE DES MAURES

Two common wildflowers on this route: Saint Bernard's-Lily (top) and Painted Orchid (a close relative to Green-winged Orchid; bottom).

Star-of-Bethlehem and, typical of these open, winter-wet environments, the tiny Yellow Centaury and Small Adder's-tongue. Closer to the road, there are Woodcock and Black Spider Orchids.

Return to the car and drive back to the junction where you turn left. Subsequently, take the first right – a small country road to Les Mayons.

8 There are various small car parks on this road, from which trails can be followed over the plain. One very good spot, where you can also take a short walk, lies on the left side of the road in an open Cork Oak forest, 1.4 kms beyond the turn. The walk is opposite the road.

Overall, this area is more densely wooded, with a thick cover of Cork Oaks and, locally, Tree Heath. There are masses of Scarce Tongue-orchids, plus lesser numbers of Dense-flowered, Lady and Lesser Butterfly Orchids. The grassy sites are home to Three-toed Skink and the river to Fire Salamander, while the butterfly fauna includes Spanish Festoon, Chapman's Green Hairstreak and Two-tailed Pasha.

Continue past Les Mayons and park at the junction towards Le Luc.

9 The area around this crossing is interesting for butterflies and orchids. We found eight species of orchids here, the most noteworthy being the Splendid Orchid* (*Ophrys splendida*), a rather rare species that is endemic to Provence.

Follow the road to Le Luc and from there to Le Cannet to complete the circuit.

Route 15: Mont Sainte Victoire

4-5 HOURS, 4 KM, ONE WAY
MODERATE-STRENUOUS

Beautiful walk to one of the world's most famous mountains. Spectacular views and a fine flora and fauna.

Habitats cliffs, flowery fields, garrigue, olive groves
Selected species Southern Early-purple Orchid, Wild Tulip, Crimean Iris, Alpine Swift, Orphean Warbler, Dartford Warbler, Bonelli's Eagle, Blue Rock Thrush, Black-eared Wheatear, Wallcreeper (w), Alpine Accentor (w), Provence Orange-tip

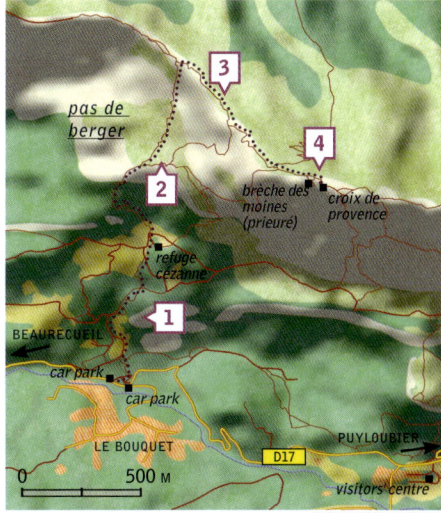

In the eyes of the world, the Mont Sainte-Victoire is the mountain of the impressionist painter Cézanne. He painted it over and over, each time capturing it in a different light.
As a wildlife site, the Mont Sainte-Victoire is akin to the Alpilles, but it is larger and higher. It is a dry limestone range, strictly Mediterranean in its flora and fauna, and one of the richest sites in bats, birds and wildflowers of dry cliff and karst.
The entire range is attractive and offers great hiking options. For this route, we've chosen for the most extreme part of the mountain: the exposed, hot and south-facing southwest, where a rich birdlife competes for your attention with breathtaking views. Note that this route is quite strenuous, especially on hot and sunny days. There is almost no shade and the white chalk rock is very bright: bring sun protection for your skin, sunglasses and plenty of water!

Starting point Car park Mont Sainte-Victoire (GPS: 43.523859, 5.564294).

Getting there From Aix-en-Provence, taking the D17 eastbound out of town, to the village of Le Thonolet. Here, continue in the direction

PRACTICAL PART

ROUTE 15: MONT SAINTE VICTOIRE

Beaurecueil and St. Antonin. Aproximately 2 kms beyond the turn to Beaurecueil, there is a car park on your left (and 100 m. further another one). Park in either one of them and follow the path to *refuge Cézanne* (yellow flashes).

1 The first section of the route leads through an open pinewood where, in spring, Serins seem to sing from every tree. Just beyond, there are olive groves and patches of open *garrigue* of the hottest and driest type, as this slope is directed towards the sun, while the porous limestone means that water disappears quickly into the bedrock. Therefore, only plants grow here that can cope with long periods of drought, such as Kermes Oak, Wild Rosemary, Prickly Juniper, Blue Aphyllanthes, Grey-leaved Cistus and Shrubby Globularia (which flowers at the end of winter). They all have leathery or hairy leaves, in either case a protection against the sun.

The climb up to the Mont Sainte-Victoire leads over the sun-drenched southern slopes (top). In spring, this is a good place to find Provence Orange-tips (bottom).

Look here and the remainder of the route for butterflies. This area is not very diverse, but does hold a good number of truly southern species – a reflection of the hot micro-climate here. Each in their own season, there is Provence Orange-tip, Spanish Festoon, Baton Blue and Marsh and Glanville Fritillaries. The better bird sites are further afield, but do look out for Sardinian and Dartford Warblers, Hoopoe and for raptors along the cliffs above you. The olive groves are home to Orphean Warbler, a fairly scarce bird in Provence.

Near the Refuge Cézanne, follow the trail *La Croix de Provence par l'Escalette (1.15 min)*. The trail climbs steeply until you arrive at a plateau. Soon thereafter, the trail splits in a *facile* (easy) and *difficile* (hard) trail to the Croix de Provence (which you see conspicuously on the crest to the right). Take the easy road, which will prove to be tough enough.

CROSSBILL GUIDES • PROVENCE

ROUTE 15: MONT SAINTE VICTOIRE

2 Just beyond the crossing, you come on a flatter area, the *Pas de Berger*. Look here for wildflowers in spring. There are many Southern Early-purple Orchids – a species that occurs only in the southern and eastern part of the Iberian Peninsula and, locally, in Provence. The familiar Early-purple Orchid grows further ahead on the trail, great for comparison. Common Jonquil, Broad-leaved Snapdragon* (*Antirrhinum latifolium*) and Crimean Iris are other attractive spring flowers here. Look out for birds as well. Orphean, Subalpine and Dartford Warblers and Tawny Pipit breed in the *garrigue*, while both Rock Thrush, Blue Rock Thrush and Black-eared Wheatear breed near the cliffs, as do Alpine Swifts and Crag Martins. Red-billed Chough, Golden, Booted, Short-toed and Bonelli's Eagle regularly patrol along the cliffs, although truth be told, none of these birds are commonly seen.

The trail climbs steeply up to the next saddle (*Pas de l'Escallete*) where it turns right, joins the blue-marked route towards the chapel and the Croix de Provence.

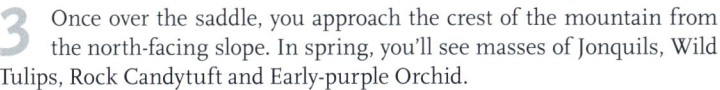

Drifts of Crimean Iris flower along the side of the trail. This plant grows in a yellow and a purple form.

3 Once over the saddle, you approach the crest of the mountain from the north-facing slope. In spring, you'll see masses of Jonquils, Wild Tulips, Rock Candytuft and Early-purple Orchid.

4 After a few zigzags up the mountain, you reach the priory and, a few metres ahead the large crucifix, the Croix de Provence. It is a remarkable construction – a seven metres tall iron cross on a concrete footing of 11 metres across. It was built between 1871 and 1875 by the Abbey of Meissonnier to thank God for sparing Provence in the Prussian War.
In the 16th century, the priory was an important pilgrimage site. Those days are over, but there still is a day of pilgrimage in the last weekend of April. Snowfinch and Wallcreeper come down from the high Alps to spend the winter around the priory and the cross.

Return via the same way.

PRACTICAL PART

Route 16: Massif de Sainte-Baume

**4 HOURS, 5.7 KM
MODERATE-STRENUOUS**

Superb, near-natural beech forest with pretty spring flora.
Witness the extreme differences of north and south oriented slopes.

Habitats oak forest, beech forest, cliffs, karst plateau
Selected species Pheasant's-eye Daffodil, Bird's-nest Orchid, Martagon Lily, Southern Early-purple Orchid, Black Woodpecker, Firecrest, Short-toed Treecreeper, Tawny Pipit, Ortolan Bunting

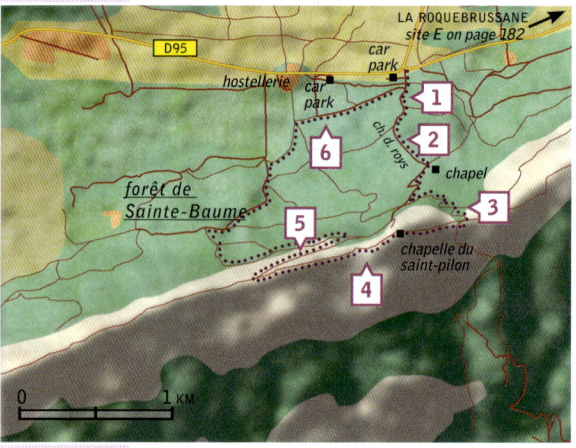

The massif de Sainte-Baume is one of the most southern limestone ranges in Provence and stands out because of its large and impressive Beech forest. The altitude (700 to 1000 m) and the steep, cool and shady north-facing slopes allow this tree of temperate forests to thrive even here in the very south of France.

This route through the Massif de Sainte-Baume promises a beautiful, wild walk through shady, tall and very old woodland with massive, mossy trunks and gnarled snags. At the top, the views are stunning. It is a fairly strenuous walk, but very much worth the effort. Along the way, you'll be able to see a flora and fauna that is more akin to the montane woodlands of the Alps than the dry Mediterranean slopes of other parts of Provence. The road over to the starting point from La Roquebrussanne is worth exploring too (see site E on page 182).

Starting point Car park at the junction of the D95 and the D80 (GPS 43.335854, 5.765751).

ROUTE 16: MASSIF DE SAINTE-BAUME

The pine stands between the road and the car park harbour Provence and Elder-flowered Orchids.

Walk up the *Chemin des Roys*, the main, broad trail uphill.

1 This first section crosses a fine, mature woodland of oaks (including some monumental specimens), Lime, Sycamore and Yew. Look and listen here and for the remainder of the wooded section of the route for Cirl Bunting and forest birds, like Short-toed Treecreeper, Nuthatch, Bonelli's Warbler, Firecrest, Great Spotted, Green and Black Woodpeckers.

In spring, the forest floor is covered with a flora that reminds of the finer forests in central Europe: Sanicle, Liverleaf, Tuberous Comfrey, Purple Gromwell, Cowslip, Wood Spurge, Angular Solomon's-seal, Spurge-laurel and Pheasant's-eye Daffodil are frequent. In summer, the flashy flowers of the Martagon Lily are common.

2 As you arrive at a well, you have entered the Beech forest. A little further, at the small shrine, go right, onto the GR-walking route. Look for Bird's-nest Orchid along this stretch.

3 Note how quickly the vegetation changes from tall beech forest, to stunted Oaks and Lime trees as you come closer to the cliff and the soil becomes thinner. On the ridge, you look out to the north, the trees become increasingly stunted.

On the ridge, turn right.

The walk up to the crest of the Sainte-Baume massif leads through a terrific old forest, which is a protected site since the Middle Ages (top). The forest has a rich spring flora with, amongst others, many Liverleafs (bottom).

PRACTICAL PART

ROUTE 16: MASSIF DE SAINTE-BAUME

View towards the limestone cliffs of Sainte-Baume (bottom). In the open oak stands you'll find many orchids. The Elder-flowered comes in two forms – the yellow and this slightly less numerous pink variety.

4 You look out over a rocky, sparsely vegetated karst plateau, radically different from the slope you just climbed, with the drought resistant Phoenician Juniper as the main shrub, and lots of White Rockroses and Blue Aphyllanthes. Look out for the Southern Early-purple Orchids as well – an orchid that is restricted to southern Spain and Provence.

The trail proceeds over the ridge to the *Chapelle du Saint-Pilon* on the highest point. Look for Tawny Pipit, both Northern and Black-eared Wheatear, Ortolan Bunting and Short-toed Eagle.

At the chapel return by the route you arrived if you don't want to do the more difficult descent.

Continue along the ridge, following the cairns and the red and white flashes of the GR, for another 1200 metres. Here, a small trail (with red markings) crosses the ridge again and turns right. The first bit of the trail is rather narrow, but this is only a small stretch.

5 You walk just beneath the crest, where, interestingly, a stunted growth of Lime trees has replaced the Beeches. There are many ferns growing here.

Once back in the forest, some 500 m further, turn left on a trail (green marks), which brings you to a broad track, where you turn right, and shortly thereafter, left. On your way down you pass a well on your left and a trail on your right, which you ignore. Instead, take the next trail right, which is just before the edge of the forest. This trail brings you back to the car park.

6 In this last section, there are massive trees again, first Beeches, then Lime and Oak trees, with a rich population of the aforementioned forest birds.

CROSSBILL GUIDES • PROVENCE

Route 17: Along the Endre river

3 HOURS, 7 KM
EASY-MODERATE

Easy walk along an unspoilt river.

Habitats River, Riverine forest, cork oak woods, maquis
Selected species Splendid Orchid, Bee-eater, Golden Oriole, Hobby, Three-toed Skink, Aesculapian Snake, Lesser Purple Emperor, Spanish Purple Hairstreak, Two-tailed Pasha, Southern Festoon, Spanish Festoon, Western Clubtail, Lesser Pincertail, Copper Demoiselle

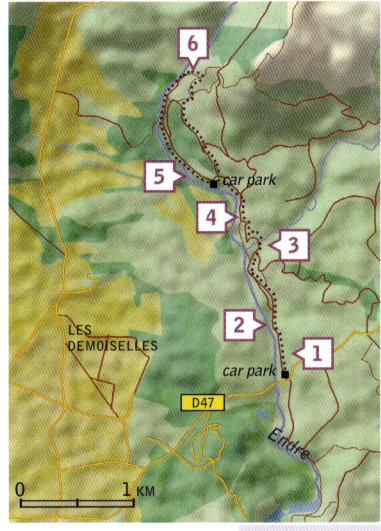

The Endre River is a rather short tributary of the Argens, which in turn flows into the Mediterranean at Fréjus. On its short course of only 30 kms, the Endre creates a superb riverine habitat with a rich wildlife.
This route starts at the bridge over the Endre at a site that is popular with locals for picnicking and bathing in summer. It then follows the river for a while to a short series of rapids, where it makes a small circuit over the hillslopes.
This is one of the easier routes for exploring the river habitat. There is something for everyone on this gentle walk: birds, butterflies, dragonflies and reptiles, plus in spring, masses of orchids.

Starting point Car Park on the D47 on the east bank of the Endre (GPS 43.504311, 6.590311). Walk the broad track that follows the bank upstream.

1 Look over the river here and in subsequent sites for birds, which include Kingfisher, Bee-eater, Hoopoe, Turtle Dove, Hobby, Little Ringed Plover, Grey Wagtail, Little and Cattle Egret.
A little away from the car park, where the roadsides have not been trampled or flattened by picnic blankets, look for orchids. Along this track there are thousands of Splendid Orchids* (*Ophrys splendida*), plus low numbers of Lizard, Giant and Woodcock Orchids. There are some Wild

ROUTE 17: ALONG THE ENDRE RIVER

Tulips, Tassel Hyacinths and two species of birthworts – Smearwort and Spanish Birthwort: the first is the larval food plant of the Southern Festoon while the second is preferred by Spanish. Both butterflies are present here, together with Spanish Purple Hairstreak, Provence Chalkhill and Adonis Blues.

2 At the first occasion, walk a trail left through the riverine woodland (with majestic Black Poplars) to the river. The forest is home to large numbers of Golden Oriole, plus a population of Lesser Spotted and Green Woodpeckers. Tread carefully and you may find Aesculapian or Montpellier Snake (both large but harmless snakes, although they may be defensive when disturbed). The river itself is home to both Grass and Viperine Snake.

The Endre River (top). This walk is excellent for finding butterflies, such as this scarce Iolas Blue (top right). Look carefully at the base of the cistus scrub and you may find the flowers of this parasitic Hypocist (bottom).

3 Next point of interest is at a sharp left bend. The soil is different here – more acidic, less permeable – hence the thick grass cover in which Three-toed Skink is at home. Check any open patches carefully as this is where it likes to sunbathe. In summer, this is a good area to look for Cardinal – one of the largest butterflies of the region. There is a trail that leads down to the river, where, in summer, the beautiful Lesser Purple Emperor can be found. Look for excrement – they often come down to take minerals from animal droppings. The river hosts dragonflies like Western Clubtail,

CROSSBILL GUIDES • PROVENCE

Lesser Pincertail and Copper Demoiselle, you have a chance on encountering Hermann's Tortoise in the scrub and European Pond Terrapin in the water.

If you are here in summer, check the flowers for the impressive Mammoth Wasp. With up to 6 cms (the females), this is the largest wasp in Europe. Fortunately, it is not aggressive to humans. The female lays her eggs on Rhinoceros Beetles (which must therefore be around too). The larvae eat the beetle from the inside out, like the Ichneumon Wasps.

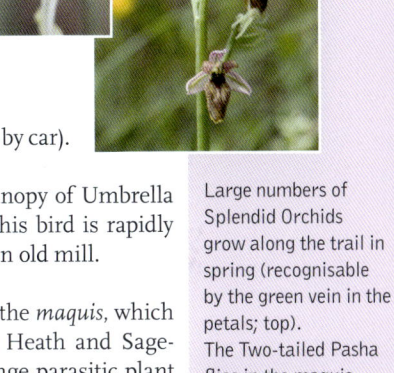

4 Just 500 metres further ahead, there is another bend to the left with another trail down to the river, which may hold the same species as described above.

At the fork, turn left to a car park (the furthest one can go by car).

5 The next stretch passes underneath a beautiful canopy of Umbrella Pines. There are still Turtle Doves around here (this bird is rapidly declining). The broad track ends at a waterfall opposite an old mill.

6 A narrow track leads up the hill. It brings you into the *maquis*, which is dominated by brooms, Strawberry Trees, Tree Heath and Sage-leaved Cistus. Beneath the latter, you may find the strange parasitic plant Hypocist, a far relative of the raflesias, which occur in the South-east Asian Jungle and are the largest flowers on earth. Another spectacular species here is the Two-tailed Pasha, which is, like the aforementioned, also the only European relative of a tropical species, this time a group of colourful tropical African butterflies.

Large numbers of Splendid Orchids grow along the trail in spring (recognisable by the green vein in the petals; top).
The Two-tailed Pasha flies in the maquis (bottom).

Turn right at the split of trails and again right when you arrive at the track to return to the main riverside track, which you follow back to the starting point.

PRACTICAL PART

ADDITIONAL SITES IN THE CÔTE D'AZUR

Additional sites in the Côte d'Azur

!
The location of the sites described here is shown on the map on page 154.

A – Île de Porquerolles

The Île de Porquerolles is the larger brother of Île Port-Cros and since 2012, part of the National Park (now called *Parc National de Port-Cros et Porquerolles*). Unlike Port-Cros, people live on Porquerolles. In terms of flora and fauna, both islands are similar. The surrounding waters are frequented by Yelkouan and (much rarer) Cory's Shearwater. There are Pallid and Alpine Swifts and all three species of Gecko. The larger size and the presence of some flat areas with reedy ponds and dense vegetation, make Porquerolles to an attractive place during bird migration periods.

You can enjoy a very fine walk when going from the village due south to *Phare du Cap d'Arme* (passing the ponds en route) and then taking the walk around the western part of the island, towards Langoustier.

The island is reached by ferries from the same ports as Île Port-Cros (see page 158).

B – Les Calanques

Les Calanques south of Marseille is France's youngest National Park. It is a spectacular place, with its white, limestone cliffs and azure sea. A *Calanque* is a rocky, steep-sloped cove, of which there are many on this coast. They were formed by rivers that cut in steep valleys in the soft bedrock. Later, as the sea level rose, the river valleys became bays on the Mediterranean coast. The white rock is also what gives the sea, so clear here, its deep blue-green colour. The exposition to the south, the dry, porous rock and near absence of fertile soil, further gives Les Calanques its wild appearance. Part of the National Park are several off-shore islands, including the Île de Frioul – see next site.

The National Park is visited annually by many tourists, most of which come to enjoy the wonderful scenery, swim in the Calanques or explore the coastline by boat. This is one of the few National Parks that is less visited by naturalists, even though there is a lot to see. The birdlife is not particularly diverse, but holds some special species, such as Pallid Swift, Cory's Shearwater and Blue Rock Thrush, which reach their highest numbers in France in this area. The Calanques offers great

ADDITIONAL SITES IN THE CÔTE D'AZUR

hiking over a fine network of trails, although it must be said that the lack of shade and it being rough underfoot can make walking tough. The coastal path connects the calanques via often steep ascents and descents over the karstic ranges. For flora and fauna, the valleys, which are not nearly as dry as the hills, are the most attractive.
You can access les Calanques on the western side at Les Goudes, which offers spectacular views over the islands, Sormiou in the centre and Cassis in the east. There are many walks in the area, including a The coast in the west, near the islands, is best for birdwatching.

A bay in les Calanques National Park.

C – Île de Frioul

Part of the Calanques National Park is the Frioul archipelago; two barren, limestone islands connected by a dam. The islands are popular with yachting tourists. The islands hold a strategic position in front of the city of Marseille (from which' old port a ferry brings you to Lioux) and are therefore riddled with forts.
The ecological fame of the Île de Frioul lies in the presence of a colony of Cory's Shearwaters. Around 400 pairs breed on the islands of Marseille collectively (most of which on the island of Riou, a bit further southeast). Pallid Swift and Blue Rock Thrush also breed on Frioul.
On the ferry you also pass the small rock island of If, dominated by a large castle. This *Château d'If* is now a national monument, but once it was a prison. It became world famous thanks to the novel *The Count of Monte Cristo* by Alexandre Dumas whose eponymous hero was imprisoned in Château d'If.
There are various walking routes on Frioul. For ferry time tables, see www.lebateau-frioul-if.fr

Careful for car theft

ADDITIONAL SITES IN THE CÔTE D'AZUR

The Dull Bee Orchid is one of several wild orchids along the Route des Crêtes.

D – Route des Crêtes

A drive over the Route des Crêtes (D 141) between Cassis and La Ciotat is easily combined with a visit to the Calanques (site B). The scenic road is signposted from the D 559 that runs through Cassis. It is a breath-taking trip up the 363 metre high *Cap Canaille* with stunning views over Cassis and the Calanques. It is a touristic road with many visitors, especially in summer. Apart from the views and the photography (in evening light it is stunning here), there are many orchids in the roadside in spring. Use the many viewpoints to park and have a stroll along the road. In the first and lower section of the road, it is mostly the *lupercalis* subspecies of Dull Bee Orchid that is abundant. Its peak flowering time is at the very end of April – a little later than at the Calanques. It grows together with a number of other species (e.g. Passion-tide and Giant Orchids). The top section of the route des Crêtes (the final kilometre to the lighthouse) is the richest. Here you can find Splendid Orchid, Passion-tide and Woodcock Orchids, masses of Painted Orchids* (*Anacamptis picta*), Narrow-leaved Helleborine and even Provence Orchid has been recorded here.

E – The D95 road between Mazaugues and Sainte-Baume

The narrow, quiet D95 country road connects the small, picturesque village of Mazaugues with Sainte Baume and is the perfect extension of a visit to this site. If you come from the east, you'll take this road to go to Sainte-Baume. If from a different direction, this stretch of road is worth the detour.

The road crosses a limestone plateau with a thin scatter of Downy Oaks, some scrub and plenty of flowery, rocky grasslands. It gradually climbs up from 400 metres in Mazaugues to almost 700 metres near Sainte-Baume, a climb that shows in the vegetation which gradually shifts to more cold-adapted plants. Crimean Iris, milkworts, spurges, Grape-hyacinth, Rosemary, various rockroses and cistuses, Feather Grass are the most eye-catching wildflowers, which are visited by numerous owl-flies (ascalaphids) and a score of butterflies. There is a good range of orchids, although not in very large numbers. Towards Sainte-Baume – the

higher part of the plateau – the trees are taller and Elder-flowered Orchids are numerous, while Woodcock, Passion-tide, Dull Bee, Pyramidal and Man Orchids occur at lower levels.
There are plenty of options for parking. The small stream (dry in summer) just before the kilometre 9 signpost (when coming from Mazaugues) is a good place to stroll around. Another good spot is at km 11, where a small walk brings you to the *Glacière Pivaut*, a small calcareous marsh.

F – Étangs de Villepey

The town of Fréjus lies in the middle of a built-up stretch of the Côte d'Azur, so it is a small miracle that the *Conservatoire du Littoral* managed to preserve the small Étangs de Villepey from development. It is a small pearl of wetlands of the estuary of the Argens river, sandwiched between holiday homes to the south and an amusement park to the north. The lagoons attract waders and some ducks in spring and autumn and holds several pairs of Moustached Warblers, plus a sizable colony of feral Rose-ringed Parakeets. Many attractive birds are seen here on a regular basis, including Booted Eagle, Greater Flamingo, Roller, Bee-eater, Kingfisher and Red-rumped Swallow. The northern part of the lake has a healthy population of European Pond Terrapin.
The central part of the area is inaccessible for visitors, but there is a hide on the lagoon that lies right next to the mouth of the Argens river. Park at the northern end of the large car park of the plage de l'Escamandre on the D559 and walk the trail up to the hide. Another site is a bit further on the D559 towards Fréjus. Just before crossing the Argens, turn left on the roundabout onto the *Chemin des Étangs*, which runs along several of the lakes.

The minor D95 road leads over a splendid plateau full of butterflies and flowers. From east to west, it slowly climbs, which means that the species gradually change (top).
The Red-rumped Swallow breeds in the Argens Valley and Étangs de Villepey (bottom).

HAUTE PROVENCE

Haute Provence

The north-eastern part of Provence is known as the Haute Provence. It is where the Alps meet the Mediterranean and where high plateaux and wild mountains are separated by warm, Mediterranean valleys. The slopes and gorges are clad in dense pine, oak and beech woods and sport an excellent range of wildflowers and butterflies.

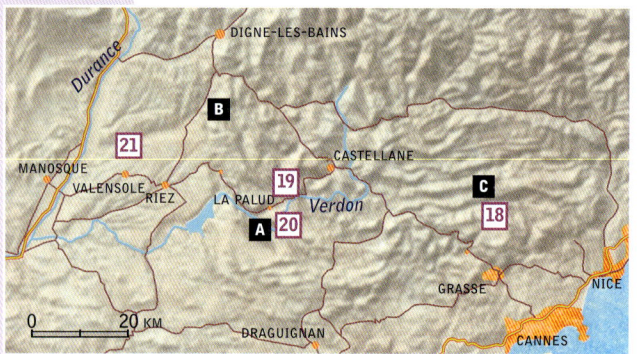

The mountains here are all limestone. There are flowery karst plateaux and scenic gorges, the most spectacular of which is the Grand Canyon du Verdon (routes 19 and 20).
Next to the scenery, the Verdon gorges' claim to fame are its colonies of (reintroduced) Griffon and Black Vultures. These massive birds (with a wingspan of 2.5 metres) pass by at an arm's length in front of the viewpoints over the gorge – a sight that will leave no-one unmoved. The Canyon du Verdon is a popular summer holiday destination, but the nearby gorges (e.g. site A and B on page 201) are much less visited and have a splendid flora and fauna too. Right next to the Gorge du Verdon lies the plain of the Valensole (route 21), which is geologically very different and is famous for having the largest concentration of lavender fields in the world. It is also an attractive site for steppe and dryland birds.

Besides mountains and the Valensole plain, the Haute Provence has many karst plateaux. The surroundings of the Gorge du Verdon is one of them. The largest is the Canjuers plain (extremely rich in wildlife, but unfortunately inaccessible because it is a military zone), the Calern plateau (route 18) and Monts d'Azur (site C on page 202). These uplands have a rich birdlife with steppe birds (e.g. Little Bustard) occurring side by side with Mediterranean and Alpine species. The same goes for butterflies and wildflowers.

The options to explore this part of Provence on foot are virtually endless. In this book we've described just a few routes on which you have the better chances of finding wildlife and wildflowers.

Route 18: Plaine de Calern

4-5 HOURS, 5 KM
EASY (WALK ONLY)

Wild karst plateau on the edge of the Alps.

Habitats limestone plateau, karst, doline, open pinewoods
Selected species Provence Snake's-head Fritillary, Elder-flowered Orchid, Early-purple Orchid, Green-winged Orchid, Pheasant's-eye Daffodil, Short-toed Eagle, Peregrine, Griffon Vulture, Tawny Pipit, Rock Thrush, Alpine Swift, Ortolan Bunting, Meadow Viper, Apollo, Black-eyed Blue, Ripart's Anomalous Blue, Spring Ringlet

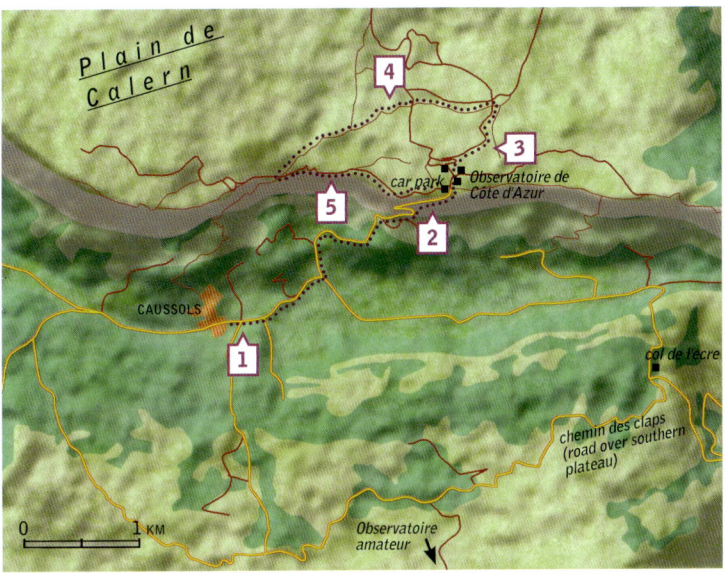

The Plaine de Calern is a high plateau that stands out like a balcony over the Côte D'Azur. It is part of the regional park of the *Préalps d'Azur*. The plateau is open and wind-beaten, craggy and potholed with dolines. The vistas are wide, with on the one side the Alps and on the other a steep cliff and a formidable view over the lower Provence with in the distance,

ROUTE 18: PLAINE DE CALERN

with good weather, the Mediterranean Sea. The flora and fauna are an interesting combination of mountain, Mediterranean and steppe species. Early-purple, Green-winged and Elder-flowered Orchid cover the plateau in thousands.
The walk we propose here is a fairly short and easy ramble over the plateau, which can easily be extended as you wish.

Starting point the hamlet of Caussols (which lies north of the village of Saint-Vallier-de-Thiey; GPS 43.741618, 6.900066).

1 In the meadows in the valley around the village, there are many butterflies, with Damon and Ripart's Anomalous Blues, Twin-spot and Knapweed Fritillary and Dusky Meadow Brown among the more remarkable species. In spring these meadows are spectacular due to the mass flowering of Pheasant's-eye Daffodil.

Follow the road east for just less than a kilometre and at the T-junction outside the village turn left onto a minor road signposted *Observatoire de la Côte d'Azur*.

2 On your way up look for Rock Thrush on the wires and Short-Toed Eagle, Peregrine and Griffon Vulture above the cliff. After two kilometres you reach the Observatoire where you park in the car park on the left.

The Calern Plateau is spectacular, open and wild.

ROUTE 18: PLAINE DE CALERN

From the car park, walk the road that leads onto the plateau towards *Cipieres* (signposted). The road bends to the left twice and after the second bend (about 250 m from the car park), go right onto a track signposted again *Cipieres*.

3 When you walk around the plateau you will notice many craters – dolines. The vegetation in these dolines is much more verdant than that of the plateau.
Dolines are formed where water has found its way into the plateau and dissolved lower layers of limestone eventually forming caves. At some point these collapsed and the hole that was left filled up with sediments from the higher plateau.
Spring visitors will immediately notice the many deep purple orchids flowering on the plateau. Careful examination shows that there are two species, both numerous: Early-purple Orchid and Green-winged Orchid. Around the observatory, there are also some yellow Elder-flowered Orchids. Other plants that occur here are Tuberous Valerian, Grass-leaved Buttercup, Provence Snake's-head (*Fritillaria involucrata*), Grape-hyacinth, Wild Lavender, Wild Peonies and various saxifrages.

Rock Thrush breeds on the cliffs beneath the observatory.

The plateau is home to many attractive birds: Ortolan Bunting, Northern Wheatear, Skylark, Woodlark, Black Redstart, Tawny Pipit and Mistle Thrush can be seen and heard here. Keep an eye out for Alpine, Common and Pallid Swifts – the latter sometimes coming in from their coastal breeding sites to hunt.

There are many small trails branching off to the left and right. Ignore them, but take the GR (marked white and red) to the left, signposted *Caussols* and marked with a pole with the number 188 on it. Follow the GR until you reach the cliff (about an hour).

4 The rich plateau habitat is similar to that of the previous point. In late spring and summer, this area is excellent for butterflies, with species like Apollo, Black-veined White, Baton Blue, Large Blue, Wall Brown and Spring Ringlet. Among the reptiles, the extremely rare and

PRACTICAL PART

ROUTE 18: PLAINE DE CALERN

hard-to-find Meadow Viper is the star species. It has a strong population here. Also, the large Ocellated Lizard is listed for the plateau, as is the hard to spot Parsley Frog.

Although GR signs are frequent, we found that it is easy to miss the trail, as it is not always clear in the open landscape. However, the buildings of the *Observatoire* stand out in the open landscape as a point of reference, so you won't get entirely lost. Once you reach the cliffs, turn left.

5 From the cliffs you look down on the village of Caussols which lies in the middle of a large plain, a polje. This has been created in the same way as the dolines on the plain, but at a much larger scale. Because the ground consists of clay it is very fertile, as a result, humans have been using the polje for ages to grow crops.
On and around the cliffs you can find various swifts, kestrels, Rock Thrush, Short-Toed Eagle and Griffon Vultures, which take advantage of the rising air from the hot, south-facing cliffs.

Two butterflies of the Calern Plain: Damon Blue (top) and Apollo (bottom).

Follow the trail along the cliffs back to the car park.

Additional remarks

If your hunger for wildlife isn't satisfied, drive the minor road (*Chemin des Claps*) over the karst plateau south of Caussols, which leads through a more wooded area with lots of rocky meadows, superb for wildflowers and butterflies, such as Black-eyed Blue and Spring Ringlet. To get there, follow the road east out of Caussols, which follows the doline valley for a while before bending sharply to the right and climbing up the plateau. Shortly after a hairpin bend and the *Col de l'Ecre*, the *Chemin des Claps* branches off to the right, signposted *Observatoire Amateur*. The road brings you all the way down to the western end of the doline (see map). Another attractive spot is the Col du Ferier, just south of Caussols, on the way to Saint-Vallier-de-Thiey.

Route 19: Grand canyon du Verdon – a first exploration

6 HOURS, 53 KM
EASY-MODERATE

One of the deepest limestone cliffs of Europe.
Vultures soaring by at close range.

Habitats cliffs, cliff forests, karst plateau, river
Selected species Griffon Vulture, Black Vulture, Egyptian Vulture, Golden Eagle, Short-Toed Eagle, Wallcreeper (winter), Wryneck, Subalpine Warbler, Chequered Blue, Baton Blue, Provence Orange-tip, Bird's-nest Orchid

The Gorge du Verdon offers some of the most awe-inspiring landscapes of France. The canyon exceeds the 700m depth at some points! The water running down in the gorge is azure blue and the cliffs glow gold in the evening light. At any time, Griffon Vultures can come soaring by at close range and with luck you might even find a Black or Egyptian Vulture, or Golden Eagle.

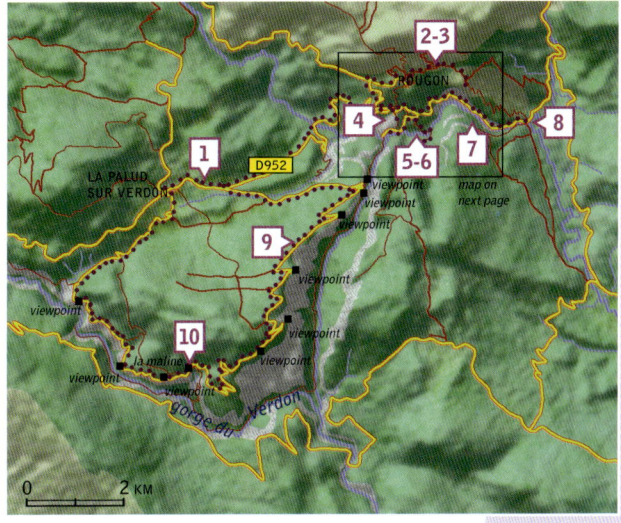

This route will lead you past some of the most stunning views of the Gorge and the different habitats that can be found around the Gorge.

Starting point La Palud sur Verdon; GPS 43.779786, 6.340218
From the village, take the D952 east.

1 Like many villages in the high Provence, La Palud is situated in a doline – a fertile plain in the otherwise rocky and inhospitable

ROUTE 19: GRAND CANYON DU VERDON – A FIRST EXPLORATION

A view into the Gorge du Verdon from Rougon.

plateau. The doline is formed by water that has dissolved the lower limestone layers, which caused the higher layers to collapse. Because this area is now lower, water with erosion material runs towards it, slowly filling it with fertile clay. This makes it perfect for agricultural activities. As you drive out of the village, note, the green pastures with, in June, the thousands of Pheasant's-eye Daffodils.

At the crossing, turn left to Rougon. Once you have reached the village, park in the car park and continue on foot to the square and viewpoint.

2 Take a moment to take in the landscape at the viewpoint, which looks into the canyon towards the east. The cliffs on the left side are where many of the vultures breed. The rocks face the south, which means that the air warms up quickly and rises in front of the cliff. Like an elevator made of air, the raptors just have to spread their wings and soar up.

Follow the path that continues from the viewpoint (not the one that goes down into the field).

3 You are now walking right above the breeding cliffs of the Griffon Vultures. Keep an

CROSSBILL GUIDES • PROVENCE

eye out since they might fly by at any time. The track itself leads through scrubland with scattered trees. You can find Wryneck, Subalpine Warbler, Whitethroat, Bonelli's Warbler, Woodlark, Cirl Bunting and Crested Tit. Continue along the track until it turns towards the left to reach the highest point where the magnificent view looks towards some cliffs with the snowy peaks of the Alps in the distance. This is an excellent vantage point to scan for raptors. Four species of Vultures have been recorded from here although only Griffon Vulture commonly occurs, Black and Egyptian Vultures are rare and the chances of finding a Bearded Vulture are very small. Other raptors include Golden and Short-toed Eagle, Peregrine and Honey Buzzard. (The best viewpoint can be found when you follow the fence on the right side of the track, towards the cliff; (careful as this is not an official viewing point).

Return to Rougon and drive back to the crossing where you first turned left. Park here at the opposite side of the road.

From the viewpoints on the Route de Crête you have close views of Red-billed Chough (top) and Griffon Vulture (bottom).

4 From the car park, walk towards the *Point Sublime* following the signposts. The viewpoint offers you the classic view of the Gorge Du Verdon. Note the tilted layers that are visible in the cliffs at some places. These result from the folding of the plateau millions of years ago.

From the viewpoint you can again see the vultures and other cliff birds mentioned at point 3.

Return to your car and continue your way eastwards on the D952. Turn right after 700 metres, following the sign towards *Belvédère de Couloir*. After 500 metres you will find a path on your left with a sign pointing towards *Pont de Tusset*. Park at the side of the road and walk this trail.

ROUTE 19: GRAND CANYON DU VERDON – A FIRST EXPLORATION

5 You pass through damp forest with open rocky places. In the forest note the blankets of moss growing on the trees – a sign of the gorge forest dampness that is in such a sharp contrast to the scorching drought on the plateau at the *Pointe Sublime*, only a few hundred metres away. On the rocky places keep an eye out for butterflies like the rare Chequered and Baton Blues and Provence Orange-tip. You can also find orchids like Bird's-nest, Violet Bird's-nest, Lady Orchid and White Helleborine. The track leads to a beautiful arched bridge from which you can see Crag Martins, Grey Wagtail and Dipper on the river. You can continue further on the other side into a damp pine forest. It is mainly interesting for its spring flowers with Liverleaf, Primrose and Spring Pea – all of which are familiar species in the temperate regions of Europe as well. The birdlife is also distinctly 'central European', with Firecrest, Coal and Crested Tits.

Return to the road and turn left to walk to the end point, from where you can visit the river again (this is where the Martel walk ends; route 20).

6 The exposed, south-facing cliffs on the side of the road are excellent for butterflies. Apart from the aforementioned Checkered and Baton Blues and Provence Orange-tip, look for Woodland Grayling, False Grayling and Great Sooty Satyr (the latter three in summer).

Return to the D952 and turn right, direction Castellane.

The Pont de Tusset over the Verdon river.

7 The next section of the road is spectacular, with massive cliffs overhanging the road. It is hard to stop here, especially in the tourist season, but if you find a spot, pull over and admire the large numbers of vultures soaring overhead.

After you pass a small bridge on the right, park the car on the right side of the road. At the other side of the bridge is a relaxing picnic spot.

ROUTE 19: GRAND CANYON DU VERDON – A FIRST EXPLORATION

8 While unwrapping your lunch, you overlook the river and several pebble banks. You have another chance at finding Dipper and Grey Wagtail. The gravel banks are large enough to support breeding Little Ringed Plover. Around the picnic spot, the flora supports Common Spotted Orchid, an orchid which is widespread and numerous in the Alps, but not in Provence. A touch of the mountain flora.

Return to La Palud Sur Verdon. One km before the village, turn left onto the *Route de Crête*.

The boldly marked Chequered Blue is perhaps the smartest-looking blue of Provence. It flies in sunny spots along the Verdon River.

9 The Route the Crête is a touristic road that takes you past some of the most impressive viewpoints of the gorge. Especially the first four viewpoints are balconies from which you look down sheer cliffs into a depth of several hundred metres – very impressive! We advise you to spend some time here as Griffon Vultures come soaring by at close range. The other vultures are only sometimes seen here, but Golden Eagle is regular. Alpine Swift, Crag Martin, Red-billed Chough, Raven and Short-toed Eagle are present here as well. From autumn to early spring, this is a superb site for Wallcreepers. The cliffs are outside the breeding range of this mysterious 'butterfly bird', but only just.

The box-strewn plateau has only few birds, but one of the most common ones is an attractive species: the Subalpine Warbler. Butterfly enthusiasts in spring should look for Spring Ringlet, while Crimean Iris and Provence Snake's-head* (*Fritillaria involucrata*) flowers at this time as well.

10 The next stop is the bar of *La Maline* (starting point of the Sentier Martel walk; see next route). It is a wonderful, laid-back place to have a drink right on the edge of the plateau. There is a small rock garden just left of the café, which is an ideal place to look for butterflies. Many if not all of the species of south-facing, rocky slopes may come here to enjoy the nectar of the flowers. Unlike the usual spots where these butterflies occur, the terrain here is easy to walk, allowing for easy access and good views.

Continuing this route takes you back to La Palud.

PRACTICAL PART

Route 20: Grand Canyon du Verdon – Sentier Martel

FULL DAY, 13.1 KM
STRENUOUS

The walk-of-walks in the Grand Canyon du Verdon.
Spectacular gorge, with wild canyon forests and paradisiacal spots on the river.

Habitats cliffs, gorge forest, scrubland, river
Selected species Primrose, Bird's-nest Orchid, Griffon Vulture, Dipper, Grey Wagtail, Common Goldenring, Small Pincertail, Great Sooty Satyr, False Ringlet, Checkered Blue, Provence Orange-tip

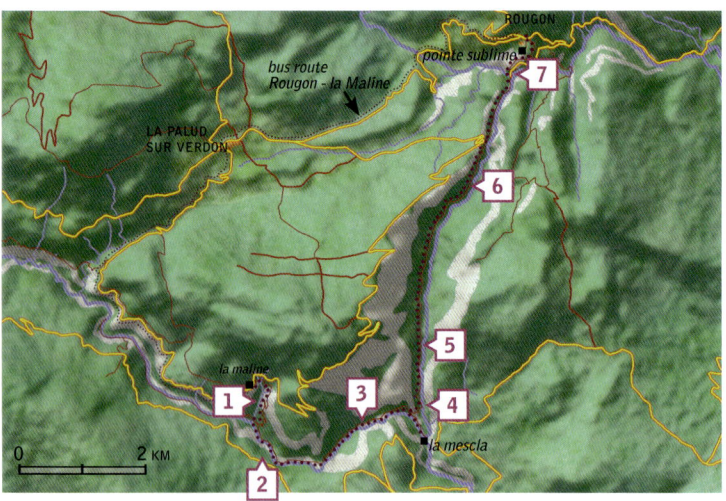

The Gorge du Verdon is also called *Le Grand Canyon* – imparting a sense of drama that is more than justified: this is, perhaps together with that of the Tarn, France's most spectacular gorge. The Martel trail traverses the largest section of the canyon. It is the route-of-routes, one that demands respect – both for its awe-inspiring landscape and for the fact that it is a strenuous walk.
The trail as described here descends into the gorge in the middle and follows the river upstream to its eastern gateway near *Point Sublime*,

Preparation and expectation

A few words on the preparation: the Henry Martel walk is definitely a strenuous one – by far the toughest route in this book. However, it doesn't take an unsurmountable effort either – anyone in a decent condition who goes well prepared and does not shy away from a bit of sweaty effort, will be able to do it. The trail is well-maintained and any of the potentially more dangerous sections are supplied with handles, handrails, fences and steps.

When hiking, keep in mind to bring sufficient water (at least 2 litres on warm days) and enough food to keep you on your feet for 7 hours. You can buy water and snacks at La Maline. Furthermore, make sure you have strong and suitable footwear, for the trail is rocky and uneven. When wet the rocks become slippery and we advise against walking this trail in rainy conditions.

The trail has large shady sections and there are various points where you can cool off in the river, but there are also exposed sections so do bring sun lotion and sunglasses. Finally, bring a torch (alternatively, a fully charged smartphone with flashlight function) to cover the 650 metre long, unlit tunnel.

View from the Martel trail in the gorge.

where you climb out of it again. Between the descent at the start and the ascent at the end, you follow the river, sometimes climbing high above it and dropping down again to its pebbly borders.

The attraction of this route lies in the spectacular cliffs, the azure river and the old gorge woodlands with its many mossy trees. Although much of the flora and fauna of the region can be seen along the trail, this is not an itinerary designed to nail certain species – for that the rough terrain asks too much of your attention. Therefore, we keep this description short and focus on the landscape instead.

Almost by definition, gorges are linear and steep, so opportunities for getting into them and

ROUTE 20: GRAND CANYON DU VERDON – SENTIER MARTEL

The descent into the gorge leads through an impressive old gorge forest.

out are infrequent and always takes effort. On the bright side, you can't get lost either.

The trick is to leave your vehicle on the one end and take a bus or taxi to the other, from which you walk back to the car. By far the easiest and most popular direction is to leave your car at the Point Sublime car park and take the bus or taxi to La Maline. In summer, busses go to the other side of the trail at La Maline (8.45 and 9.30; € 6.00 pp in 2017), during the rest of the year, you need to take a taxi (€ 33.00 carrying up to 8 people. Book in advance (0033 (0)668181313; English and French spoken).

Starting point Café La Maline (GPS 43.746273, 6.344701)

1 The first section of the trail is the descent; first gentle but increasingly steep as you proceed. During much of this careful-where-you-step-trail, your eyes will be glued to the ground, but if you glance up from time to time, you'll notice the micro-climate change as you go down: from hot and exposed to damper, shadier and generally more benign. There are some massive trees on this stretch.

2 Once down, rest and enjoy the river. Dipper and Grey Wagtail may fly by (although they are more common further upstream) and

Small Pincertail and Common Goldenring are frequent dragonflies.

3 The section up to *La Mescla* leads mostly through beautiful woodland. Note the diversity of trees and bushes here, which reflect the variety of environmental conditions: shallow and deep soils, wet and dry, sunny and shady. There are Common and Field Maples, Lime, Ash and Elm trees, Willow, Whitebeam, Hawthorn, Dogwood, Box and Holly, to name the most prominent species.

4 Just after the side trail to the viewpoint of la Mescla, the Verdon makes a sharp turn. This is scenically one of the most spectacular parts. There are several steep climbs, followed by a spectacular descent down a flight of 219 steps, known as the *Brèche Imbert*. They were built in the 1920s by the local villagers who hauled over 5 tons of wood and metal into the gorge to build these ladders. They were renovated in 2012.

The *Brèche Imbert* – 219 steps straight down to the river.

5 The next part is fairly level and easy-going, albeit with long, exposed sections. If it is not too hot, you can enjoy the spectacular sights of the vultures above your head.

6 In 1905 there were plans to build a large hydro-electric dam in the Gorge du Verdon. Thankfully, this project was abandoned as it would have been an ecological disaster. The tunnels on this section of the trail are a remainder of that enterprise. There is one of 132 m long and another of no less than 650 m – pitch-dark and wonderfully cool. There are several small balconies with superb views over the cliffs.

7 After the tunnels it is but a small stretch to the car park of Couloir Samson (see point 4 of route 19), from where a final ascent of 150 m brings you back to the car park of Point Sublime. Note that this last section is again hot and exposed.

Route 21: The Valensole Plain

3-4 HOURS, 42 KM

Birds of the steppes and arable fields.
The classic views of lavender fields with the Alps in the background.

Habitats fields, lavender fields, pastures, stream
Selected species Chamois, Short-toed Eagle, Rock Sparrow, Montagu's Harrier, Hen Harrier, Roller, Hoopoe, Calandra Lark, Spectacled Warbler

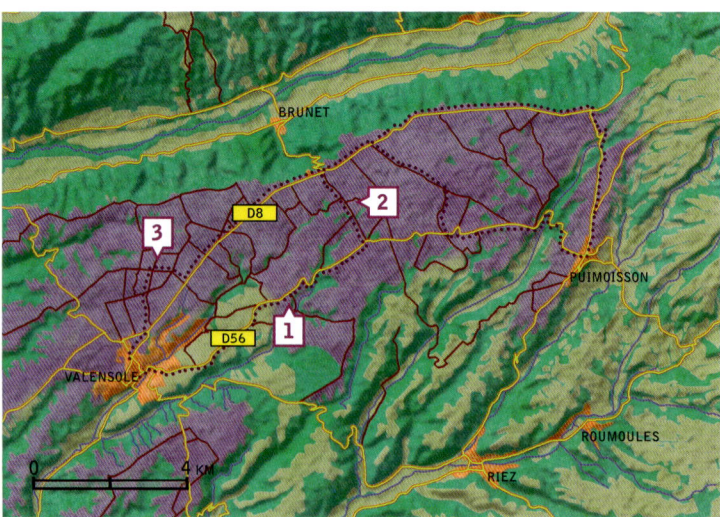

Come in spring and the Valensole plain has a spectacular emptiness. This upland plateau is different from the other, higher plateaux in the region – instead of rocky karst, it consists of cereal and lavender fields, which stand out spectacularly with the high Alps in the background. Therefore, if you come in late June and July, you find the plain full with visitors for the lavender fields.
This route is attractive for more than just the landscape though. The birdlife is very rich as well. The treeless plain is somewhat like an upland version of the Crau – important for steppe birds like various species

ROUTE 21: THE VALENSOLE PLAIN

of larks, harriers and even the odd Roller and Little Bustard. Their numbers are not very high, but with some luck and dedication, you can find quite a few species. Yet at the same time, the plateau is close enough to the Alps to find Chamois grazing on the fields on a quiet evening.

The Plaine de Valensole has the largest concentration of lavender fields in the Provence.

The Valensole plain is laced by river valleys. Unlike the gorges elsewhere, these are pretty green valleys with thyme scrub that attract masses of butterflies. This route combines a visit to the plains and these valleys.

Starting point Valensole village
From the village centre, follow the signs *Riez*. Just after you've crossed the bridge on the edge of the village, turn left onto the D56 towards Puimoisson.

1 This quiet country climbs out of the valley of Valensole and crosses the level plain with cereal and lavender fields. In rotation, fields are left fallow or planted with Lucern (alfalfa) or Sainfoin to improve the soil for another year of crops. The fallow fields are vital for birds. Stop at regular intervals to look and listen for Skylark (common), Crested, Short-toed and Calandra Larks (scarce). Tawny Pipit occurs here too, as well as Quail, Stone Curlew and Little Bustard (the latter often in alfalfa fields). On the wires, Bee-eater, Corn Bunting, Linnet, Goldfinch and Rock Sparrow are regular, but look out too for the rare Ortolan Bunting and Turtle Dove. In recent years, Black-headed Bunting, a birds from south-eastern Europe, has bred on the Valensole Plain. Like Corn Bunting, it often sits on

PRACTICAL PART

ROUTE 21: THE VALENSOLE PLAIN

A Short-toed Eagle scans the fields for snakes – its favourite prey.

electricity wires. Among the raptors, Black Kite is common, and Buzzard and Short-toed Eagle frequent. From time to time, a Griffon Vulture or Golden Eagle from the nearby Gorge du Verdon may fly over as well. Over the fields, all three harriers may be seen hunting: Montagu's, Hen and Marsh, the latter two mostly during migration periods.

After several kilometres, the road snakes down a small wooded valley and climbs up on the other side. Another 900 metres further, the road bends left and then right and in that bend there is a broad track that branches off to the left. Follow it to the D8.

2 This is the heartland of the lavender fields – spectacular when in flower in early summer. An ornithological oddity of these fields is the presence of a small population of Spectacled Warblers – outside the Camargue and Mediterranean littoral, this is the only French population of this rare bird. Be aware that Sardinian Warbler also occurs here.

The lavender and thymes attracts Knapweed, Glanville, Spotted and Marsh Fritillaries, Large Blue and Brown Argus.

Turn right on the D8 and turn the second right again through the lavender fields back to the D56. Once there, turn left to Puimoisson. In the village, turn left and to Valensole.
From this junction, drive 11 kms and then turn right onto a dirt track opposite of *les Bargegiers*. At the second crossing of dirt tracks, turn left and proceed parallel to the D8 back to Valensole.

3 This section leads you over well-maintained dirt tracks with lots of lavender fields. The same birds as before can be found here. Look carefully near stone sheds and ruins, because Rock Sparrow, Little Owl and Hoopoe breed here. In addition, scan the rows of lavender for perching Spectacled Warblers, Stonechats and during migration, Wheatear and Whinchat.

Additional sites in Haute Provence

A – Southern road in the Gorge du Verdon

In our route selection in the Canyon du Verdon we have focussed on the north side of the gorge. However, the road that passes on the southern side is attractive as well. Following the D71 road from Comps-sur-Artuby to Aiguines, you pass along some spectacular viewpoints, such as *Balcon de la Mescla* and *Belvédère Aiguines*. Both have breath-taking views over the gorge, and both (but especially *Mescla*) offer views of Griffon Vultures and, with a little luck, Black Vulture, Golden Eagle and Alpine Swift.

The section of the road east of the *Balcon* leads through a bushy plateau with Box and small pines. It is worth stopping here and stroll around, to look for Subalpine Warbler, butterflies (which in spring include the rare Spring Ringlet), orchids, Provence Snake's-head* (*Fritillaria involucrata*) and Crimean Iris.

The section west of the viewpoints is higher and leads through Beech woods with flowery meadows, again worth exploring for wildflowers and butterflies.

Orchid enthusiasts may want to explore the roadsides of the D 957 on the western side of the gorge, north of the Lac de Sainte Croix, where Lady Orchid, White Helleborine, Small Spider Orchid, Late Spider Orchid and the local endemic *Ophrys pseudoscolopax* all grow.

! The location of the sites described here is shown on the map on page 184.

The Gorge du Verdon seen from the viewpoint on the southern road.

B – Gorges du Trevans

Of course the Gorge du Verdon is the main attraction of this area, and the one with the most dramatic landscape. For that reason, it is also rather crowded, especially in summer. The Gorges du Trevans are less well known, and much quieter, without

ADDITIONAL SITES IN HAUTE PROVENCE

losing much of the dramatic gorge landscape. It is therefore the perfect alternative to the Gorge du Verdon.
To get there, take the D901 road to the village of Estoublon, where you turn right directly after the bridge (when coming from the south) onto the road signposted *Gorges du Trevans*. Follow this road for 5 kms to the car park. From there, a trail leads to the entrance of the gorge. Here you will find a large map of the trails in the area. All of them are attractive for wildlife, but the one leading through the two gorges is arguably the most scenic. Note that all of these trails are moderately difficult and definitely not suited to walk with rainy weather. Whichever route you choose, always keep an eye out for the sky, as Griffon, Black and Egyptian Vultures and Golden Eagles are frequent. On the cliffs of the gorge, Eagle Owls breed. Wherever the trail crosses the stream, look for dragonflies, notably Common Goldenring, Small Pincertail and demoiselles.

C – Col de Bleine and Monts d'Azur

North of the Plateau of Calern lies, on the doorstep of the Maritime Alps, the valley and village of Gréolières. From here the narrow D2 snakes up to yet another limestone plateau, that of the Monts d'Azur. Here are, besides the beautiful scenery, two attractions. One is the Réserve des Monts d'Azur rewilding area – a nature park where European Bisons and Przewalski Horses have been introduced, which can be observed in an enclosure. There are also Red and Roe Deer, Chamois and Wild Boar, while Lynx and Wolf pass through the area occasionally.
A visit to the Monts d'Azur reserve (which has a restaurant and ecolodges as well) is a rather luxurious and pricey affair. There are various options of guided routes, including with horse carriage, but you can also book a 2 hour walking trip (€ 22). For more information, see **www.wildlife-nature-reserve.com**.
A very different naturalist experience you have, when you continue on the D2 a few kilometres further and arrive at the *Col de Bleine* (1439 m). The open Austrian Pinewood and many flowery grasslands are excellent for butterflies, such as Great Sooty Satyr, Pearly Heath, Spotted Fritillary, Dryad and Piedmont Ringlet.

A Spotted Fritillary; one of the common butterflies on the Col de Bleine.

CROSSBILL GUIDES • PROVENCE

Vauclúse

The lovely region of the Vaucluse lies, roughly between the Luberon massif in the south and the Ventoux in the north, the Rhône Valley in the west and the Durance river in the east. The centre of the region consists of a limestone plateau that rises in altitude to approximately 1000 m towards the east. The plateau is little populated, but west of it, there are many small (and beautiful) villages.

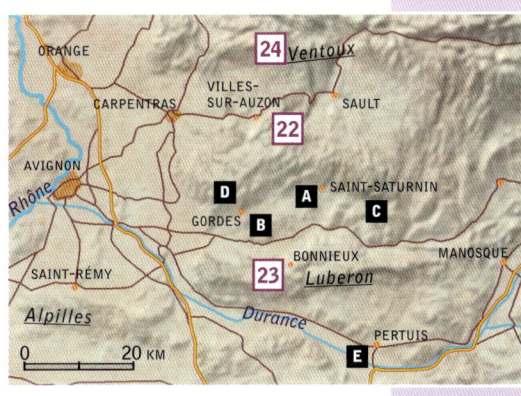

Picturesque is the word that comes to mind when travelling through the Vaucluse. Poppy strewn fields and vineyards and the famous rows of lavender alternate with shrubby chalk downs and woodlands. Pretty medieval villages look as from a painting as they sit on top of a cliff. It is all very pleasant and beautiful.

Pleasant is also the word to describe a naturalist's day in the region. There are many butterflies and wildflowers, orchids in particular, and often they are found right in the side of the road. With Bee-eaters, a few Rollers, Hoopoes and Cirl Buntings, the Vaucluse has a good range of birds, but many of them are much scarcer than you'd think from the ample amount of seemingly good habitat. On our preparatory trips we've found Rollers, Bee-eaters, Hoopoes, Eagle Owls, Golden and Short-toed Eagles and even Egyptian Vulture, but always ones or twos – never in high numbers.

One of the great attractions of the Vaucluse is the Mont Ventoux (route 24) where birds, plants and butterflies of high altitudes can be seen with relative ease. On the plain, the limestone gorges woodlands and grasslands are the places to go (route 22). Additionally, we've described several sites (A to E on page 217-218), sometimes just on the side of some small country road, that are good sites for orchids and butterflies.

Olive trees in a sea of poppies – the Vaucluse excels in lovely landscapes.

PRACTICAL PART

Route 22: Car route through the Vaucluse

FULL DAY, 70 KM

The lovely Vaucluse countryside.
Lots of sites to ramble, particularly attractive for wildflowers and butterflies.

Habitats grasslands, lavender fields, scrub, cliffs, Mediterranean woodland
Selected species Burnt Orchid, Fly Orchid, Lesser Butterfly Orchid, Crag Martin, Blue Rock Thrush, Short-toed Eagle, Eagle Owl, Egyptian Vulture, Cirl Bunting, Stonechat, Western Green Lizard, Wall Lizard, Spanish Festoon, Southern Swallowtail, Chequered Blue, Southern White Admiral

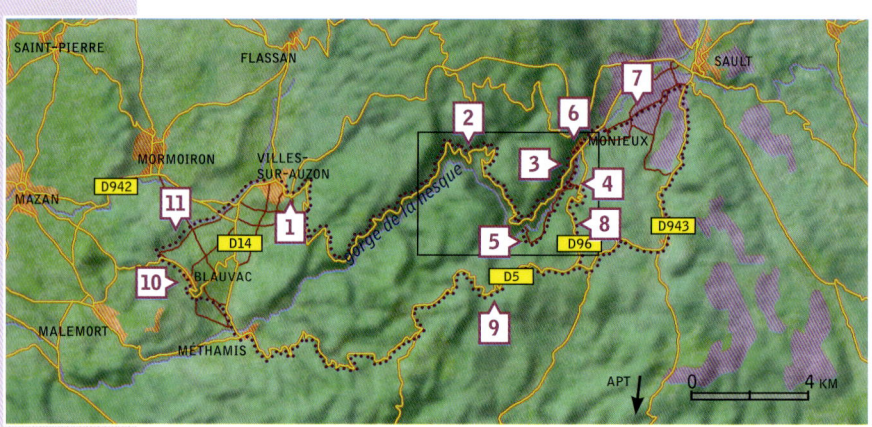

An image of the Provence countryside is often one of the Vaucluse: deep purple lavender fields, sunflowers, an abandoned terracotta shed, small oak woodlands, a medieval village and mountains in the distance – *La douce France* in other words. That's precisely what you'll get on this car route, plus plenty of wildlife stops to enjoy the birds, the orchids and masses of butterflies.

This route crosses the limestone plateau of the Vaucluse near the Gorge of the Nesque river – a bonsai version of the Gorge du Verdon, but nevertheless impressive. The gorge as well as the surrounding woodlands and fields are the destination for this route.

ROUTE 22: CAR ROUTE THROUGH THE VAUCLUSE

Starting point Villes-sur-Auzon (GPS 44.057720, 5.234134)

Getting there From Carpentras, head east to Mazan and continue along the D942 to Villes. In the village, turn right following the Gorge de la Nesque signs. Once outside the village (and on the Gorge de la Nesque road) there is a crossing, where Monieux and Sault are signposted. Park here explore the track that runs parallel to the D942.

1 The dry grasslands next to the road are superb for butterflies from mid May all through the summer. Among the more remarkable butterflies are Spanish Festoon, Southern Swallowtail, Southern White Admiral, Dingy Skipper, Black-eyed and Baton Blues, Pearl-bordered Fritillary, Provence Orange-tip, Cleopatra, Ilex Hairstreak and Southern Gatekeeper. You can also find the first of orchids of the route here: Violet Bird's-Nest, Lizard and Pyramidal Orchids, White and Narrow-leaved Helleborines.

Continue along the D942 into the gorge.

2 You are entering the foothills of the Mont Ventoux, where the river Nesque has cut through the soft limestones. The terrain is not high, but the river gorge is nothing short of dramatic.

A Weaver's Fritillary in a lavender field beneath Sault.

Although the road is narrow, there are various car parks from where you look over the gorge. Look for Crag Martin, Alpine Swift, Subalpine Warbler, Blue Rock Thrush, Short-toed Eagle and Egyptian Vulture. The latter does not breed annually, but we found a pair here in 2017. Along the way, note the weird 'crash barrier' of small pollarded Holm Oaks that lines the road.

On the other side of the gorge, just before km post 58, there is a track to the left, where there is a quarry. Park here.

ROUTE 22: CAR ROUTE THROUGH THE VAUCLUSE

3 The dry quarry is another excellent spot to look for butterflies like Baton, Adonis and Checkered Blues. In spring evenings, you may hear the soft calls from the Midwife Toads.

In Monieux, turn right to *Plan d'Eau* and park at the small reservoir.

4 The reservoir (where some Great Reed Warblers breed and Kingfisher is often present) is fringed with reeds and trees. It looks a little like a city park, which stands out oddly next to the wild gorge de la Nesque and traditional landscape around Monieux.
It pays to be here at dusk, as the local Eagle Owls fly out of the gorge over the lake to go out hunting. The flowery fields are a riot of butterflies in summer (Great Banded Grayling, Southern White Admiral, Sooty Copper, Blue-spot and Ilex Hairstreak, to name but a few).
On foot, follow the footpath into the gorge (direction *St. Hubert, La Peisse*), for a beautiful, short (2.5 km one way) walk.

An Eagle Owl in the Gorge de la Nesque, looking down on the footpath near Plan d'Eau.

5 The walk starts out near the river but soon climbs the hill. You are surrounded by young woodland and Box woods, with here and there a large old tree with a massive crown that reminds of times that these rocky, limestone plateaux were much more barren and used to graze sheep. The scattered trees were the only shaded spots. There are several dry meadows which are again attractive for butterflies. Check the crags in the cliffs carefully as well – in 2017 we stumbled upon the Eagle Owl shown on the photo here.

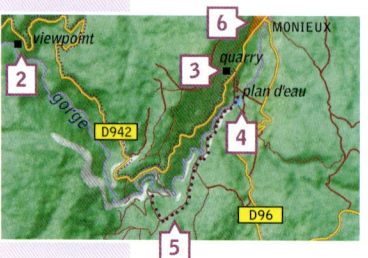

Continue the trail to the edge of the cliff (follow *Chapelle Saint-Michel*), from which you have wonderful views and again a good chance on cliff birds.

Return to Plan d'eau and drive to Monieux.

6 Monieux is worth a visit in itself. It is an intact and well-maintained medieval village.

CROSSBILL GUIDES • PROVENCE

ROUTE 22: CAR ROUTE THROUGH THE VAUCLUSE

On the slope above the houses are some ruins on a dry, south-facing cliff. A steep trail just west from the church will bring you to them. It is again a good site for butterflies, with, among others, Chequered Blue and Great Sooty Satyr.

In Monieux you have a choice. In summer, we advise to follow the loop through the Lavender fields south of Sault; in spring, the dry plateau is more exciting because of its orchids. Point 6 here describes the lavender fields; point 7 the shorter road over the plateau.

7 Leave Monieux in direction Sault and after a few hundred metres, turn right at Le Moulin. Subsequently, take the first left and cross the lavender fields until you reach Sault.
No summer visit to the Vaucluse is complete without a visit to the lavender fields for which the region is famous (see page 57). The lavender not only attracts people but also masses of butterflies – the purple flowers are true nectar factories and attract masses of butterflies. Here, there are lots of Queen of Spain and Weaver's Fritillaries and Long-tailed Blue, but anything may turn up here.

The road ends at the D943 just south of Sault (which is worth the short detour). Turn right towards Saint-Saturnin-les-Apt. You climb further up on the plateau until you reach the hamlet of St Jean (6 km), beyond which you go straight following the D 943 direction Apt. At the next junction, bear right onto the D5 to Méthamis.

8 In spring, opt for the direct route out of Monieux via the D96, direction St Hubert and Méthamis (note the many Pheasant's-eye Daffodils in the meadows). After 5.5 km the D96 connects with the local D5 road.
This stretch of road is peaceful and quiet and crosses the Vaucluse plateau with its box bushes and limestone grassland. Anywhere along this road is good for orchids. At around 800 metres altitude, the Mediterranean species are replaced by temperate-European species like Lesser Butterfly, Burnt, Green-winged and Fly Orchid. It is hard to pinpoint precisely where they grow but we found them along the final two kilometres before arriving at the junction with the D5.

At the T-junction, turn right.

ROUTE 22: CAR ROUTE THROUGH THE VAUCLUSE

9 The road continues over the plateau. You can make regular stops at viewpoints, from which you have gorgeous views to the Mont Ventoux in the north. As you proceed, you slowly descend from the Vaucluse plateau into the hot lowlands.

Cross the village of Méthamis and turn right onto the D14 signposted Villes-sur-Auzon. Then, after 2.4 kms, turn left to Blauvac, signposted by an old stone sign.

10 The last stop on this route through the Provençal Idylle is the village of Blauvac. Situated on a hill with views to either side, this is again a pretty hamlet. From the central square, you look out over the hills on all sides. On the village walls there are lots of Red Valerian where you can find, in theory, three species of Swallowtail butterflies: Scarce, Common and Southern Swallowtail, although the latter is uncommon. There are also lots of Hummingbird and Broad-bordered Bee Hawk-moths. From the village, there are several trails that explore the hillside.

The Egyptian Vulture is a regular breeding bird of the Gorge de la Nesque (top).
View from the road to Méthamis with the Mont Ventoux in the back (bottom).

Proceed. After 900 metres from the square of Blauvac, turn right on the *Chemin des Arnaud*. Subsequently, go right again and at the next two crossings, just go straight until you arrive on the main D942. Turn right to return to Villes-sur-Auzon.

11 This final stretch leads once again through a pretty mosaic landscape of woodlands, flowery grasslands, vineyards and cherry groves.

CROSSBILL GUIDES • PROVENCE

Route 23: Walking in the Montagne du Luberon

6 HOURS, 11 KM
EASY-MODERATE

Pretty walk through wooded hills.
Lots of orchids and butterflies in spring.

Habitats flowery fields, downy oak woodland
Selected species Drome Orchid, White Helleborine, Passion-tide Orchid, Lady Orchid, False Woodcock Orchid, Violet Bird's-nest, Short-toed Eagle, Purple-shot Copper, Spanish Festoon, Spanish Fritillary

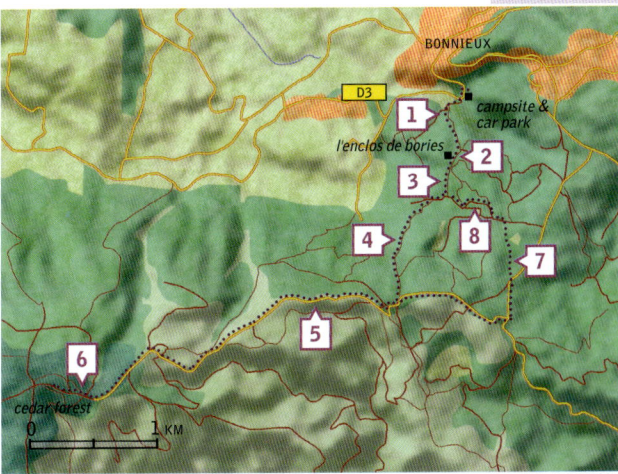

The mountains of the Luberon extend from Cavaillon to Manosque on the north bank of the Durance. It is a continuation of the Alpilles, but higher, wilder and more densely wooded, with on its edges some beautiful villages. Much of the Luberon is rather difficult to visit. The area south of Bonnieux is the exception. This route crosses a shady area of Downy Oak forest with small, flowery fields that are superb for orchids and butterflies. Don't forget to visit the village of Bonnieux itself, which is considered to be (one of) the most beautiful villages of the Vaucluse. The village dates back to the Roman days, when there was an important trade route here. When the Pope resided in Avignon (see page 66), Bonnieux was the domicile of many bishops.

Starting point Bonnieux camp site (GPS 43.820575, 5.308981)

ROUTE 23: WALKING IN THE MONTAGNE DU LUBERON

The car park near the campsite is situated on the D3 just outside the village in the direction of Lacoste.

From the car park take the the track up to *l'Enclos de Bories*. Ignore the first track left and at the hairpin, continue towards *l'Enclos*.

1 You enter a woodland of Downy and Holm Oaks with lots of Box and Shrubby Scorpion-vetch which will be your habitat for much of this route. Western Green Lizards are frequent along the trail and you should be able to pick up your first butterflies: Little Blue and Provence Orange-tip. The birdlife is not particularly rich, but Bonelli's Warbler, Cirl Bunting and Serin should be present in large numbers.

Ignore the side trail to a car park and proceed uphill.

The Atlas Cedars in the Bois des Cèdres are brought up from Morocco and planted in the Luberon. The forest isn't rich in wildlife, but is nevertheless very scenic (top). In one of the fields Drome and Passiontide Orchids flower in May, plus what is probably the hybrid between those two species (bottom).

2 You'll soon come to the site of *l'Enclos de Bories*, a restored ancient Provençal village. Entrance to the site is € 5 but the trail that runs through it is public. Follow it until you come to some flowery fields a bit further on.

3 The fields are superb for butterflies. We found Glanville, Knapweed, Spanish, Pearl-bordered and Twin-spot Fritillaries, Provence Orange-tip, Black-eyed, Little and Osiris Blues in spring, and there is bound to be more present here. Further on the route, there will be more of these fields which are worth checking.

The track arrives at a T-junction. Turn right here and a little further on, just before the track becomes private, a trail turns left, signposted *Bois the Cèdres*.

ROUTE 23: WALKING IN THE MONTAGNE DU LUBERON

4 This long(ish), somewhat strenuous but pretty trail runs uphill through dense woodland. On both sides of the trail are mossy rocks with Maidenhair Spleenwort and Rustyback Ferns.

You arrive at the road towards *Bois the Cèdres*. Here you have a choice – turn right to the Ceder forest (3 kms) or left to return.

5 Turning right, you continue over a small tarmac road over the ridge of the Luberon chain. The ground is rocky, and dry, with little soil. You'll find the typical flora of Mediterranean dry limestone rock, with the Blue Aphyllanthes, White and Hoary Rockroses, Grey-leaved Cistus, Shrubby Globularia and the shiny blue flowers of Beautiful Flax. With luck you may spot a Short-toed Eagle or some Alpine Swifts overhead, or a Subalpine or Sardinian Warbler which breed in the Kermes Oak shrub on the ridge.

Take some time to watch the butterflies in the small fields along the path. There are many different species, including Scarce Swallowtail (top) and the Burnet *Zygaena rhadamanthus*.

6 It is not far until the road gives way to the *Bois de Cèdres*, or forest of the Cedar Trees. The lofty trees are Atlas Cedars, undoubtedly introduced from Morocco, when it was still a French colony. The parklike woodland is pretty rather than rich in wildlife, although Firecrest, Goldcrest, Coal and Crested Tits and Short-toed Treecreeper add some avian flavour to this otherwise quiet area.

Walk on for as long as you like. Then return and continue past the trail to Bonnieux. The road comes to a Y junction. About 100 metres further, you arrive at some fields, where electrical wires pass overhead. Enter these fields following the electrical wires as your reference point. The best entry point is to walk beneath the wires and turn right on a track next to the 4th pole.

PRACTICAL PART

ROUTE 23: WALKING IN THE MONTAGNE DU LUBERON

Part of the route leads through a mossy forest of Downy Oak (top). There are many ferns (Rustyback, Maidenhair Spleenwort) growing on the old stone walls along the path (bottom).

7 These fields form the most attractive part of this route. There are plenty of butterflies and orchids. On the patches of thyme (great nectar flowers), look for Purple-shot Copper, Large Blue (summer) and Spanish Festoon, plus the aforementioned butterflies. Among the orchids, it is the spectacular and endemic Drome Orchid that takes the cake, plus a stable population of the hybrid between Drome and Passion-tide Orchid. But there are many more species to be found, including False Woodcock Orchid* (*Ophrus pseudoscolopax*) and, in June, Lizard and Pyramidal Orchids. Note that the orchids are rather local and it requires some searching to find all of them.

Continue downhill following the electrical wires. Ignore the first crossing and at the next dirt track, go left. Take the next right and follow it until you return to the trail towards l'Enclos.

8 This section has again many woodlands with flowery fields, again with the same rich variety of butterflies.

Route 24: The summit of the Mont Ventoux

5-6 HOURS, 5.5 KM, ONE WAY
MODERATE

Bizarre limestone landscape of Provence's most famous mountain. An 'island' of high mountain species in the lowland Vaucluse. Stunning views of the Alps and surrounding lowlands.

! Weather conditions may change rapidly on the mountain.

Habitats bare rock, juniper scrub, scots pine forest
Selected species Golden Primula, Silver Eryngo, Rhaetian Poppy, Narcissus-flowered Leek, Chamois, Citril Finch, Crossbill, Rock Thrush, Rock Bunting, Golden Eagle, Snow Finch (winter), Alpine Accentor (winter), Meadow Viper, Apollo, Dusky Heath, Provençal Fritillary

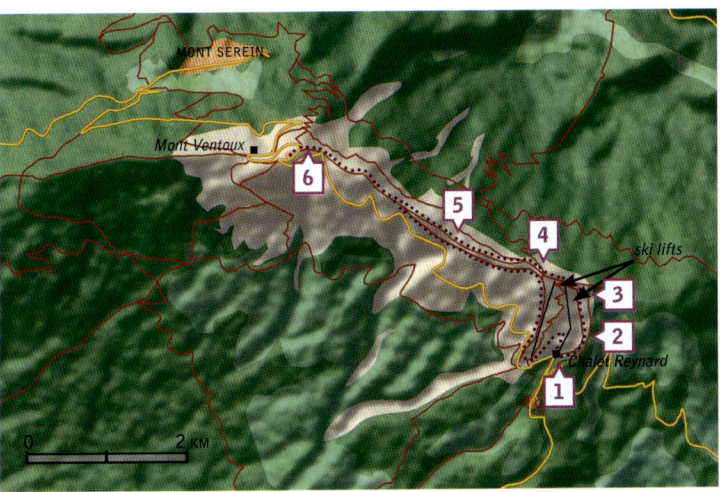

The legendary Mont Ventoux is like a Santiago de Compostella to cyclists. With its 1912 metres and with a 26 km road that climbs virtually non-stop to the peak, it is an irresistible mountain to climb. The Mont Ventoux lies isolated, a little away from the Alps (it is geologically speaking part of the Pyrenees rather than the Alps; see pages 16-17). Precisely these characteristics – an isolated high mountain with perfect access to the upper slopes – is what makes it superb for naturalists as well.

PRACTICAL PART

ROUTE 24: THE SUMMIT OF THE MONT VENTOUX

For the most part, the Mont Ventoux is densely wooded. Downy Oak grows on the low slopes and Beech and Scots Pine further up. The summit area in contrast, is bare and rocky, with scattered stunted trees and bushes. It is here that you'll find most of the special flora and fauna. This walk covers the best parts of the high slopes.

To make the most out of your visit, make sure you select your day carefully. Clear and windfree days are the best ('Windfree' on the Mont Ventoux is relative; its name literally translates the ever-windy mountain). Also, make sure you start early as it is bound to become crowded with cyclists and day-trippers during the course of the morning.

Starting point Chalet Reynard
(GPS 44.152181, 5.318840)

Getting there from Sault, follow the road up to the Mont Ventoux. Six km before the actual summit, the chalet lies on the right side of the road.

1 Chalet Reynard is situated on the treeline, with woodland just below and a scatter of stunted pines, junipers and bare rock further up. This zone is rich in birds and you might very well pick up your first Citril Finches around the car park. We found them often sitting on the road, flying up to the trees whenever a car or cyclist approaches. Crossbill, Dunnock (within in Provence only breeding here), Mistle Thrush,

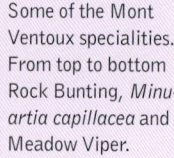

Some of the Mont Ventoux specialities. From top to bottom Rock Bunting, *Minuartia capillacea* and Meadow Viper.

CROSSBILL GUIDES • PROVENCE

ROUTE 24: THE SUMMIT OF THE MONT VENTOUX

Black Redstart, Serin, Woodlark, Firecrest, Coal and Crested Tits are other birds around the chalet. In winter, Snow Finch can be seen here too.

Follow the track up the slope that starts on the right side of the Chalet.

2 This section remains excellent for birds, which show themselves best on spring mornings. In addition to the aforementioned, there are Rock Bunting, Linnet, Raven and Rock Thrush. Check the wires of the ski lift, which are a popular singing post. Keep an eye out for large raptors too. Golden Eagle is not uncommon here.

3 As the trail bends around the corner, it follows a gully between wooded slopes. This sunny, sheltered spot is ideal for butterflies in summer, such as Dusky Heath, Purple-shot Copper, Grayling and the first Apollos. The ground-hugging, brightly yellow Golden Primula is a common sight on the side of the trail in spring, and you'll find the first of the tall Silver Eryngos here later in the year.

4 You pass underneath two ski lifts. At the second, your view of the peak opens up. At this elevation the trees have given up and only the oddly rounded patches of junipers remain. The ground appears bare, but look carefully as a number of Alpine plants thrive here. Most flower in (early) summer: Creeping Globularia, Rock-jasmine, Lesser Meadow-rue, Alpine Bluebell, Mountain Germander, Saxifrage Catchfly, the sandwort *Minuartia capilacea*, Lesser Catmint, Mont Cenis Pansy, Purple Saxifrage and others. This is also the habitat of the rare and endangered Meadow Viper (see page 105). Among the birds, Northern Wheatear is common, while in winter, look for Alpine Accentors.

Two ski trails lead up to the top, lined by blue and red poles respectively. Follow the red ones up and the blue ones down.

5 The red ski trail follows the ridge from which on clear days the views over the Alps are breath-taking (At the pass on the summit is a table naming the peaks in front of you). A scatter of stunted trees here means you still have a chance on the birds noted for points 1 and 2. The sheltered spots between the trees are attractive butterfly haunts, with, next to the aforementioned, lots of Queen-of-Spain and Provençal Fritillaries and large numbers of Apollos. Also, there is a chance on spotting Chamois on these slopes, so keep an eye out for them as well.

PRACTICAL PART

ROUTE 24: THE SUMMIT OF THE MONT VENTOUX

6 The final ascent leads through a bleak stony desert. In July, there are a number of interesting plants flowering here, such as Rhaetian Poppy, the spectacular Narcissus-flowered Leek* (*Allium narcissiflorum*), Seguier's Crowfoot, Round-headed Rampion, the endemic candytuft *Iberis candolleana*, and the toadflax *Linaria striata*. Some of these are specialists of the highest peaks of the Alps and of the high Arctic, which is remarkable as the Mont Ventoux peak is much lower and more influenced by the Mediterranean climate. However, the climate on the peak is just as extreme as in these Arctic sites: the extreme drought narrows the growing season to late spring and early summer – a period just as short as in the Arctic.

In winter, this area and the area around the peak is where Alpine Accentor is often found.

When the weather is good, the path to the top is easy walking (top). Keep an eye out for Chamois along the way (bottom).

Return via the blue poles which eventually lead you back to the road. Here you can either follow the road for 800 m back to Chalet Reynard, or follow the trail left to the start of the ski lift. From there, follow the trail left (not the one that follows the ski lift cables) that connects with the trail above Chalet Reynard (see map). This latter trail is longer and more demanding than simply following the road, but leads through more good birding habitat.

Additional remarks Station du Mont Serein underneath the Ventoux on the north slope has meadows and coniferous forest and is another excellent spot to search for woodland birds including Citril Finch, and for the rare Meadow Viper.

Additional sites in the Vaucluse

A – Roadside spots near St Aturnin les Apt

There are many excellent roadside spots for butterflies and wildflowers in the Vaucluse. Without claiming to have found the best, here are some that we found very attractive.

The first is the area northwest of Saint-Saturnin-lès-Apt. If you take the D943 direction Sault from Saint-Saturnin, you first arrive at a dual bridge over a beautiful river gorge with a rich Mediterranean vegetation. Beyond it, turn onto the small country road to Lioux. There are some fine grasslands with orchids along this road (e.g. Small Spider, Late Spider, False Woodcock, Fragrant and Military Orchids). Lioux itself is a tiny hamlet at the base of a magnificent cliff. Further on, the road connects with the D4 and if you head south here, you pass some wonderful poppy fields (in spring) and more roadside spots with plenty of orchids.

! The location of the sites described here is shown on the map on page 203.

The village of Lioux lies beneath an impressive cliff.

B – Fields of Gordes

South of the D2 between the town of Gordes and Rousillon (which are both beautiful and famous medieval villages) lies a fertile plain with fields, vineyards and some small rivers with thick riverine vegetation. This region has some attractive birds. Next to Hoopoes, Bee-eaters, Corn Buntings and Stonechats, this is a good area to search for Rollers. The fields are easy to view from the many minor roads, such as the D104 and the D169, both near the hamlet of Les Bartagnons.

C – Le Colorado

The basin between the Vaucluse Plateau and the Luberon mountains has a special geology, with soft sandstone in splendid ochre and terracotta colours. For hundreds

ADDITIONAL SITES IN THE VAUCLUSE

The famous Abbeye de Senanque.

of years, ochre was quarried near the village Rousillon about 15 kms further west (the mines can still be visited there). Even more beautiful is the old quarry known as *Le Colorado de Rustrel*, near the latter-named village. There is a 4 km waymarked trail through the site. Le Colorado is well signposted from the D22 between Apt and Gignac, just south of Rustrel. Entrance is free, but to park you need to pay € 5.

The main attraction are the sandy cliffs with their bright, ochres, brick-reds and whites (see page 18), but the trail has much more to offer. Water seeps out of the ground in various places, allowing a lush woodland to grow with a dense vegetation of Giant Horsetail and many small streams where butterflies come down to drink (e.g. Meleager's Blue, Scarce Swallowtail). For a site that advertises itself as *Le Sahara*, it is perhaps surprising that dense, verdant woodland is a main attraction for naturalists.

D – Gordes and Abbeye de Senanque

The village of Gordes and the Abbey of Senanque are famous attractions in the Vaucluse – Gordes for being so beautifully situated on the flank of a steep hill (and for being the place where many movie stars and French celebrities go) and Senanque for being a wonderful, original monastery situated in a narrow, wooded valley with beautiful lavender fields in front of it.

If you drive from Gordes to the Abbey and on to Venasque a little further north (yet another superbly conserved medieval village on top of a cliff), you pass through fine downy oak woodland with grassy fields and a dry limestone gorge, which, for naturalists, are great places to look around. There are plenty of orchids (including the rare and attractive Drome Orchid) and other wildflowers, the usual rich array of butterflies (e.g. Provence Orange-tip, Cleopatra, Cardinal and Provence Chalk-hill Blue) and the usual lizards and snakes which are as ever, rather hard to track down. The roads connecting these sites are quiet and offer lots of places to stop and explore, giving a 'day of culture' a fine naturalist lining.

E – Durance

Of all the great ecological sites of Provence, the Durance is probably the hardest to visit. You follow it for several kilometres when you take the A51 motorway, but good access is hard. Yet it is an important river for birds, wildflowers and insects. One good, if somewhat forlorn place to visit the Durance is near the town of Pertuis.

To get there, turn off the motorway 51 at exit 15, Pertuis. At the roundabout, don't go right to Pertuis, but straight on a small road, signposted *Les Gravières*. The road turns into a very potholed track and passes a narrow iron gate (take great care going through it!), before you arrive at a long and straight dead-end road that runs parallel to the river. To avoid speeding, the tarmac is cut up at regular intervals, but if you're careful, you can drive it.

Birdwatching – nature in general – is one of the great things this road offers. But the seclusion and lack of traffic is appealing to other people as well. Apart from birdwatching, this is a place where driving schools set out circuits for learner motorists. All in all, this place edges towards being tacky, but the wildlife makes up for that.

Kingfishers are common along the Durance.

For naturalists there are good views over the river and a number of reed-fringed, water-filled quarries, where Little and Great Crested Grebes, Night Heron, Little and Great White Egret and Kingfisher can be seen. Nightingales and Cetti's Warbler sing from within the vegetation, while Golden Orioles, Turtle Doves and Green Woodpeckers can be found in the taller trees. In the roadside, there are masses of Passiontide Orchids in April-mid May, while in June, Lizard Orchids are numerous. This stretch of river is also excellent for dragonflies. Look for Mercury Bluet, White-tailed Skimmer, Banded Darter, Copper Demoiselle, White Featherleg and Common Clubtail.

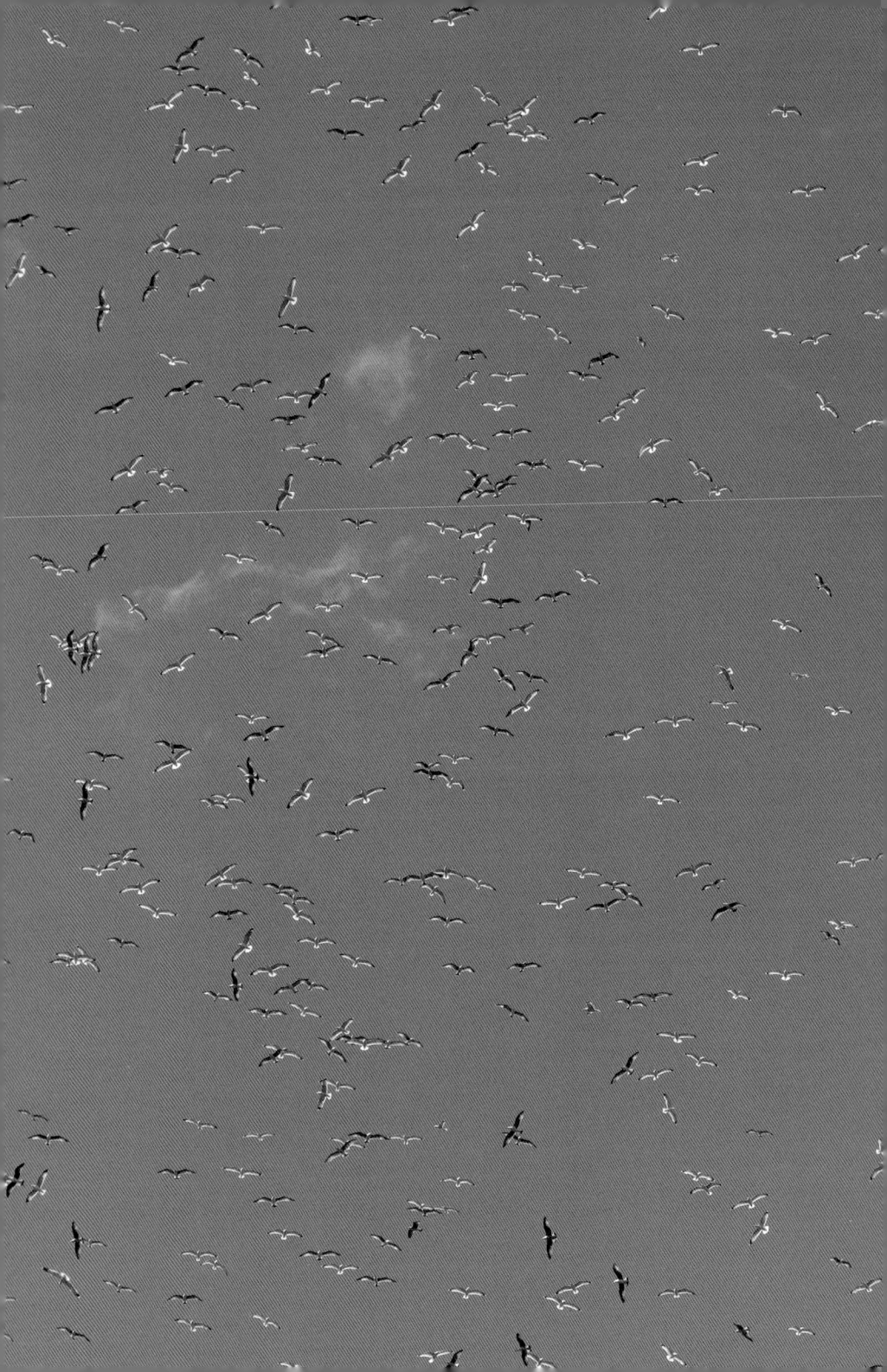

TOURIST INFORMATION & OBSERVATION TIPS

Travel

Travelling to and in Provence by public transport
Provence is very easy to get to by public transport. Coming from Paris, Avignon is the main hub, from where you can easily take a train or bus deeper into the region. A TGV train takes you from Paris *Gare de Lyon* to Avignon in only 3½ hours (or in 4½ hours to Marseille), where you can rent a car or continue by bus or train to any of the other cities in Provence. For train tickets and departure times, check **www.oui.sncf.fr**. There are also cheap long distance bus services, such as Flixbus (**www.flixbus.com**), Ouibus (**www.ouibus.com**) or Eurolines (**www.eurolines.com**).
Bus services within Provence are generally good, although buses to smaller villages are not very frequent. Your best starting point on the web is **www.info-ler.fr**. Here you can buy tickets and download maps showing bus and train services.

Travelling to and in Provence by car
Most visitors to Provence and Camargue will go by car. Via the *Route du Soleil* you can easily dash down to Avignon, from where motorways will bring you further into the region. The car is by far the easiest way to explore the region and to get to the starting points of the routes in this book.
Roads are generally in good condition. France, more than other south European countries, has a very fine network of roads, with many little travelled country roads to connect tiny hamlets with one another. You can stop and stroll pretty much wherever you like, which makes an exploration by car a real adventure.
Driving these small roads is an invitation to potter along at a relaxed pace, especially in the mountains. If you want to travel quickly, then the toll roads are excellent (but pricey) and put most parts of Provence within easy reach. The main ones are the *Route du Soleil* which follows the Rhône Valley and forks north of Avignon into a western branch (the A9) towards Nîmes and Montpellier, south (A7) to Marseille and east (A8) to Aix-en-Provence and Nice. From Aix, another toll road (A 51) heads northeast, following the Durance river to Manosque and Gap.
The traffic is generally not too busy, but there are some exceptions. The summer season, especially 'Black Saturday' (the name given to the last Saturday of July and, less often, the first Saturday of August), when the French start their summer holiday and traffic on the motorways is awful. Outside the holiday periods, only in and around the main cities are there frequent traffic jams in mornings and afternoons.

Finally, the built-up coastal road along the Côte d'Azur is very busy in summer – the combination of numerous villas and holiday homes, beach traffic and sinuous mountain roads is a recipe for traffic jams.

Planning your trip

When to go
With so many different habitats, Provence is an attractive destination at all times of the year, but if a favourite season must be chosen, then it is most likely May or June. Here is a description of Provence throughout the year.

December to February
The dead of winter is far from dead in Provence. The coast is the most attractive part, with tens of thousands of wintering birds in the Camargue and the Hyères salt pans. Among them are plenty of flamingos, waders, ducks and herons, but also rarities like Spotted Eagle (several individuals each year). In the Gorge du Verdon, the Alpilles and various other mountains, there are Wallcreepers and Alpine Accentors.

March - early April
The first signs of spring can be seen in late February. The region becomes more attractive by the day. On sunny days (which is the majority) out of the wind, it is wonderfully pleasant and warm. All the winter birds are still present and the first wildflowers appear. Some of the early orchids (Giant Orchid, Western Spider Orchid*; *Ophrys exaltata*) come into bloom, narcissi blossom and there are some butterflies on the wing. The first sign of bird migration comes in the form of waders and swallows, but also the Great Spotted Cuckoo is early. Higher up in the mountains, wildflowers have yet to bloom, but the woodpeckers call and thrushes and larks are singing.

April
The lowland Provence bursts into flower – orchids pop up everywhere, the early butterflies like festoons and Provence Hairstreak are on the wing. The woodlands higher up in the mountains develop a carpet of spring wildflowers. Amphibians and reptiles gradually become active. In the Camargue and elsewhere on the coast, migration is in full swing. While some of the winter visitors are still lingering, the Hoopoe's, Short-toed Eagles, Lesser Kestrels and other birds are pouring in.

May
Perhaps the finest of all months is May when birds are in full song, reptiles are active, there are many butterflies about and many flowers burst into life. Better still,

it's when temperatures are agreeable and campsites and restaurants are opening, but still quiet. The coastal marshes are brimming with life as both breeding birds and large numbers of migrants are present. The birds that nest in the region are still singing and displaying, making even the shy species relatively easy to see. Frogs are calling everywhere and in places, the Yellow Irises carpet the marshes. The scrublands in Provence are in full flower. The orchid flora reaches its peak, with masses of tongue-orchids in the Plaine des Maures and all sorts of bee orchids in the limestone areas. All the spring butterflies are on the wing now.

June

In June, the Mediterranean lowland is undeniably becoming hot. Grasses have finished blooming and turn yellow. The new plants that come into bloom have a more robust appearance – thistles and Round-headed Leeks. Birds are gradually becoming less visible as they are tending their young (although there is still a lot around). Meanwhile, the larger insects appear: large grasshoppers and bush-crickets, mantids, dragonflies and, of course, it's when the cicada chorus starts to sing on the hot afternoons. In the mountains on the karst plateaus flowers are still in full bloom and butterflies appear everywhere. Towards the end of the month, the Lavender fields wash the horizon purple.

July and August

Early July is excellent. There are interesting dragonflies in the lowlands, young birds start to move around (hence becoming more visible), the number of mountain butterflies peaks and the lavender and sunflowers are blooming. Early on there are plenty of tourists already, but it isn't yet the main season. That changes in mid-July, when more people are present by the day and nature is increasingly less visible. Note that because of fire hazard, many dry woodlands in the lowlands are now closed to visitors (see page 227).

September

By late August, the peak holiday season is over and nature too is preparing for autumn. It also marks the start of the migration season. Waders pass through during this time of the year, and later on in month, the raptors pass through. There are still some interesting flowers to be found as, for instance, the spectacular Sea Daffodil is in bloom.

October

During October, migration continues in full swing. In Camargue particularly, each day brings something new. Check every bush and remember to keep an eye on the sky, as raptors soar by. Away from the coast, it is becoming wonderfully quiet, but days are generally still warm and sunny, and there are still reptiles, butterflies and other insects around. October makes for a wonderful month for hiking.

November
In November, the main wave of migratory birds has passed through, but there are still some around. The wintering birds start arrive in force with increasing chances on Wallcreepers, Alpine Accentors and other winter visitors. The first half of November is particularly attractive for the autumn colours, particularly the Beech forests and the sansouires, with their glassworts which have turned bright red by now.

Weather and temperatures
The climate in Provence shows two distinct faces; Lowland Provence enjoys a mild Mediterranean climate, whereas the highlands (not surprisingly) have much more of a mountain climate. In addition, there is the mistral, that both provides a much appreciated 'cool summer breeze' on hot days and a bitterly cold wind in winter.
Spring is the least predictable time of the year. In lowland Provence, there is as much chance of days with temperatures not above the 15 °C as there is of one of 25 °C when you can enjoy life lazing on a terrace. The mistral only exaggerates this, and it is not uncommon to wear gloves and a winter coat during a hike. In the mountains, it is still cold at night. Only from May onwards do temperatures really start to rise.
Summers are dry and can be very hot. Temperatures easily reach 35°C, and in some years might even surpass the 40°C. In the mountains, temperatures are more bearable, but even here you need to be a warmth-loving creature to enjoy the weather.
Autumn, and especially October, can be mild and beautiful one day, and bring downpours the next. Downpours is not exaggerated, as some years there is flooding and damage due to storms. Finally, winter is wonderfully mild along the coast, and gets colder as you move away from the sea, up into higher altitudes.

Accommodation
Provence has accommodation on offer for everybody. It is one of the best areas to go camping, as the climate is favourable and campgrounds are numerous. Note that there are enormous differences between camp sites. For those who travel on a tight budget, there are very basic campgrounds available only equipped with a shower and a toilet. These are often the municipal camps (Camping municipal), run by the town hall (however, there are luxurious municipal camps too). For those seeking some more luxury, you can also find sites equipped with swimming pools, discos and organised family entertainment. Keep in mind that Provence is, especially in summer, a popular destination for family holidays, and many camp sites focus on families specifically. If you enjoy the idea of camping, but not the inconveniences that come with living in a tent, most campgrounds also offer mobile homes and chalets.

Most villages also have some other form of accommodation, ranging from simple B&Bs to five-star hotels. In addition, there are the 'gîtes rural', small (to sometimes large) fully equipped houses in rural areas. For more information and booking see (www.gites-de-france-paca.com).

Convenient Travel and Safety Issues

Annoyances and hazards
Except for the summer sun, the natural world doesn't pose much of a threat to the traveller in the Camargue or Provence. The only seriously venomous snake is the Asp Viper, but it lives such a secluded life that you should consider an encounter with an Asp Viper a rare privilege. In some summers, the Camargue can be full of mosquitoes. They emerge from in mid-spring and can become a nuisance in summer in some years so bring insect repellent (also for sale in pharmacies, which you'll find in every town and village).
Perhaps the biggest inconvenience during summer is discovering that your hike or route is closed (see page 227). In addition, the Route des Crêtes (site D on page 182) is closed during fierce winds.
Provence is flooded with tourists during summer, which makes 'peace and quiet' quite hard to find. Autumn, winter and spring visitors to the western part of the region (especially Camargue and La Crau) are wise to bring wind and weatherproof clothes to withstand the fierce and cold mistral wind (see page 24). Also be aware of downpours and consequent flooding.

Private property issues
When it comes to private property, land-owners in southern France are fiercely protective, sometimes bordering on the paranoid. Most houses have a guard dog, and not infrequently public tracks are suddenly barred as the land has apparently been bought by somebody. In principle, private property is marked with a sign 'propreriété privée, défense d'entrer' (private property, access forbidden).
Unfortunately, it is not always clear if an area or a track is private, and if private, if one has the right of way. Private property signs at the start of a track are an obvious indication that continuing means you're trespassing. Since you can buy these signs at € 10 at the local bricolage, it is not hard to imagine there are a lot of unjustified private property signs. Conversely, some landowners seem to expect ramblers to simply know the boundaries of their property and are offended when, unwarned, you enter 'their' track (you'll never know if it is indeed theirs). And then there are private property signs that are directed towards the land next to the track that, in principle, mean that you are allowed on the track but that you can't wander into the field.

We advise strongly against entering private property without the owner's consent. Not only is it forbidden, it also violates somebody's private space and in extreme cases you might even be putting yourself in harm's way. If access is unclear or if it seems you have the right to access and you see someone, our advice is to be the first to strike a conversation and ask politely for permission (in French, obviously). If you don't get it, leave. There is no point in arguing about it; the only thing you'll achieve is ruining your day.

Responsible Tourism

'Take nothing but your photo, leave nothing but your footprint', is the well-known phrase that summarises the nature of responsible tourism. It goes without saying that, as a visitor to a nature reserve, you have a responsibility to leave your surroundings and everything in it undisturbed. Apart from the obvious, in Provence there are some specific things to keep in mind.

When going into the field, it is important to respect private property (see above). Many local landowners will see you as representatives of, even ambassadors for, nature conservation. If you do not respect the private property rights of landowners, this reflects negatively on nature conservation as a whole. In recent years, there have been increasing problems with tourists entering Lavender and sunflower fields, often harvesting whole bushes of Lavender without paying or asking for permission.

Some shy birds are under pressure, most notably birds of the Crau and several eagles. When making a trip in La Crau, keep a low profile. Never leave the tracks! If you encounter Little Bustards or Stone Curlew near the road, do not leave your car, because, by doing so, you will frighten or flush them. Other vulnerable birds breed on ledges in rock faces. Be careful when, approaching rocky slopes, that you do not disturb the nests of breeding birds. In addition, there are breeding colonies, which should not be approached as this might disturb hundreds of birds.

Wherever you go, go *bio*. The term for nature friendly farming is *agriculture biologique*, the sign to look out for is the green 'bio' logo. The decline of flora and wildlife in Provence is largely tied to the change of land use in the past decades. Intensification and land abandonment, the use of fertilizers, herbicides and pesticides is for a large part responsible for the decline of the insects, the flora and the birdlife (see page 71). As a visitor, buying local organic produce is the best way to have a positive contribution to local biodiversity. There are also many local markets where farmers sell their produce, which is another good way to buy the food that's produced with care for the land and environment.

Furthermore, visit nature info centres, buy in their goods, support or become a member of these organisations. This is not just a financial matter, it is also a mandate for these organisations to continue to do their important work.

Ecotourism code of conduct
We appeal to every naturalist, birdwatcher and nature photographer to abide by this code of conduct in the interests of birds, wildlife and their environment.

1. Learn patterns of animal behaviour – know when not to interfere with an animal's life cycle.
2. Acquaint yourself with the fragility of the ecosystem – stay on trails that are intended to lessen impact.
3. When out in the field, use good judgement – treat the wildlife, plants and places as if you were their guest.
4. Treat other observers and photographers courteously – ask before joining others already in an area.
5. Keep your distance from birds to avoid stressing them or exposing them to danger, exercise restraint and caution during observation, photography, sound recording or filming. Use appropriate lenses to photograph wild animals – if an animal shows stress, move back and use a longer lens.
6. Keep well back from burrows, nests, colonies, roosts, display areas and important feeding sites. Do not handle birds, chicks or eggs unless for permitted research activities.
7. Before advertising the presence of a rare species of plant or animal, evaluate the potential for disturbance including to its surroundings and other people in the area, and proceed only if access can be controlled, disturbance minimized, and, where applicable, permission has been obtained from private land-owners. Unless officially publicised, the sites of rare nesting birds should be divulged only to the proper conservation authorities.
8. Do not enter private property without the owner's explicit permission.
9. Tactfully inform others if you observe them engaging in inappropriate or harmful behaviour – many people unknowingly endanger themselves and animals. If this doesn't help, report inappropriate behaviour to proper authorities.
10. Be a role model – educate others by your actions; enhance their understanding.
11. Support the protection of important bird habitat.

Walking in Provence

Provence offers countless opportunities for exploration and is probably one of the best areas for hiking in the Mediterranean. There is a well-maintained network of tracks, and it would probably take more than a lifetime to walk them all. Walking is, besides being enjoyable, also the best way to see wildflowers, reptiles, amphibians, butterflies, and other small wildlife. Most tracks will surprise you in some unexpected way or another. You might suddenly find yourself before a stunning view, or stumble upon a rare orchid. We once came face to face with an Eagle Owl on a cliff and had an Egyptian Vulture soaring overhead five minutes later. Both a complete surprise. So it is worth exploring on your own and finding new trails.

Go prepared though. Take enough food and above all water with you. In some villages there are fountains with drinking water, where you can fill up your water bottles. To know whether the water is drinkable, look for a sign stating *'eau potable'* (drinkable water). If not drinkable, the fountain will most likely have a sign *'eau non potable'*. However, sometimes there is no sign, in which case you probably also should not take the risk (or ask one of the locals whether the water is drinkable).

The tracks and trails are generally in good state and well-marked. However, during summer many tracks are closed to the public to prevent wildfires (you can check beforehand at **www.myprovence.fr/en/enviedebalade** – all paths in red zones are closed). Make sure you wear suitable footwear and layered clothing, so you can take off or put on a layer according to the ambient weather conditions. Take the sun seriously, especially in the warmer months. In summer, avoid going out in the middle of the day. Check the itinerary to see if there are large, exposed areas, such as grasslands or scrublands. Wear a sun hat or cap and preferably UV-blocking clothing, which is light and protects the skin. Finally, realise that the sun is not only hot and dehydrating, it is also extremely bright. It is the constant strain on the eyes that is one of the causes of heat stroke, so bring a good pair of sunglasses and a hat which will shade your face.

There is no great danger from biting or stinging insects, but ticks are present so make sure to check after every hike. In addition, in some years mosquitos can be numerous, in which case insect repellent is a life-saver. There are many Wild Boar in the area. Although they only come near the tracks in the evening and try to avoid contact with humans, occasionally you might suddenly cross their path. In those cases, just stand still and enjoy the unique encounter – they won't harm you as long as you don't scare them.

Another thing to keep in mind is that you shouldn't bring a dog with you in La Crau or any place with sheep or cattle. There are usually guard dogs around, and they are not keen on other dogs, nor are the cattle, especially bulls and cows with calves. So, for your own safety, that of your dog and for the well-being of the sheep and cattle – leave your dog at home.

Another no-go is an open fire. The forest fire risk is enormous, and people are permanently on guard when it comes to the dangers of forest fire. Even when you are extremely cautious and responsible, just avoid the risk and stress for the local people and simply never make a fire. In addition, you might save yourself a €500 fine and a hard time explaining in French what you were thinking of ...

Finally, mobile phone coverage is not perfect, but you do have reception in many places. So do bring your mobile with you in case of an emergency, but don't rely on it too much. When going on long walks, go with company or, if you are alone, tell others (e.g. hotel staff) of your plans. It is also worth downloading a map app on your smartphone such as maps.me (see below), which shows you your position and the trails in the area without an internet connection. This is your best preparation against getting lost.

Whalewatching trips

The Mediterranean Sea is an excellent place to see whales and dolphins, although they are always elusive. With luck you might see them from the cliffs of the Calanques or Île Port-Cros, but the best way to find them is to go out onto the sea.
Whale-watching is a sensitive issue. It is popular and there is a pressure on whale-watching companies to get closer to the animals than is good for the animals. The best places for watching marine mammals now form the Pelagos Marine reserve and as part of the reserve agreement, authorities have created a certificate for operators who follow a set of rules for ethical whale-watching: the High Quality Whale Watching label (see **www.whale-watching-label.com**). Currently, within the area of this book, the following operators from these ports offer services under this label and we strongly encourage you to book your tour with one of these:
Bandol (**www.atlantide1.com**), Hyères (**www.espacemer.fr** and **www.verticalhorizon.com**), Port-Fréjus (**www.lechantdesdauphins.com**), Sanary-sur-Mer (**www.decouverteduvivant.fr**), Mandelieu-la-Napoule (**www.nature-essentielle.fr**) and Six-Fours (**www.sea-adventure.net**). There are half- and full-day tours available. Several of these organisations also offer research or conservation programs.

Additional information

Recommended reading

Apart from the usual guidebooks and field guides, we recommend the following resources, books and websites.

Maps One of the best maps around is the open source and free app maps.me. Once you've downloaded the app, zoom in on Provence to download the map. Once you have it, you can use it without internet connection. In paper, the Michelin and IGN small-scale maps (1:100,000/150,000) give a useful overview to the area. However, for site details it is essential to buy the IGN blue series at the larger scale of 1:25,000, sometimes referred to as *Carte de Randonnée*, available at local newsagents and bookshops. These show all GRs as well as many other public footpaths.

Walking There several walking guides to Provence, such as the Cicerone, Rother and Sunflower guides. These books have different and usually more walking routes than this book, but lack (usually entirely) information on landscape and nature. It pays to visit the local tourist office, which usually has some guides with interesting local walks available, often with additional information on culture, landscape, flora and fauna (usually in French).

Flora There are several good wildflower guides available on the flora of Provence. The only complete one is the *Flore de la France méditerranéenne continentale* by Jean-Marc Tison, Henri Michaud, Philippe Jauzein (ISBN 9782909717906). However, it's bone dry, has only line drawings and is only available in French. If you don't mind any of that, but prefer a book with a wider coverage, opt for the *Flora Gallica – flore de France* by Jean-Marc Tison and Bruno de Foucault (ISBN 9782366620122). A less specialist option is the *Guides des fleurs sauvages de Méditerranée Occidentale*, by Chris Thorogood (ISBN 9782603025611), which offers more images and a selection of species that can be found, but is still only available in French. A non-specialist option would be the *Field guide to the wild flowers of the western Mediterranean* by Chris Thorogood (2016; ISBN 9781842466162). It takes you a long way but is nevertheless much less complete than the aforementioned books. German readers could try *Kosmos Mittelmeerflora* by I. and P. Schönfelder.
For Orchids specifically we would advise the recently published *Orchids of Europe and the Mediterranean* by Rolf Kuehn, Henrik Pedersen and Phillip Cribb (ISBN: 9781842466698). This guide follows a different taxonomy than previous orchid field guides, which makes identification simpler. Another book that will suit orchid lovers is *Les Orchidées de France, Belgique et Luxembourg* (Parthenope Collection; ISBN 2914817118). It is an Atlas with descriptions of all the orchids within the area.
Reptiles and Amphibians We recommend the new *Reptiles and Amphibians of Britain and Europe* by Jeroen Speybroek, Wouter Beukema et al. (Bloomsbury; ISBN-13: 9781408154595) which has replaced the now out-dated guide from Harper-Collins as the new standard guide for European reptiles and amphibians.
Mammals The standard field guide for European mammals is *Mammals of Europe, North Africa and the Middle East* by Stéphane Aulagnier et al (Helm; ISBN-13: 9781408113998) which adequately covers the region. This can be supplemented by *Tracks and Signs of the Animals and Birds of Britain and Europe* by Lars-Henrik Olsen (Princeton University Press; ISBN-13: 9780691157535).
Birds The definitive European field guide is *Collins Bird Guide* by Lars Svensson (Harper Collins; ISBN-13: 9780007268146). For more detailed information, one could use the *Atlas des oiseaux de France Métropolitaine* (Nidal Issa and Yves Muller; EAN13 : 9782603018781), a two-volume atlas on the birds of France that also includes winter visitors, or the *Atlas des oiseaux nicheurs de Provence-Alpes-Côte d'Azur* (LPO-PACA; ISBN 9782603016220) which covers the breeding birds of the region. Note that these are not the kind of books that you want to be dragging around. The online resources **www.observado.org** and **www.ebird.org**) allow you to see what other visitors have seen in Provence, including dates, numbers, maps and bar charts for both individual species and 'hotspots' in Provence (and across the

world). Another valuable resource is Xeno-canto (**www.xeno-canto.org**) which has recordings of the songs and calls of all the species you'll likely to find in Provence.

Butterflies and dragonflies The standard guides for butterflies are *Butterflies of Europe* by Tristan Lafranchis (ISBN 9782952162005; also available in Dutch) and *Collins Butterfly Guide* by Tolman & Lewington (Harper Collins; ISBN-13: 9780007279777) whilst for dragonflies we recommend *A Field Guide to the Dragonflies of Britain & Europe* by Dijkstra & Lewington (British Wildlife Publishing; ISBN-13: 780953139941). Wildguides releases a new photographic guide to European dragonflies in 2020 (ISBN 9780691168951).

Other insects are covered in the brand new (2017) and excellent *Photographic Guide to Insects of Southern Europe and the Mediterranean* by Paul D Brock (Pub. NatureBureau; ISBN-13: 9781874357797).

Another good buy is the Papillons de jour – Atlas de Provence-Alpes-Côte d'Azur by André Chauliac and colleagues (ISBN: 9782909717654). Parthenope has an atlas of the dragonflies of France: *Les libellules de Provence-Alpes-Côte d'Azur* (ISBN: 9782366621853).

Observation tips

Nearby destinations worth a visit

Provence has enough wildlife and flowers to keep you spell-bound for weeks, or even years. However, there are a few areas not far from its borders to the northeast, northwest and southwest that offer habitats and species that you will not find within the region.

To the east, you will find the departement of *les Alpes Maritimes*. The area is unique as from the Mediterranean Sea you quickly ascend into the Alps. As a result, the region harbours a spectacular flora, perhaps even richer than that of Provence. From there, you can enter the Alps, which offer completely different habitats to explore.

To the northwest, crossing the Rhône river, you enter the famous Cévennes. This area is, much like the Alpes Maritimes, appreciated for its flora and its butterflies. The landscape is dominated by schists, karstic formation, dramatic gorges and granite plateau – highly versatile in other words. Also, the culture is completely different from that of Provence, and it is less overrun by tourists in summer, and those who do go there, almost always come for its nature.

Southwest of Provence, the French Mediterranean coast continues. The Languedoc is lower and flatter than Provence. Although the flora largely remains the same (but also offers some interesting new species), the area has some excellent birding sites. Many of the species that can be found in Camargue and La Crau occur here too, but there are also some birds that are generally found on the Iberian Peninsula (e.g. Thekla's Lark).

Finding snakes, spiders, scorpions and the like

Turning stones is rather like unwrapping Christmas gifts: it is exciting, highly addictive and there is always one more ahead that must conceal something good. Mostly you will find ants and their nests, but every now and then there are scorpions, tarantulas and snakes. Toads and lizards are other possibilities.

Turning flat stones of over 20 by 20 centimetres yields the best results. Lift them up to one side, turn them over and step back. Be aware that some animals have a painful sting or bite. Always turn them over towards yourself and never hold the stone you turned in your hand, because the animal might be underneath it and crawl up.

Turning stones is very invasive for the animals that live beneath them. Many of them worked hard to create an underground nest. Therefore, make sure that you don't disturb the subterranean life too long and place the stone back in exactly as you found it. Note that snakes and lizards become more active during the course of May. A late April visitor may not see a single snake while a late May visitor could see one every day.

Finding orchids

Orchids are numerous in Provence, but this does not mean that they are easy to find if you do not know where to look. The first thing you should realise is that orchids are not the most resilient plants nature has brought forth. They have no protection against grazing, meaning that they quickly disappear when there are too many goats and sheep. What's more, many species of orchids are weak competitors that are easily pushed out by other plants if the vegetation is left to develop.

The result is that whilst they grow everywhere, they're usually alone or in small clumps. They are usually not numerous... except along roadsides. There, the grazing pressure is very low and the frequent mowing seems to be enough to keep the competitors at bay.

If you have never searched for orchids before, pictures (including those in this guidebook) can be very deceiving, because the flowers seem very large. The larger spikes of Early-purple and Giant Orchids are very conspicuous, but the flowers of the *Ophrys*-genus are little gems for which you need to develop an eye.

Limestone soils harbour different species than acidic soils. In general, the limestone areas are the richest in orchids, but the Hercynian Provence (Plaine des Maures and Massif des Maures) are a notable exception to this. Tongue-orchids prosper particularly well on the acidic soils, and Provence has a lot of them, with the most impressive one – the Scarce Tongue-orchid – being fairly numerous on the Plaine des Maures. Other orchids occur all over Provence, mostly concentrated in the low mountain ranges, each harbouring its own unique set of orchids.

Birdwatching list

The numbers between the brackets () refer to the routes from page 119 onwards:

Swans, geese and ducks Mute Swan is a common breeding bird of freshwater lakes (e.g. 2, 4). Greylag Goose is a scarce breeding bird of the Rhône, that is common in winter (e.g. 2, 4). Sometimes small numbers of Bewick's Swan, Bean, Barnacle and White-fronted Geese are among them.
Shelduck is a common breeding bird of the saline lagoons (3, 5, 6, 7, 11; site A on page 151). Wigeon, Gadwall, Teal, Shoveler, Mallard, Tufted Duck, Pintail, Red-crested Pochard and Common Pochard winter in large numbers (2, 3, 4, 5). Ferruginous Duck is a scarce winter bird. Gadwall, Shoveler, Mallard and Red-crested Pochard also breed in low numbers. At Sea, Red-breasted Merganser is frequent and Eider scarce (4).
Partridges Red-legged Partridge is frequent, especially in La Crau (8). Quail breeds in cereal fields in the lowlands (2, 4, 9, 21). Pheasant occurs throughout the lowlands in low numbers.
Grebes Both and Great Crested and Little Grebe are locally common in wetlands (2, 4, 5, 9; site E on page 153, F on page 183 and E on page 219). Black-necked Grebe winters on the coast of the Camargue (4, 5) and Étang de Berre (one of the largest wintering sites in Europe).
Shearwaters, Gannets and Storm-petrels Both Yelkouan and Cory's Shearwaters are found around islands off the coast (12; mostly Yelkouan, and site C on page 181; mostly Cory's). Gannet is common off the coast in winter (4, 12, site C on page 181). European Storm-petrel is a very rare breeding bird of the coastal islands of the Calanques.
Cormorants Cormorants are frequent in large lagoons, especially in winter (e.g. 3, 6). Shag is found around islands of the coast (12; site C on page 181; mostly in winter).
Storks, flamingos, spoonbills and ibises White Stork is only found in the freshwater zone of the Rhône delta, where it is easy to see (e.g. 2, 4, 5, 9). Greater Flamingo is very common in the saline part of the Camargue and the salinas of Hyères (2, 3, 5, 6, 7 and 11). The largest colony can be seen from a distance on route 7. Spoonbill is mostly seen on 2, 3, 4 and 6; the breeding birds are augmented in winter. Glossy Ibis are very numerous, especially on 1, 2, 3, 4.
Herons, egrets and bitterns Night and Squacco Heron are among the more uncommon species (2, 3, 4, 9); Night Heron is found mostly in wooded areas and along the rivers like the Durance (site E on page 219); Squacco Heron in small ponds and rice paddies. Grey Heron is frequent in all marshes and along the larger rivers, also those far away from the coast. Purple Heron is locally common in large reedbeds (2, 3, 4, 5, 9). Great White Egret breeds in Scamandre (4), Vigueirat

(9) and other large marshes. It is very numerous in winter. Little Egret is common throughout, especially in the salt marshes and along the rivers, such as the Durance. Cattle Egret is common in the *pelouses* and *sansouires*, following the horses and cattle (1, 2, 3, 4, 5, 9 and site B on page 151). Great and Little Bittern inhabit the large reedbeds and are mostly seen at Scamandre (4) and Vigueirat (9).

Vultures Egyptian Vulture is a rare breeding bird of the lower, rocky mountain ranges (best 10, 19, 22, site B on page 201). Reintroduced Griffon Vultures occur in very specific areas, where they are easy to see (19, 20). Sometimes, you see them on the Ventoux, Valensole and Caussols as well. Black Vulture, another reintroduction, is only seen with relative ease in the Verdon (19). Occasionally, Bearded Vultures of the Alps are seen here too.

Eagles Short-toed Eagle is widespread and mostly seen on the plateau (9, 10, 13, 14, 18, 19, 21, 22). Booted Eagle is very rare and only sometimes found in the wet Crau and northern Camargue (9). Golden Eagle breeds in the mountains and can be seen in many places, with a higher probability on 19, 24. Bonelli's Eagle is a breeding bird of remote, dry, rocky sierras, mostly the Alpilles (10). Osprey, Spotted and White-tailed Eagles winter in low numbers in the Camargue, mostly around Étang de Vaccarès (2, 3, 5).

Other birds of prey Common Buzzard and Black Kite are the most numerous raptors; Buzzard occurs throughout and Black Kite mostly in the lowlands (1-9, 13, 14, 17). Red Kite is a winter bird of the Crau and Rhône (8, 9, B and E on pages 151-153). Honey Buzzard is widespread but fairly scarce on plateaux above 500 m (best 19, 21, 22). Both Sparrowhawk and Goshawk are widespread in woodlands. Marsh Harrier is common all over the Camargue and Crau, sometimes seen in Villepey (F on page 183) and Valensole (21). Montagu's Harrier is best seen on the Valensole plain (21). Hen Harrier is seen in winter in the lowlands.

Falcons and kestrels Lesser Kestrel breeds in La Crau (8). Kestrel is widespread but never numerous in open agricultural plains, both low and high. Hobby is a widespread breeding bird of river valleys (2, 9, 17, site E on page 219). Peregrine breeds in two different areas: the high mountains (18, 19) and on coastal cliffs (12, sites A, B, C and D on pages 180-182). It winters in the Camargue. Merlin winters in the Camargue and Crau.

Rails, crakes and gallinules Purple Gallinule breeds in Étang de Scamandre (4). Coot and Moorhen are common in all marshes. Water Rail breeds in large reedbeds (2, 4, 9). Other rails are scarce on passage.

Cranes and Bustards Common Crane has become quite numerous in winter in the Camargue (2, 4, 5, 9). Little Bustard is fairly common but elusive in La Crau (best 9 and site B on page 151, occasionally 8). It also breeds in Valensole (21) and Caussols (18) but they are very hard to find there.

Waders, Stone Curlew and Collared Pratincole Waders of saline and brackish mudflats include Oystercatcher (frequent), Avocet (common), Black-winged Stilt (common), Common Sandpiper (frequent), Dunlin (common), Sanderling (frequent), Curlew (scarce), Red Knot (frequent), Little Stint (frequent), Curlew Sandpiper (frequent), Redshank (common), Spotted Redshank (frequent), Greenshank (scarce), Bar-tailed Godwit (scarce), Grey Plover (scarce), Kentish Plover (common) and Ringed Plover (scarce). They are best seen on 3, 6, 7 and 11.

In freshwater marshes, Wood Sandpiper, Black-tailed Godwit, Black-winged Stilt, Snipe, Common Sandpiper and Lapwing are the most numerous waders. Look for them on routes 1, 2, 3 and 5. Golden Plover and (less frequently) Dotterel winter in La Crau (8, 9, site B on page 151).

Little Ringed Plover is a fairly common breeding bird along the larger rivers. Stone Curlew breeds in good numbers in la Crau (8, 9, site B on page 151) and lesser numbers in Valensole (21). Collared Pratincole is a rare and irregular breeder of the northern Camargue and around Étang de Vaccarès (2, 3).

- **Gulls and terns** Yellow-legged Gull is the common large gull along the coast. Black-headed Gull is common along the rivers and marshes. Large colonies of Mediterranean Gull breed in the Camargue (2, 3, 5). Slender-billed Gull breeds in the salt pans (best 6 and 7, also 11). Common and Lesser Black-backed Gull winter in the delta.

  Little, Sandwich and Common Terns breed on small islands in the coastal lagoons (3, 6, 7); Common Tern also breeds along the Durance. Gull-billed Tern is another Camargue species (2, 3, 5, 7). Whiskered Tern is a common passage migrant and irregular breeder. You see it mostly over the rice paddies (2, 3, 5), sometimes joined by Black and White-winged Tern. Sandwich Tern is frequent on the coast in winter (4, 7).
- **Sandgrouse** Pin-tailed Sandgrouse breeds but is hard to spot in La Crau (8). Sandgrouse are mostly detected by their flight call.
- **Pigeons and doves** Feral/Rock Pigeons breed in the cliffs and canyons (e.g. 22). Wood Pigeon and Stock Dove are common in the woodlands. Collared Dove is common in the villages. Turtle Dove is in general decline but still breeds in good numbers in riparian habitat (e.g. 17 and site E on page 151 and E on page 219).
- **Cuckoos** Common Cuckoo is common throughout. Great Spotted Cuckoo is most frequently seen in the northern Camargue (2).
- **Owls** Little Owl is a declining bird that used to be common, widespread and easy to see. Now it is most frequent in La Crau (site B on page 151). Barn owl, Tawny Owl, Long-eared Owl are all common in their preferred habitat. Listen for Scops Owl in rural areas and villages near Mediterranean woodland (e.g. Île Port-Cros, Massif des Maures, Alpilles). Eagle Owl is widespread in certain gorges in the Mediterranean Sierras (Alpilles; 10, Gorge de la Nesque; 22, Mont Sainte-Victoire; 15).

Tengmalm's Owl is an Alpine species with a small population in the forests of the Mont Ventoux (24).

Nightjars Nightjar is common in open woodlands on dry plains (13, 14, 15, 16, 22, 23; Calanques).

Swifts Common Swift is common throughout. Pallid Swift breeds in coastal cliffs and hunt along the coastal ranges (11, 12, sites A, B, C, D). For Alpine Swift, try routes 10, 12, 13, 15, 18, 19, 22).

Bee-eater, Roller and Hoopoe Roller occurs in La Crau and the northern Camargue (2, 9, 21 and site E on page 153 and B on page 217). Hoopoe is found in roughly the same areas, but is much more widespread. Bee-eater is frequent throughout the lower parts of Provence, but most common in the Camargue (e.g. route 5, 7). A beautiful colony can be viewed in Marais du Vigueirat (9). Kingfisher breeds along all major rivers (3, 4, 17, 22, site F on page 183, site E on page 153 and site E on page 219).

Woodpeckers Great Spotted and Green Woodpeckers are widespread. Black Woodpecker is a bird of Beech forests (16, 24). Lesser Spotted Woodpecker is an uncommon breeding bird of mature forest, mostly along rivers (e.g. 17, site E on page 153). Wryneck is fairly widespread in open dry woodlands and half overgrown plateaux in the mountains (19, 22).

Larks Skylark breeds on open plateaux and in lowland *pelouses* and *sansouires* (e.g. 3, 5, 8, 9, 18). Woodlark is common on plateaux with scattered trees (18, 19, 22). Crested Lark is uncommon in dry lowland plains, often along the road (2, 5, 8, 9, 21). Calandra and Short-toed Larks are respectively scarce and rare in La Crau and Valensole (8, 9, 21).

Swallows and martins Swallow and House Martin are common throughout. Sand Martin occurs along the Durance (site E on page 219). Crag Martin is common around cliffs (e.g. 10, 13, 15, 19, 22). Red-rumped Swallow is a scarce breeding bird of river valleys (e.g. Durance, Argens; site F on page 183).

Pipits and wagtails Tawny Pipit is an uncommon breeding bird of dry plains (8, 9, 10, 16, 21). Richard's Pipit is a rare but regular winter bird in La Crau. Tree Pipit is common in open woodlands. Meadow and Water Pipits are winter birds on the coastal lowlands.

White Wagtail is common throughout. Grey Wagtail is common on all rivers with pebbles and shingle banks. Yellow Wagtail breeds in the *sansouires* and is very numerous here during migration (3, 5, 6, 7).

Dipper and accentors Dipper occurs on all fast-flowing mountain streams (19, 20). Dunnock breeds on the Mont Ventoux (24). Alpine Accentor winters in the lower mountains (e.g. Les Beaux; site D on page 153).

Wren and Robin Both are numerous in woodlands.

Thrushes Song Thrush is a frequent winter visitor and breeding bird of the Beech forests (16, 24). Mistle Thrush is common and widespread in open pine forests (18, 19, 24); Ring Ouzel sometimes breeds on the Mont Ventoux. Blackbird is common throughout. Blue Rock Thrush breeds on coastal dry cliffs (10, 12, 15, 19, 22 site A, B and C on page 180-181 and site D on page 153). Rock Thrush replaces Blue Rock Thrush in the higher areas (18, 24). Fieldfare and Redwing are widespread winter birds.

Nightingale, chats, wheatears, redstarts and allies Nightingale is a very common summer visitor to damp areas with bushes. Black Redstart is a common and widespread breeding bird of villages and rocky mountain slopes. Redstart is numerous in open woodlands. Bluethroat winters in low numbers in the Camargue. Stonechat is a frequent breeding bird of dry terrain. Whinchat is found here on passage. Northern Wheatear breeds in a few isolated places (e.g. 8, 16, 18, 24) and is widespread on passage. Black-eared Wheatear is a scarce breeding bird of open, rocky areas (10, 15, 16, 18).

Warblers Zitting Cisticola (Fan-tailed Warbler) is rather common in damp meadows (1-9, 11). Cetti's Warbler is common along well-vegetated streams and bramble thickets in the lowlands. Savi's, Great Reed, Reed Warbler and Moustached Warblers breed in reedbeds (1, 2, 4, 5, 11, and site F page 183). Moustached and Savi's are much less common than the other two, and have their core populations in Scamandre (4) and Vigueirat (9).

Melodious Warbler is typical of riversides and scrub of the lower mountains. Bonelli's Warbler breeds in mountain woodland where it is common throughout. Chiffchaff and Blackcap are common throughout. Sardinian Warbler is common in Mediterranean scrubland and even more so in the tamarisks of the Camargue. Western Orphean Warbler is a complicated bird to find, breeding in south-facing mountain slopes with scattered trees, olive groves and low bushes (e.g. 15). Dartford Warbler prefers low, dense scrub and is more common and widespread (10, 11, 12, 14, 15). Subalpine Warbler prefers similar terrain on higher altitude (often in Box scrub; 10, 13, 19, 22). Spectacled Warbler breeds in *sansouires* (6) and the lavender fields of Valensole (21). Whitethroat occupies hedges and bushes in farmland higher in the mountains (19).

Goldcrest and Firecrest Firecrest breeds commonly in coniferous and mixed open woods. Goldcrest breeds in coniferous forest in the Mont Ventoux only (24).

Flycatchers Pied Flycatcher occurs as migrant throughout the area. Spotted Flycatcher is a surprisingly scarce breeding bird of open woodlands.

Tits Great, Blue and Long-tailed Tits are frequent throughout well-wooded parts of Provence. Crested Tit also occurs throughout but is more associated with stands of coniferous trees. Coal and Willow Tits are found in coniferous woods in the Vaucluse (24). Penduline Tit winters in the Camargue and Bearded Tit breeds in reedbeds here (1, 2, 4, 9).

Nuthatch and creepers Nuthatch and Short-toed Treecreeper are common in the woodlands. Wallcreeper is a winter visitor to many of the south-facing mountains (e.g. 19 and site D on page 153).
Shrikes Woodchat Shrike is a scarce bird of lowland plains (best 14). Red-backed Shrike is a scarce bird of shrubby plateaux (14, 18, 19, 22). Lesser Grey Shrike breeds in the wet Crau (9), but may have gone extinct there. Iberian Grey Shrike is a scarce breeding bird of the northern Camargue, Alpilles and Crau.
Crows and allies Jay, Magpie, Jackdaw and Carrion Crow are all common in their habitat. Raven is fairly common in the mountains (18, 19, 24). Rook breeds in the Rhône valley around Avignon. Red-billed Chough breeds in the Gorge du Verdon (19) and migrates south in winter.
Starling and oriole Starling is common throughout. Golden Oriole is common in riverside forest and mountain forests (from early May onwards).
Sparrows House Sparrow is common. Tree Sparrow breeds in agricultural lowlands (Camargue (2), Durance and Argens valleys). Rock Sparrow is very local and breeds mostly on the Valensole plain (21).
Finches and allies Chaffinch, Greenfinch, Goldfinch, Serin and Linnet are all common or fairly common in their preferred habitat. Crossbill and Bullfinch breed in the coniferous forests in the high mountains, mostly Ventoux (24). Citril Finch breeds on the Mont Ventoux (24). In winter, Siskin, Hawfinch, Bullfinch and Brambling visit the lower forests, while White-winged Snowfinch can be seen on the Mont Ventoux (24).
Buntings Cirl Bunting is a common breeding bird of the agricultural plains and open forests of the lowlands (e.g. 2, 9, 10, 11, 13, 14). Ortolan Bunting and Rock Bunting breed in the mountains and prefer the open pinewoods near cliffs and open pastures (18, 19, 24). Ortolan Bunting also breeds in small-scale agricultural land (13 to 16). Corn Bunting breeds in dry plains and agricultural land and is fairly common throughout. Reed Bunting breeds in low numbers in the larger reedbeds of the Camargue (most 4, 9). Yellowhammer winters on agricultural fields. A handful of Black-headed Bunting, a bird of dry fields, have bred in recent years (mostly Valensole 21) but this bird has yet to establish a sustainable population.

ACKNOWLEDGEMENTS

This book is made with the help of many people – authors, experts in the fields of ecology, nature conservation or a specific group of species. And sometimes vital information or a good idea came through a spontaneous conversation with a fellow rambler, a shepherd in the field or a helpful employee of the tourist office. Of all these people, we want to mention a few in particular.

We thank Axel Wolff of the *Reserve Naturelle Nationale des Coussouls de Crau* for checking and correcting the information and routes of the Crau reserve. David Simpson, naturalist, tour guide and author of the Crossbill Guide to Dordogne proofread large sections of the guidebook and gave us a ton of helpful suggestions – Thanks a million, David. We thank the butterfly specialists and local residents Pieter and Brigitte Kan who kindly showed us some spectacular species and great places. Due to their help we could describe the route along the Endre River. Finally, we would like to thank Marjolein de Groen and Peter Jordaan, not for anything regarding the content of this guide particularly, but for your helping the Crossbill Guides Foundation through a logistic bottleneck in the period this book was written.

Finally, there is the Crossbill Guides team, without whom we'd never be able to make these guidebooks: John Cantelo – thanks for your proofreading and additional research for the guide. Botanist Kim Lotterman compiled the species list and checked the flora sections of the book. Horst Wolter made the fine illustrations for this book. Oscar Lourens did the lay-out and Brian Clews' eagle eyes spotted the last errors in the manuscript.

Thank you all for your help in making this book.

Dirk Hilbers, Albert Vliegenthart, Constant Swinkels, March 2020

PICTURE CREDITS

In the references that follow, the numbers refer to the pages and the letters to the position on the page (t=top, c=centre, b=bottom, with l and r indicating left and right).

CEN-PACA / Toutain, Yann: 42 (t)
Crossbill Guides / Hilbers, Dirk: cover, 4 (3rd, 4th), 5 (2nd, 3rd), 10, 13, 15, 17, 18, 20, 24 (t), 28 (t+b), 29 (t), 30 (t), 32 (b), 34, 35, 36, 37 (t), 38, 40 (t), 44, 47, 49, 50, 51 (t), 52, 53, 54 (t), 55, 57, 60, 61, 62, 64, 69, 70, 71 (b), 73, 77 (t+b), 78 (t), 80 (t), 81 (t+b), 84 (t), 85, 86 (t+b), 87 (t+b), 90, 96 (tl), 102, 110 (t), 113, 116, 120 (b), 124 (b), 126 (b), 128, 130 (t), 132, 136 (b), 138 (b), 141 (b), 145, 146, 148, 149 (c), 152, 156, 157 (t+b), 159, 160 (t), 161, 163 (t+b), 165 (t+b), 167, 168, 169 (b), 170 (t+b), 172 (t), 173 (t+b), 175 (t+b), 176 (t+b), 178 (bl), 179 (all), 181, 182, 183 (t), 186, 190, 191 (b), 192, 195, 196, 197, 199, 200, 201, 205, 208 (b), 210 (t), 211 (b), 212 (t+b), 214 (c), 216 (t+b), 218
Crossbill Guides / Vliegenthart, Albert: cover, 4 (2nd from top), 14 (t+b), 46, 48 (t+b), 51 (b), 56, 59, 82 (t+b), 108 (t+b), 109, 110 (b), 114, (t+b), 126 (t), 142, 172 (b), 178 (tl+tr), 188 (t), 191 (t), 193, 202, 203, 211 (t), 217
Crossbill Guides / Swinkels, Constant: cover, 24 (b), 30 (b), 31, 41, 54 (b), 58, 78 (b), 80 (b), 84 (b), 86 (c), 87 (c), 88, 98, 103, 107, 111, 123, 124 (t), 133, 139 (b), 144 (t), 149 (t+b), 153, 160 (b), 169 (t), 191 (b), 206, 210 (b), 220
Crossbill Guides / ten Cate, Bouke: cover, 134, 144 (b), 187, 188 (b), 214 (t+b)
Felix, Rob: 42 (b)
Fikkert, Cor: cover spine
Folkers, Jack: 4 (t), 5 (b), 32 (t), 37 (b), 40 (tl+bl), 71 (t), 72, 94, 95, 96 (tr+b), 97 (t+b), 99, 124 (m), 127 (t), 130 (b), 136 (t), 138 (t), 139 (t), 141 (t), 183 (b), 208 (t)
Hills, Lawrie: 105 (t+c+b), 120 (t), 122
Lourens, Leo: 5 (t)
Saxifraga / Dekker, Hans: 106
Saxifraga / Zekhuis, Mark: 29 (b)
Saxifraga / Felix, Rob: 164
Smits, Stijn: 74, 91, 93, 100, 127 (b), 219

All illustrations by Horst Wolter of the Crossbill Guides Foundation.

SPECIES LIST & TRANSLATION

The following list comprises all species mentioned in this guidebook and gives their scientific, German and Dutch names. It is not a complete checklist of the species of Provence and Camargue. Some names have an asterisk (*) behind them, indicating an unofficial name. See page 7 for more details.

Flora

English	Scientific	German	Dutch
Adder's-tongue, Small	Ophioglossum azoricum	Azoren-Natterzunge	Azorenaddertong
Anemone, Broad-leaved	Anemone hortensis	Stern-Anemone	Steranemoon
Aphyllanthes, Blue	Aphyllanthes monspeliensis	Blaue Binsenlilie	Blauwe bieslelie
Ash, Manna	Fraxinus ornus	Manna-Esche	Pluim-es
Aspen, Trembling	Populus tremula	Espe	Ratelpopulier
Asphodel, Hollow-stemmed	Asphodelus fistulosus	Röhriger Affodill	Holle affodil*
Asphodel, Summer	Asphodelus aestivus	Kleinfrüchtiger Affodill	Gewone affodil
Balm, Bastard	Melittis melissophyllum	Immenblad	Bijenblad
Baneberry	Actaea spicata	Christophskraut	Christoffelkruid
Beech	Fagus sylvatica	Buche	Beuk
Bellflower, Rampion	Campanula rapunculus	Rapunzel-Glockenblume	Rapunzelklokje
Bindweed, Sea	Convolvulus soldanella	Strandwinde	Zeewinde
Bird's-nest, Violet	Limodorum abortivum	Violetter Dingel	Paarse aspergeorchis
Bird-in-a-bush	Corydalis solida	Gefingerter Lerchensporn	Vingerhelmbloem
Bird's-nest, Yellow	Monotropa hypopitys	Fichtenspargel	Stofzaad
Birthwort, Common	Aristolochia clematitis	Osterluzei	Pijpbloem
Birthwort, Spanish	Aristolochia pistolochia	Pistolochia-Osterluzei	Zuidelijke pijpbloem*
Bladder-senna	Colutea arborescens	Blasenstrauch	Europese blazenstruik
Box	Buxus sempervirens	Buchsbaum	Buxus
Butcher's-broom	Ruscus aculeatus	Stechender Mäusedorn	Stekelige muizendoorn
Buttercup, Grass-leaved	Ranunculus gramineus	Grasblättriger Hahnenfuss	Grasbladige boterbloem*
Buttercup, Jersey	Ranunculus paludosus	Kerbel-Hahnenfuss	Kervelboterbloem*
Candytuft, Rock	Iberis saxatilis	Felsen-Schleifenblume	Rots-scheefbloem*
Catchfly, Saxifrage	Silene saxifraga	Steinbrech-Leimkraut	Steenbreeksilene
Catchfly, Small-flowered	Silene gallica	Französisches Lichtnelke	Franse silene
Catchfly, Sweet-William	Silene armeria	Nelken-Leimkraut	Pekbloem
Cat-mint, Lesser	Nepeta nepetella	Kleine Katzenminze*	Kittenkruid*
Cedar, Atlas	Cedrus atlantica	Atlaszeder	Atlasceder
Centaury, Common	Centaurium erythraea	Echtes Tausentguldenkraut	Echt duizendguldenkruid
Centaury, Seaside*	Centaurium maritimum	Gelbes Tausendguldenkraut	Geel duizendguldenkruid
Centaury, Yellow	Cicendia filiformis	Fadenenzian	Draadgentiaan
Chamomile, Sea*	Anthemis maritimus	Meer-Hundskamille*	Zeekamille*
Chestnut, Sweet	Castanea sativa	Edelkastanie	Tamme kastanje
Cistus, Grey-leaved	Cistus albidus	Weissliche Zistrose	Viltige cistusroos*
Cistus, Montpellier	Cistus monspeliensis	Montpellier-Zistrose	Montpellier cistusroos*
Cistus, Narrow-leaved	Cistus monspelliensis	Montpellier-Zistrose	Montpellier cistusroos*
Cistus, Sage-leaved	Cistus salviifolius	Salbeiblättrige Zistrose	Saliebladige cistusroos*
Clover, Starry	Trifolium stellatum	Sternklee	Sterklaver
Comfrey, Tuberous	Symphytum tuberosum	Knoten-Beinwell	Knolsmeerwortel
Coris	Coris monspeliensis	Stachelträubchen	Blauwe coris*
Cottonweed	Otanthus maritimus	Strand-Filzblume	Katoenkruid*

TOURIST INFORMATION & OBSERVATION TIPS

English	Scientific	German	Dutch
Cowslip	Primula veris	Wiesen-Schlüsselblume	Gulden sleutelbloem
Crane's-bill, Bloody	Geranium sanguineum	Blutroter Storchschnabel	Bloedooievaarsbek
Crowfoot, Seguier's	Ranunculus seguieri	Seguier-Hahnenfuss	Seguiers ranonkel*
Cudweed, Narrow-leaved	Filago gallica	Französisches Filzkraut	Frans viltkruid
Cupidone, Blue	Catananche caerulea	Blaue Rasselblume	Blauwe strobloem
Daffodil, Pheasant's-eye	Narcissus poeticus	Weisse Narzisse	Witte narcis
Daffodil, Sea	Pancratium marimum	Strandlilie	Zeenarcis
Dogwood	Cornus sanguinea	Blutroter Hartriegel	Rode kornoelje
Elm	Ulmus sp.	Ulme	Iep
Eryngo, Field	Eryngium campestre	Feld-Mannstreu	Echte kruisdistel
Eryngo, Silver	Eryngium spinalba	Silber-Mannstreu	Zilveren kruisdistel*
Fern, Rustyback	Ceterach officinarum	Milzfarn	Schubvaren
Fen-sedge, Great	Cladium mariscus	Schneide	Galigaan
Fir, Silver	Abies alba	Weisstanne	Gewone zilverspar
Flax, Beautiful	Linum narbonense	Französischer Lein	Frans vlas
Flax, Campanulate*	Linum campanulatum	Glocken-Lein	Klokjesvlas*
Flax, French	Linum trigynum	Französische Lein	Dicht vlas*
Flax, Upright	Linum strictum	Steifer Lein	Stijf vlas
Foxglove, Straw	Digitalis lutea	Kleinblütiger Fingerhut	Geel vingerhoedskruid
Garlic, Rosy	Allium roseum	Rosen-Lauch	Roze look
Germander, Felty	Teucrium polium	Polei-Gamander	Viltgamander*
Germander, Mountain	Teucrium montanum	Berg-Gamander	Berggamander
Germander, Wall	Teucrium chamaedrys	Echter Gamander	Echte gamander
Germander, Yellow	Teucrium flavum	Gelber Gamander	Gele gamander
Glasswort, Bushy*	Sarcocornia fruticosa	Strauchige Gliedermelde	Struikzeekraal
Glasswort, Common	Salicornia europaea	Gewöhnlicher Queller	Kortarige zeekraal
Glasswort, Perennial	Sarcocornia perennis	Ausdauernde Gliedermelde	Overblijvend zeekraal*
Globularia, Creeping	Globularia repens	Kriechende Kugelblume	Kruipende kogelbloem*
Globularia, Heart-leaved	Globularia cordifolia	Herzblättrige Kugelblume	Hartbladige kogelbloem
Globularia, Shrubby	Globularia alypum	Strauchkugelblume	Struikkogelbloem*
Grape, Sea	Ephedra distachya	Gewöhnliches Meerträubel	Gewone zeedruif*
Grass, Feather	Stipa pennata	Echtes Federgras	Gewoon vedergras*
Grass, Neptune	Posidonia oceanica	Neptungras	Neptunusgras
Greenweed, Spanish	Genista hispanica	Spanischer Ginster	Spaanse brem
Gromwell, Purple	Lithospermum purpurocaeruleum	Blauer Steinsame	Blauw parelzaad
Ground-pine	Ajuga chamaepitys	Gelber Günsel	Akkerzenegroen
Hawthorn	Crataegus monogyna	Eingriffeliger Weissdorn	Eenstijlige meidoorn
Heath, Tree	Erica arborea	Baumheide	Boomhei
Hellebore, Green	Helleborus viridis	Grüne Nieswurz	Wrangwortel
Helleborine, Narrow-leaved	Cephelanthera longifolia	Schwertblättriges Waldvöglein	Wit bosvogeltje
Helleborine, Small-leaved	Epipactis microphylla	Kleinblättrige Stendelwurz	Kleinbladige wespenorchis
Helleborine, White	Cephalanthera damasonium	Weisses Waldvöglein	Bleek bosvogeltje
Holly	Ilex aquifolium	Stechpalme	Hulst
Holly, Sea	Eryngium maritimum	Stranddistel	Blauwe zeedistel
Honeysuckle, Evergreen	Lonicera implexa	Windende Geissblatt	Altijdgroene kamperfoelie*
Honeysuckle, Japanese	Lonicera japonica	Japanisches Geissblatt	Japanse kamperfoelie
Hyacinth, Grape	Muscari neglectum	Weinbergs-Traubenhyazinthe	Troshyacint
Hyacinth, Tassel	Muscari comosum	Schopfige Traubenhyazinthe	Kuifhyacint

Hypocist	Cytinus hypocistis	Zistrosenwürger	Gele hypocist
Iris, Crimean	Iris lutescens	Gelbliche Schwertlilie	Gele dwerglis*
Iris, Sea	Iris (spuria ssp.) maritima	Meer-Schwertlilie	Zeelis*
Iris, Yellow	Iris pseudacorus	Sumpf-Schwertlilie	Gele lis
Ironwort, Simplebeak	Sideritis romana	Römisches Gliedkraut	Romeins ijzerkruid
Jerusalem-sage, Iberian*	Phlomis lychnitis	Filziges Brandkraut	Viltbrandkruid*
Joint-pine, Large	Ephedra major	Grosse Meerträubel	Grote zeedruif*
Jonquil, Common	Narcissus jonquilla	Jonquille	Jonquille
Juniper, Phoenician	Juniperus phoenicea	Phönizischer Wacholder	Phoenicische jeneverbes
Juniper, Prickly	Juniperus oxycedrus	Stechwacholder	Spaanse jeneverbes
Jupiter's-beard	Anthyllis barba-jovis	Jupiterbart	Jupitersbaard
Lavender, French	Lavandula stoechas	Schopflavendel	Kuiflavendel
Leek, Narcissus-flowered	Allium narcissiflorum	Narzissenblütiger Lauch	Prachtlook*
Leek, Round-headed	Allium sphaerocephalon	Kugel-Lauch	Kogellook
Leek, Yellow	Allium flavum	Gelber Lauch	Gele look
Lettuce, Blue	Lactuca perennis	Blauer Lattich	Blauwe sla
Lettuce, Purple	Prenanthes purpurea	Hasenlattich	Hazensla
Lily, Martagon	Lilium martagon	Türkenbund-Lilie	Turkse lelie
Lily, St. Bernard's	Anthericum liliago	Astlose Graslilie	Grote graslelie
Lily, Turban	Lilium pomponium	Seealpen-Lilie	Rode lelie*
Lime	Tilia spec.	Linden	Linde
Lineseed, Mediterranean	Bellardia trixago	Bunte Bellardie	Bellardia
Liverleaf	Anemone hepatica	Leberblümchen	Leverbloempje
Madder, Field	Sherardia arvensis	Ackerröte	Blauw walstro
Maple, Field	Acer campestre	Feld-Ahorn	Spaanse aak
Meadow-rue, Alpine	Thalictrum alpinum	Alpen-Wiesenraute	Alpenruit
Meadow-rue, Lesser	Thalictrum minus	Kleine Wiesenraute	Kleine ruit
Medick, Sea	Medicago marina	Strand-Schneckenklee	Zeerupsklaver
Mercury, Dog's	Mercurialis perennis	Wald-Bingelkraut	Bosbingelkruid
Mezereon	Daphne mezereum	Gewöhnlicher Seidelbast	Rood peperboompje
Mezereon, Mediterranean	Daphne gnidium	Herbst-Seidelbast	Herfstpeperboompje*
Milk-vetch, Montpelier	Astragalus monspessulanus	Französischer Tragant	Montpellier hokjespeul
Milkwort, Chalk	Polygala calcarea	Kalk-Kreuzblümchen	Kalkvleugeltjesbloem
Milkwort, Common	Polygala vulgaris	Gewöhnliches Kreuzblümchen	Gewone vleugeltjesbloem
Mustard, Buckler	Biscutella laevigata	Glatt-Brillenschötchen	Glad brilkruid
Oak, Cork	Quercus suber	Korkeiche	Kurkeik
Oak, Downy	Quercus pubescens	Flaum-Eiche	Donzige eik
Oak, Holm	Quercus ilex	Stein-Eiche	Steeneik
Oak, Kermes	Quercus coccifera	Kermes-Eiche	Hulsteik
Orchid, Bird's-nest	Neottia nidus-avis	Nestwurz	Vogelnestje
Orchid, Black Spider	Ophrys incubacea	Schwarze Ragwurz	Zwarte spinnenophrys
Orchid, Burnt	Neotinea ustulata	Brand-Knabenkraut	Aangebrande orchis
Orchid, Champagne	Anacamptis champagneuxii	Dreiknollen-Knabenkraut	Blesharlekijn
Orchid, Common Spotted	Dactylorhiza fuchsii	Fuchs' Knabenkraut	Bosorchis
Orchid, Common Tongue	Serapias lingua	Einschwieliger Zugenstendel	Gewone tongorchis
Orchid, Dense-flowered	Neotinea maculata	Gefleckte Keuschorchis	Nonnetjesorchis
Orchid, Drome	Ophrys drumana	Drome-Ragwurz	Drome orchis
Orchid, Dull Bee	Ophrys fusca	Braune Ragwurz	Bruine orchis
Orchid, Early Spider	Ophrys sphegodes	Grosse Spinnen-Ragwurz	Spinnenorchis
Orchid, Early-purple	Orchis mascula	Mannliches Knabenkraut	Mannetjesorchis
Orchid, Elder-flowered	Dactylorhiza sambucina	Holunder-Knabenkraut	Vlierorchis
Orchid, False Woodcock	Ophrys pseudoscolopax	Falsche Schnepfen-Ragwurz*	Valse snippenorchis*

TOURIST INFORMATION & OBSERVATION TIPS

Orchid, Fly	Ophrys insectifera	Fliegen-Ragwurz	Vliegenorchis
Orchid, Fragrant	Gymnadenia conopsea	Mücken-Händelwurz	Grote muggenorchis
Orchid, Giant	Himantoglossum robertianum	Riesen-Knabenkraut	Hyacinthorchis
Orchid, Green-winged	Anacamptis morio	Kleines Knabenkraut	Harlekijn
Orchid, Heart-flowered Tongue	Serapias cordigera	Herzförmiger Zungenstendel	Brede tongorchis
Orchid, Lady	Orchis purpurea	Purpur-Knabenkraut	Purperorchis
Orchid, Late Spider	Ophrys fuciflora	Hummel-Ragwurz	Hommelorchis
Orchid, Lesser Butterfly	Platanthera bifolia	Weisse Waldhyazinthe	Welriekende nachtorchis
Orchid, Lizard	Himantoglossum hircinum	Bocksorchis	Bokkenorchis
Orchid, Loose-flowered	Anacamptis laxiflora	Lockerblütiges Knabenkraut	IJle moerasorchis
Orchid, Man	Orchis anthropophora	Ohnsporn	Poppenorchis
Orchid, Meadow*	Anacamptis palustris	Sumpf-Knabenkraut	Moerasorchis
Orchid, Military	Orchis militaris	Helm-Knabenkraut	Soldaatje
Orchid, Painted	Anacamptis picta	Lockerblutiges Kleines Knabenkraut	Slanke harlekijn
Orchid, Passion-tide	Ophrys passionis	Oster-Ragwurz	Paasorchis*
Orchid, Provence	Orchis provincialis	Provence-Knabenkraut	Stippelorchis
Orchid, Provence Tongue*	Serapias olbia	Südfranzösischer Zungenständel	Franse tongorchis*
Orchid, Pyramidal	Anacamptis pyramidalis	Hundswurz	Hondskruid
Orchid, Scarce Tongue	Serapias neglecta	Verkannter Zungenständel	Vergeten tongorchis
Orchid, Small Spider	Ophrys araneola	Kleine Spinnen-Ragwurz	Vroege spinnenorchis
Orchid, Southern Early-purple	Orchis olbiensis	Hyères-Knabenkraut	Kleine mannetjesorchis
Orchid, Splendid*	Ophrys splendida	Prächtige Ragwurz	Prachtorchis*
Orchid, Western Spider	Ophrys exaltata	Ausgebreitete Ragwurz	Westelijke spinnenorchis*
Orchid, Woodcock	Ophrys scolopax	Schnepfen-Ragwurz	Snippenorchis
Orchid, Yellow Bee	Ophrys lutea	Gelbe Ragwurz	Gele orchis
Pansy, Mont Cenis	Viola cenisia	Mont Cenis-Stiefmütterchen	Cenis-viooltje*
Pea, Spring	Lathyrus vernus	Frühlings-Platterbse	Voorjaarslathyrus
Peony, Common	Paeonia officinalis	Echte Pfingstrose	Wilde pioenroos
Pine, Aleppo	Pinus halepensis	Allepo-Kiefer	Aleppoden
Pine, Austrian	Pinus nigra	Schwarzkiefer	Zwarte den
Pine, Maritime	Pinus pinaster	Strandkiefer	Zeeden
Pine, Scots	Pinus sylvestris	Waldkiefer	Grove den
Pine, Umbrella	Pinus pinea	Pinie	Parasolden
Plant, Curry	Helichrysum stoechas	Mittelmeer-Strohblume	Mediterrane strobloem
Poplar, Black	Populus nigra	Schwarzpappel	Zwarte populier
Poplar, White	Populus alba	Silber-Pappel	Witte abeel
Poppy, Rhaetian	Papaver alpinum ssp. rhaeticum	Rhätischer Alpen-Mohn	Rhaetische klaproos
Primrose	Primula vulgaris	Stengellose Schlüsselblume	Stengelloze sleutelbloem
Primula, Golden	Vitaliana primuliflora	Goldprimel	Goudmansschild*
Purslane, Sea	Atriplex portulacoides	Portulak-Salzmelde	Gewone zoutmelde
Rampion, Round-headed	Phyteuma orbiculare	Kugelige Teufelskralle	Bolrapunzel
Rocket, Sea	Cakile maritima	Europäischer Meersenf	Zeeraket
Rock-jasmine, Alpine	Androsace alpina	Alpen-Mannsschild	Alpenmansschild
Rockrose, Hoary	Helianthemum canum	Graues Sonnenröschen	Klein zonneroosje*
Rockrose, Spotted	Tuberaria guttata	Geflecktes Sonnenröschen	Gevlekt zonneroosje

Rockrose, White	Helianthemum apenninum	Weisses Sonnenröschen	Wit zonneroosje
Rosemary, Wild	Rosmarinus officinalis	Rosmarin	Rozemarijn
Rustyback	Asplenium ceterach	Milzfarn	Schubvaren
Saltwort, Opposite-leaved	Salsola soda	Soda- Salzkraut	Sodakruid*
Samphire, Golden	Inula crithmoides	Salz-Alant	Zeealant
Sanicle	Sanicula europaea	Sanikel	Heelkruid
Saxifrage, Meadow	Saxifraga granulata	Knöllchen-Steinbrech	Knolsteenbreek
Saxifrage, Purple	Saxifraga oppositifolia	Gegenblättriger Steinbrech	Zuiltjessteenbreek
Scorpion-vetch, Shrubby	Coronilla valentina	Valencia-Kronwicke	Mediterraan kroonkruid
Sea-blite, Annual	Suaeda maritima	Strand-Sode	Klein schorrenkruid
Sea-blite, Shrubby	Suaeda vera	Strauch-Sode*	Struikschorrenkruid*
Sea-lavender	Limonium spec.	Strandflieder	Lamsoor
Smearwort	Aristolochia rotunda	Rundblättrige Osterluzei	Rondbladige pijpbloem
Snake's-head, Provence*	Fritillaria involucrata	Gegenblättrige Schachblume	Provencaalse Kievitsbloem
Snapdragon, Broad-leaved*	Antirrhinum latifolium	Breitblättriges Löwenmaul	Breedbladige leeuwenbek*
Snowflake, Spring	Leucojum vernum	Frühlings-Knotenblume	Lenteklokje
Solomon's-seal, Angular	Polygonatum odoratum	Wohlriechende Weisswurz	Welriekende salomonszegel
Spleenwort, Maidenhair	Asplenium trichomanes	Braunstieliger Streifenfarn	Steenbreekvaren
Spurge, Cypress	Euphorbia cyparissias	Zypressen-Wolfsmilch	Cypreswolfsmelk
Spurge, Mediterranean	Euphorbia characias	Palisaden-Wolfsmilch	Zwartbloemige wolfsmelk*
Spurge, Sea	Euphorbia paralias	Strand-Wolfsmilch	Zeewolfsmelk
Spurge, Seguier's	Euphorbia seguieriana	Steppen-Wolfsmilch	Zandwolfsmelk
Spurge, Tree	Euphorbia dendroides	Baum-Wolfsmilch	Boomwolfsmelk
Spurge, Wood	Euphorbia amygdaloides	Mandelblättrige Wolfsmilch	Amandelwolfsmelk
Spurge-laurel	Daphne laureola	Lorbeer-Seidelbast	Zwart peperboompje
Star-of-Bethlehem	Ornithogalum umbellatum	Dolden-Milchstern	Gewone vogelmelk
Stock, Sad	Matthiola fruticulosa	Kleine Levkoje	Struikviolier
Stock, Three-horned	Matthiola tricuspidata	Dreihörnige Levkoje	Driehoornige violier*
Stonecrop, Pale	Sedum sediforme	Felsen-Fetthenne	Rotsvetkruid*
Stonecrop, Reflexed	Sedum rupestre	Gewöhnliche Felsen-Fetthenne	Tripmadam
Strawberry, Wild	Fragaria vesca	Wald-Erdbeere	Bosaardbei
Swallow-wort	Vincetoxicum hirundinaria	Weisse Schwalbenwurz	Witte engbloem
Sycamore	Acer pseudoplatanus	Bergahorn	Gewone esdoorn
Tamarisk, French	Tamarix gallica	Französische Tamariske	Franse Tamarisk
Thistle, Acanthus-leaved Carline	Carlina acanthifolia	Akanthusblättrige Eberwurz	Gouddistel
Thistle, Golden	Scolymus hispanicus	Spanische Golddistel	Spaanse gouddistel
Thistle, Illyrian	Onopordum illyricum	Illyrische Eselsdistel	Illyrische wegdistel
Thistle, Mediterranean	Galactites tomentosus	Milchfleckdistel	Galactites*
Thyme, Common	Thymus vulgaris	Echter Thymian	Echte tijm
Toadflax, Alpine	Linaria alpina	Alpen-Leinkraut	Alpenleeuwenbek
Tree, Judas	Cercis siliquastrum	Gemeiner Judasbaum	Europese judasboom
Tree, Plane	Platanus sp.	Platane	Plataan
Tree, Strawberry	Arbutus unedo	Erdbeerbaum	Aardbeiboom
Tulip, Wild	Tulipa sylvestris	Weinberg-Tulpe	Bostulp
Valerian, Red	Centranthus ruber	Rote Spornblume	Spoorbloem
Valerian, Tuberous	Valeriana tuberosa	Knolliger Baldrian	Knolvaleriaan*
Viper's-bugloss, Italian	Echium italicum	Italienischer Natternkopf	Italiaans slangekruid
Virgin's-bower	Clematis flammula	Brennende Waldrebe	Scherpe clematis
Whitebeam	Sorbus aria	Echte Mehlbeere	Meelbes
Yellow-wort	Blackstonia perfoliata	Durchwachsener Bitterling	Zomerbitterling
Yew	Taxus baccata	Eibe	Taxus

Mammals

English	Scientific	German	Dutch
Badger	Meles meles	Dachs	Das
Bat, Geoffroy's	Myotis emarginatus	Wimperfledermaus	Ingekorven vleermuis
Beaver	Castor fiber	Bieber	Bever
Bison, European	Bison bonasus	Wisent	Wisent
Boar, Wild	Sus scrofa	Wildschwein	Wild zwijn
Chamois	Rupicapra rupicapra	Gemse	Gems
Coypu	Myocaster coypus	Nutria	Beverrat
Deer, Red	Cervus elaphus	Rothirsch	Edelhert
Deer, Roe	Capreolus capreolus	Reh	Ree
Dolphin, Bottlenose	Tursiops truncatus	Grosstümmler	Tuimelaar
Dolphin, Common	Delphinus delphis	Delphin	Gewone dolfijn
Dolphin, Risso's	Grampus griseus	Rundkopfdelfin	Gramper, Grijze dolfijn
Dolphin, Striped	Stenella coeruleoalba	Streifendelfin	Gestreepte dolfijn
Dormouse, Edible	Glis glis	Siebenschläfer	Relmuis
Dormouse, Garden	Eliomys quercinus	Gartenschläfer	Eikelmuis
Dormouse, Hazel	Muscardinus avellanarius	Haselmaus	Hazelmuis
Fox	Vulpes vulpes	Rotfuchs	Vos
Genet	Genetta genetta	Ginsterkatze	Genetkat
Lynx, European	Lynx lynx	Luchs	Lynx
Marten, Beech	Martes foina	Steinmarder	Steenmarter
Marten, Pine	Martes martes	Baummarder	Boommarter
Mouflon	Ovis (ammon) musimon	Mufflon	Moeflon
Mouse, Algerian	Mus spretus	Algerische Hausmaus	Algerijnse muis
Otter	Lutra lutra	Fischotter	Otter
Rabbit	Oryctolagus cuniculus	Wildkaninchen	Konijn
Shrew	Soricidae	Spitzmäuse	Spitsmuizen
Vole, Mediterranean Pine	Microtus duodecimcostatus	Mittelmeer-Kleinwühlmaus	Provençaalse woelmuis
Weasel	Mustela nivalis	Mauswiesel	Wezel
Whale, Fin	Balaenoptera physalus	Finnwall	Gewone vinvis
Whale, Pilot	Globicephala melas	Grindwal	Griend
Whale, Sperm	Physeter macrocephalus	Pottwall	Potvis
Wildcat	Felis silvestris	Wildkatze	Wilde kat
Wolf	Canis lupus	Wolf	Wolf

Birds

English	Scientific	German	Dutch
Accentor, Alpine	Prunella collaris	Alpenbraunelle	Alpenheggemus
Avocet	Recurvirostra avosetta	Säbelschnäbler	Kluut
Bee-eater	Merops apiaster	Bienenfresser	Bijeneter
Bittern, Great	Botaurus stellaris	Rohrdommel	Roerdomp
Bittern, Little	Ixobrychus minutus	Zwergdommel	Woudaapje
Blackbird	Turdus merula	Amsel	Merel
Blackcap	Sylvia atricapilla	Mönchsgrasmücke	Zwartkop
Bluethroat	Luscinia svecica	Blaukehlchen	Blauwborst
Brambling	Fringilla montifringilla	Bergfink	Keep
Bullfinch	Pyrrhula pyrrhula	Gimpel	Goudvink
Bunting, Black-headed	Emberiza melanocephala	Kappenammer	Zwartkopgors
Bunting, Cirl	Emberiza cirlus	Zaunammer	Cirlgors
Bunting, Corn	Miliaria calandra	Grauammer	Grauwe gors
Bunting, Ortolan	Emberiza hortulana	Ortolan	Ortolaan

Bunting, Reed	*Emberiza schoeniclus*	Rohrammer	Rietgors
Bunting, Rock	*Emberiza cia*	Zippammer	Grijze gors
Bustard, Little	*Tetrax tetrax*	Zwergtrappe	Kleine trap
Buzzard, Common	*Buteo buteo*	Mäusebussard	Buizerd
Buzzard, Honey	*Pernis apivorus*	Wespenbussard	Wespendief
Chaffinch	*Fringilla coelebs*	Buchfink	Vink
Chiffchaff	*Phylloscopus collybita*	Zilpzalp	Tjiftjaf
Chough, Red-billed	*Pyrrhocorax pyrrhocorax*	Alpenkrähe	Alpenkraai
Cisticola, Zitting	*Cisticola juncidis*	Cistensänger	Graszanger
Coot	*Fulica atra*	Blässhuhn	Meerkoet
Cormorant	*Phalacrocorax carbo*	Kormoran	Aalscholver
Crane	*Grus grus*	Kranich	Kraanvogel
Crossbill	*Loxia curvirostra*	Fichtenkreuzschnabel	Kruisbek
Crow, Carrion	*Corvus corone*	Aaskrähe	Zwarte kraai
Cuckoo, Common	*Cuculus canorus*	Kuckuck	Koekoek
Cuckoo, Great Spotted	*Clamator glandarius*	Häherkuckuck	Kuifkoekoek
Curlew	*Numenius arquata*	Grosser Brachvogel	Wulp
Curlew, Stone	*Burhinus oedicnemus*	Triel	Griel
Dipper	*Cinclus cinclus*	Wasseramsel	Waterspreeuw
Dotterel	*Charadrius morinellus*	Mornellregenpfeifer	Morinelplevier
Dove, Collared	*Streptopelia decaocto*	Türkentaube	Turkse tortel
Dove, Stock	*Columba oenas*	Hohltaube	Holenduif
Dove, Turtle	*Streptopelia turtur*	Turteltaube	Tortelduif
Duck, Ferruginous	*Aythya nyroca*	Moorente	Witoogeend
Duck, Tufted	*Aythya fuligula*	Reiherente	Kuifeend
Dunlin	*Calidris alpina*	Alpenstrandläufer	Bonte strandloper
Dunnock	*Prunella modularis*	Heckenbraunelle	Heggenmus
Eagle, Bonelli's	*Hieraaetus fasciatus*	Habichtsadler	Havikarend
Eagle, Booted	*Hieraaetus pennatus*	Zwergadler	Dwergarend
Eagle, Golden	*Aquila chrysaetos*	Steinadler	Steenarend
Eagle, Greater Spotted	*Aquila clanga*	Schelladler	Bastaardarend
Eagle, Short-toed	*Circaetus gallicus*	Schlangenadler	Slangenarend
Eagle, White-tailed	*Haliaeetus albicilla*	Seeadler	Zeearend
Egret, Cattle	*Bubulcus ibis*	Kuhreiher	Koereiger
Egret, Great White	*Ardea alba*	Silberreiher	Grote zilverreiger
Egret, Little	*Egretta garzetta*	Seidenreiher	Kleine zilverreiger
Eider	*Somateria mollissima*	Eiderente	Eider
Falcon, Eleonora's	*Falco eleonorae*	Eleonorenfalke	Eleonora's valk
Falcon, Red-footed	*Falco vespertinus*	Rotfussfalke	Roodpootvalk
Fieldfare	*Turdus pilaris*	Wacholderdrossel	Kramsvogel
Finch, Citril	*Serinus citrinella*	Zitronengirlitz	Citroenkanarie
Firecrest	*Regulus ignicapillus*	Sommergoldhähnchen	Vuurgoudhaantje
Flamingo, Greater	*Phoenicopterus roseus*	Flamingo	Europese flamingo
Flycatcher, Pied	*Ficedula hypoleuca*	Trauerschnäpper	Bonte vliegenvanger
Gadwall	*Anas strepera*	Schnatterente	Krakeend
Gallinule, Purple	*Porphyrio porphyrio*	Purpurhuhn	Purperkoet
Gannet	*Morus bassanus*	Basstölpel	Jan-van-gent
Godwit, Bar-tailed	*Limosa lapponica*	Pfuhlschnepfe	Rosse grutto
Godwit, Black-tailed	*Limosa limosa*	Uferschnepfe	Grutto
Goldcrest	*Regulus regulus*	Wintergoldhähnchen	Goudhaan
Goldfinch	*Carduelis carduelis*	Distelfink	Putter
Goose, Barnacle	*Branta leucopsis*	Weisswangengans	Brandgans
Goose, Bean	*Anser fabalis*	Saatgans	Rietgans
Goose, Greyleg	*Anser anser*	Graugans	Grauwe gans

English	Scientific	German	Dutch
Goose, White-fronted	Anser albifrons	Blässgans	Kolgans
Goshawk	Accipiter gentilis	Habicht	Havik
Grebe, Black-necked	Podiceps nigricollis	Schwarzhalstaucher	Geoorde fuut
Grebe, Great Crested	Podiceps cristatus	Haubentaucher	Fuut
Grebe, Little	Tachybaptus ruficollis	Zwergtaucher	Dodaars
Greenfinch	Carduelis chloris	Grünling	Groenling
Greenshank	Tringa nebularia	Grünschenkel	Groenpootruiter
Gull, Black-headed	Chroicocephalus ridibundus	Lachmöwe	Kokmeeuw
Gull, Common	Larus canus	Sturmmöwe	Stormmeeuw
Gull, Lesser Black-backed	Larus graellsii	Heringsmöwe	Kleine mantelmeeuw
Gull, Mediterranean	Ichthyaetus melanocephalus	Schwarzkopfmöwe	Zwartkopmeeuw
Gull, Slender-billed	Chroicocephalus genei	Dünnschnabelmöwe	Dunbekmeeuw
Gull, Yellow-legged	Larus michahellis	Weisskopfmöve	Geelpootmeeuw
Harrier, Hen	Circus cyaneus	Kornweihe	Blauwe kiekendief
Harrier, Marsh	Circus aeruginosus	Rohrweihe	Bruine kiekendief
Harrier, Montagu's	Circus pygargus	Wiesenweihe	Grauwe kiekendief
Hawfinch	Coccothraustes coccothraustes	Kernbeisser	Appelvink
Heron, Grey	Ardea cinerea	Graureiher	Blauwe reiger
Heron, Night	Nycticorax nycticorax	Nachtreiher	Kwak
Heron, Purple	Ardea purpurea	Purpurreiher	Purperreiger
Heron, Squacco	Ardeola ralloides	Rallenreiher	Ralreiger
Hobby	Falco subbuteo	Baumfalke	Boomvalk
Hoopoe	Upupa epops	Wiedehopf	Hop
Ibis, Glossy	Plegadis falcinellus	Braunsichler	Zwarte ibis
Ibis, Sacred	Threskiornis aethiopicus	Heiliger Ibis	Heilige ibis
Jackdaw	Corvus monedula	Dohle	Kauw
Jay	Garrulus glandarius	Eichelhäher	Gaai
Kestrel	Falco tinnunculus	Turmfalke	Torenvalk
Kestrel, Lesser	Falco naumanni	Rötelfalke	Kleine torenvalk
Kingfisher	Alcedo atthis	Eisvogel	IJsvogel
Kite, Black	Milvus migrans	Schwarzmilan	Zwarte wouw
Kite, Red	Milvus milvus	Rotmilan	Rode wouw
Knot, Red	Calidris canutus	Knutt	Kanoet
Lapwing	Vanellus vanellus	Kiebitz	Kievit
Lark, Calandra	Melanocorypha calandra	Kalanderlerche	Kalanderleeuwerik
Lark, Crested	Galerida cristata	Haubenlerche	Kuifleeuwerik
Lark, Short-toed	Calandrella brachydactyla	Kurzzehenlerche	Kortteenleeuwerik
Lark, Thekla	Galerida theklae	Theklalerche	Theklaleeuwerik
Linnet	Carduelis cannabina	Bluthänfling	Kneu
Magpie	Pica pica	Elster	Ekster
Mallard	Anas platyrhynchos	Stockente	Wilde eend
Martin, Crag	Ptyonoprogne rupestris	Felsenschwalbe	Rotszwaluw
Martin, House	Delichon urbicum	Mehlschwalbe	Huiszwaluw
Martin, Sand	Riparia riparia	Uferschwalbe	Oeverzwaluw
Merganser, Red-breasted	Mergus serrator	Mittelsäger	Middelste zaagbek
Merlin	Falco columbarius	Merlin	Smelleken
Moorhen	Gallinula chloropus	Teichhuhn	Waterhoen
Nightingale	Luscinia megarhynchos	Nachtigal	Nachtegaal
Nightjar	Caprimulgus europaeus	Ziegenmelker	Nachtzwaluw
Nuthatch	Sitta europaea	Kleiber	Boomklever
Oriole, Golden	Oriolus oriolus	Pirol	Wielewaal
Osprey	Pandion haliaetus	Fischadler	Visarend
Ouzel, Ring	Turdus torquatus	Ringdrossel	Beflijster
Owl, Barn	Tyto alba	Schleiereule	Kerkuil

English	Scientific	German	Dutch
Owl, Eagle	Bubo bubo	Uhu	Oehoe
Owl, Little	Athene noctua	Steinkauz	Steenuil
Owl, Long-eared	Asio otus	Waldohreule	Ransuil
Owl, Scops	Otus scops	Zwergohreule	Dwergooruil
Owl, Tawny	Strix aluco	Waldkauz	Bosuil
Owl, Tengmalm's	Aegolius funereus	Raufusskauz	Ruigpootuil
Oystercatcher	Haematopus ostralegus	Austernfischer	Scholekster
Parakeet, Rose-ringed	Psittacula krameri	Halsbandsittich	Halsbandparkiet
Partridge, Red-legged	Alectoris rufa	Rothuhn	Rode patrijs
Peregrine	Falco peregrinus	Wanderfalke	Slechtvalk
Petrel, European Storm	Hydrobates pelagicus	Sturmschwalbe	Stormvogeltje
Pheasant	Phasianus colchicus	Fasan	Fazant
Pigeon, Feral	Columba livia f. domestica	Stadttaube	Stadsduif
Pigeon, Rock	Columba livia	Felsentaube	Rotsduif
Pigeon, Wood	Columba palumbus	Ringeltaube	Houtduif
Pintail	Anas acuta	Spiessente	Pijlstaart
Pipit, Meadow	Anthus pratensis	Wiesenpieper	Graspieper
Pipit, Richard's	Anthus richardi	Spornpieper	Grote pieper
Pipit, Tawny	Anthus campestris	Brachpieper	Duinpieper
Pipit, Tree	Anthus trivialis	Baumpieper	Boompieper
Pipit, Water	Anthus spinoletta	Bergpieper	Waterpieper
Plover, Golden	Pluvialis apricaria	Goldregenpfeifer	Goudplevier
Plover, Grey	Pluvialis squatarola	Kiebitzregenpfeifer	Zilverplevier
Plover, Kentish	Charadrius alexandrinus	Seeregenpfeifer	Strandplevier
Plover, Little Ringed	Charadrius dubius	Flussregenpfeifer	Kleine plevier
Plover, Ringed	Charadrius hiaticula	Sandregenpfeifer	Bontbekplevier
Pochard, Common	Aythya ferina	Tafelente	Tafeleend
Pochard, Red-crested	Netta rufina	Kolbenente	Krooneend
Pratincole, Collared	Glareola pratincola	Rotflügel-Brachschwalbe	Vorkstaartplevier
Quail	Coturnix coturnix	Wachtel	Kwartel
Rail, Water	Rallus aquaticus	Wasserralle	Waterral
Raven	Corvus corax	Kolkrabe	Raaf
Redshank	Tringa totanus	Rotschenkel	Tureluur
Redshank, Spotted	Tringa erythropus	Dunkler Wasserläufer	Zwarte ruiter
Redstart	Phoenicurus phoenicurus	Gartenrotschwanz	Gekraagde roodstaart
Redstart, Black	Phoenicurus ochruros	Hausrotschwanz	Zwarte roodstaart
Redwing	Turdus iliacus	Rotdrossel	Koperwiek
Robin	Erithacus rubecula	Rotkehlchen	Roodborst
Roller	Coracias garrulus	Blauracke	Scharrelaar
Rook	Corvus frugilegus	Saatkrähe	Roek
Sanderling	Calidris alba	Sanderling	Drieteenstrandloper
Sandgrouse, Pin-tailed	Pterocles alchata	Spiessflughuhn	Witbuikzandhoen
Sandpiper, Common	Actitis hypoleucos	Flussuferläufer	Oeverloper
Sandpiper, Curlew	Calidris ferruginea	Sichelstrandläufer	Krombekstrandloper
Sandpiper, Wood	Tringa glareola	Bruchwasserläufer	Bosruiter
Serin	Serinus serinus	Girlitz	Europese kanarie
Shag	Phalacrocorax aristotelis	Krähenscharbe	Kuifaalscholver
Shearwater, Cory's	Calonectris borealis	Kanarensturmtaucher	Kuhls pijlstormvogel
Shearwater, Yelkouan	Puffinus yelkouan	Mittelmeer-Sturmtaucher	Yelkouanpijlstormvogel
Shelduck, Common	Tadorna tadorna	Brandgans	Bergeend
Shoveler	Anas clypeata	Löffelente	Slobeend
Shrike, Iberian Grey	Lanius meridionalis	Südlicher Raubwürger	Zuidelijke klapekster
Shrike, Lesser Grey	Lanius minor	Schwarzstirnwürger	Kleine klapekster
Shrike, Red-backed	Lanius collurio	Neuntöter	Grauwe klauwier

English	Scientific	German	Dutch
Shrike, Woodchat	*Lanius senator*	Rotkopfwürger	Roodkopklauwier
Siskin	*Carduelis spinus*	Erlenzeisig	Sijs
Skylark	*Alauda arvensis*	Feldlerche	Veldleeuwerik
Snipe	*Gallinago gallinago*	Bekassine	Watersnip
Snowfinch, White-winged	*Montifringilla nivalis*	Schneesperling	Sneeuwvink
Sparrow, House	*Passer domesticus*	Haussperling	Huismus
Sparrow, Rock	*Petronia petronia*	Steinsperling	Rotsmus
Sparrow, Tree	*Passer montanus*	Feldsperling	Ringmus
Sparrowhawk	*Accipiter nisus*	Sperber	Sperwer
Spoonbill	*Platalea leucorodia*	Löffler	Lepelaar
Starling	*Sturnus vulgaris*	Star	Spreeuw
Starling, Spotless	*Sturnus unicolor*	Einfarbstar	Zwarte spreeuw
Stilt, Black-winged	*Himantopus himantopus*	Stelzenläufer	Steltkluut
Stint, Little	*Calidris minuta*	Zwergstrandläufer	Kleine strandloper
Stonechat	*Saxicola torquata*	Schwarzkehlchen	Roodborsttapuit
Stork, White	*Ciconia ciconia*	Weissstorch	Ooievaar
Swallow	*Hirundo rustica*	Rauchschwalbe	Boerenzwaluw
Swallow, Red-rumped	*Cecropsis daurica*	Rötelschwalbe	Roodstuitzwaluw
Swan, Bewick's	*Cygnus bewickii*	Zwergschwan	Kleine zwaan
Swan, Mute	*Cygnus olor*	Höckerschwan	Knobbelzwaan
Swift, Alpine	*Tachymarptis melba*	Alpensegler	Alpengierzwaluw
Swift, Common	*Apus apus*	Mauersegler	Gierzwaluw
Swift, Pallid	*Apus pallidus*	Fahlsegler	Vale gierzwaluw
Teal	*Anas crecca*	Krickente	Wintertaling
Tern, Black	*Chlidonias niger*	Trauerseeschwalbe	Zwarte stern
Tern, Caspian	*Hydroprogne caspia*	Raubseeschwalbe	Reuzenstern
Tern, Common	*Sterna hirundo*	Flussseeschwalbe	Visdief
Tern, Gull-billed	*Gelochelidon nilotica*	Lachseeschwalbe	Lachstern
Tern, Little	*Sternula albifrons*	Zwergseeschwalbe	Dwergstern
Tern, Sandwich	*Thalasseus sandvicensis*	Brandseeschwalbe	Grote stern
Tern, Whiskered	*Chlidonias hybrida*	Weissbart-Seeschwalbe	Witwangstern
Thrush, Blue Rock	*Monticola solitarius*	Blaumerle	Blauwe rotslijster
Thrush, Mistle	*Turdus viscivorus*	Misteldrossel	Grote lijster
Thrush, Rock	*Monticola saxatilis*	Steinrötel	Rode rotslijster
Thrush, Song	*Turdus philomelos*	Singdrossel	Zanglijster
Tit, Bearded	*Panurus biarmicus*	Bartmeise	Baardman
Tit, Blue	*Cyanistes caeruleus*	Blaumeise	Pimpelmees
Tit, Coal	*Periparus ater*	Tannenmeise	Zwarte mees
Tit, Crested	*Lophophanus cristatus*	Haubenmeise	Kuifmees
Tit, Great	*Parus major*	Kohlmeise	Koolmees
Tit, Long-tailed	*Aegithalos caudatus*	Schwanzmeise	Staartmees
Tit, Penduline	*Remiz pendulinus*	Beutelmeise	Buidelmees
Tit, Willow	*Poecile montanus*	Weidenmeise	Matkop
Treecreeper, Short-toed	*Certhia brachydactyla*	Gartenbaumläufer	Boomkruiper
Vulture, Bearded	*Gypaetus barbatus*	Bartgeier	Lammergier
Vulture, Black	*Aegypius monachus*	Mönchsgeier	Monniksgier
Vulture, Egyptian	*Neophron percnopterus*	Schmutzgeier	Aasgier
Vulture, Griffon	*Gyps fulvus*	Gänsegeier	Vale gier
Wagtail, Grey	*Motacilla cinerea*	Gebirgsstelze	Grote gele kwikstaart
Wagtail, White	*Motacilla alba*	Bachstelze	Witte kwikstaart
Wagtail, Yellow	*Motacilla flava*	Schafstelze	Gele kwikstaart
Wallcreeper	*Tichodroma muraria*	Mauerläufer	Rotskruiper
Warbler, (Western) Subalpine	*Sylvia cantillans cantillans*	Westliche Weissbart-Grasmücke	Westelijke baardgrasmus

English	Scientific	German	Dutch
Warbler, Bonelli's	*Phylloscopus bonelli*	Berglaubsänger	Bergfluiter
Warbler, Cetti's	*Cettia cetti*	Seidensänger	Cetti's zanger
Warbler, Dartford	*Sylvia undata*	Provencegrasmücke	Provençaalse grasmus
Warbler, Great Reed	*Acrocephalus arundinaceus*	Drosselrohrsänger	Grote karekiet
Warbler, Melodious	*Hippolais polyglotta*	Orpheusspötter	Orpheusspotvogel
Warbler, Moustached	*Acrocephalus melanopogon*	Mariskensänger	Zwartkoprietzanger
Warbler, Reed	*Acrocephalus scirpaceus*	Teichrohrsänger	Kleine karekiet
Warbler, Sardinian	*Sylvia melanocephala*	Samtkopf-Grasmücke	Kleine zwartkop
Warbler, Savi's	*Locustella luscinioides*	Rohrschwirl	Snor
Warbler, Spectacled	*Sylvia conspicillata*	Brillengrasmücke	Brilgrasmus
Warbler, Western Orphean	*Sylvia hortensis*	Orpheusgrasmücke	Orpheusgrasmus
Wheatear, (Northern)	*Oenanthe oenanthe*	Steinschmätzer	Tapuit
Wheatear, Black-eared	*Oenanthe hispanica*	Mittelmeer-Steinschmätzer	Blonde tapuit
Whinchat	*Saxicola rubetra*	Braunkehlchen	Paapje
Whitethroat	*Sylvia communis*	Dorngrasmücke	Grasmus
Wigeon	*Anas penelope*	Pfeifente	Smient
Woodlark	*Lullula arborea*	Heidelerche	Boomleeuwerik
Woodpecker, Black	*Dryocopus martius*	Schwarzspecht	Zwarte specht
Woodpecker, Great Spotted	*Dendrocopos major*	Buntspecht	Grote bonte specht
Woodpecker, Green	*Picus viridis*	Grünspecht	Groene specht
Woodpecker, Lesser Spotted	*Dendrocopos minor*	Kleinspecht	Kleine bonte specht
Wren	*Troglodytes troglodytes*	Zaunkönig	Winterkoning
Wryneck	*Jynx torquilla*	Wendehals	Draaihals
Yellowhammer	*Emberiza citrinella*	Goldammer	Geelgors

Reptiles and Amphibians

English	Scientific	German	Dutch
Frog, Agile	*Rana dalmatina*	Springfrosch	Springkikker
Frog, Common	*Rana temporaria*	Grasfrosch	Bruine kikker
Frog, Graf's Hybrid	*Rana kl. grafi*	Grafscher Hybridfrosch	Graf's bastaardkikker
Frog, Iberian Water	*Pelophylax perezi*	Iberischer Wasserfrosch	Iberische groene kikker
Frog, Marsh	*Rana ridibunda*	Seefrosch	Meerkikker
Frog, Parsley	*Pelodytes punctatus*	Westlicher Schlammtaucher	Groengestipte kikker
Frog, Stripeless Tree	*Hyla meridionalis*	Mittelmeer-Laubfrosch	Mediterrane boomkikker
Frog, Tyrrhenian Painted	*Discoglossus sardus*	Sardischer Scheibenzüngler	Tyrrheense schijftongkikker
Gecko, Leaf-toed	*Euleptes europaea*	Europäischer Blattfingergecko	Bladvingergekko
Gecko, Moorish	*Tarentola mauritanica*	Maurischer Gecko	Muurgekko
Gecko, Turkish	*Hemidactylus turcicus*	Europäischer Halbfinger	Europese tjiktjak
Lizard, Ocellated	*Timon lepidus*	Perleidechse	Parelhagedis
Lizard, Wall	*Podarcis muralis*	Mauereidechse	Muurhagedis
Lizard, Western Green	*Lacerta bilineata*	Westliche Smaragdeidechse	Westelijke smaragdhagedis
Newt, Alpine	*Triturus alpestris*	Bergmolch	Alpenwatersalamander
Newt, Palmate	*Lissotriton helveticus*	Fadenmolch	Vinpootsalamander
Psammodromus, Spanish	*Psammodromus hispanicus*	Spanischer Sandläufer	Spaanse zandloper
Salamander, Strinati's Cave	*Speleomantes ambrosii*	Strinati Höhlensalamander	Ligurische grottensalamander
Salamander, Fire	*Salamandra salamandra*	Feuersalamander	Vuursalamander
Skink, Western Three-toed	*Chalcides striatus*	Westliche Erzschleiche	Gestreepte hazelskink

English	Scientific	German	Dutch
Slider, Red-eared	Trachemys scripta	Rotwangen-Schmuckschildkröte	Roodwangschildpad
Snake, Aesculapian	Zamenis longissimus	Äskulapnatter	Esculaapslang
Snake, Grass	Natrix natrix	Ringelnatter	Ringslang
Snake, Ladder	Elaphe scalaris	Treppennatter	Trapslang
Snake, Montpellier	Malpolon monspessulanus	Eidechsennatter	Hagedisslang
Snake, Southern Smooth	Coronella girondica	Girondische Glattnatter	Girondische gladde sla
Snake, Viperine	Natrix maura	Vipernatter	Adderringslang
Snake, Western Whip	Coluber viridiflavus	Gelbgrüne Zornnatter	Geelgroene toornslang
Spadefoot, Western	Pelobates cultripes	Messerfuss	Iberische knoflookpad
Terrapin, European Pond	Emys orbicularis	Europäische Sumpfschildkröte	Europese moeras-schildpad
Toad, Common	Bufo bufo	Erdkröte	Gewone pad
Toad, Midwife	Alytes obstetricans	Geburtshelferkröte	Vroedmeesterpad
Toad, Natterjack	Epidalea calamita	Kreuzkröte	Rugstreeppad
Toad, Spiny	Bufo spinosus	Mittelmeer-Erdkröte	Westelijke gewone pac
Toad, Yellow-bellied	Bombina variegata	Gelbbauchunke	Geelbuikvuurpad
Tortoise, Hermann's	Testudo hermanni	Griechische Landschildkröte	Griekse landschildpad
Turtle, Green	Chelonia mydas	Suppenschildkröte	Soepschildpad
Turtle, Loggerhead	Caretta caretta	Unechte Karettschildkröte	Dikkopschildpad
Viper, Asp	Vipera aspis	Aspisviper	Aspisadder
Viper, Meadow	Vipera ursinii	Wiesenotter	Weideadder
Worm, Slow	Anguis fragilis	Blindschleiche	Hazelworm

Invertebrates

English	Scientific	German	Dutch
Admiral, Southern White	Limenitis reducta	Blauschwarzer Eisvogel	Blauwe ijsvogelvlinder
Antlion, Giant	Palpares libelluloides	Libellenähnliche Ameisenjungfer	Reuzenmierenleeuw
Apollo	Parnassius apollo	Apollofalter	Apollovlinder
Argus, Brown	Aricia agestis	Kleiner Sonnenröschen-Bläuling	Bruin blauwtje
Argus, Scotch	Erebia aethiops	Graubindiger Mohrenfalter	Zomererebia
Beauty, Camberwell	Nymphalis antiopa	Trauermantel	Rouwmantel
Bee, Violet Carpenter	Xylocapa violacea	Holzbiene	Houtbij
Beetle, European Rhinoceros	Oryctes nasicornis	Nashornkäfer	Neushoornkever
Beetle, Stag	Lucanus cervus	Hirschkäfer	Vliegend hert
Blue, Adonis	Polyommatus bellargus	Himmelblauer Bläuling	Adonisblauwtje
Blue, Amanda's	Polyommatus amandus	Vogelwicken-Bläuling	Wikkeblauwtje
Blue, Baton	Pseudophilotes baton	Graublauer Bläuling	Klein tijmblauwtje
Blue, Black-eyed	Glaucopsyche melanops	Schwarz-Auge Bläuling*	Spaans bloemenblauw
Blue, Chapman's	Polyommatus thersites	Kleine Esparsetten-Bläuling	Esparcetteblauwtje
Blue, Chequered	Scolitantides orion	Fetthennen-Bläuling	Vetkruidblauwtje
Blue, Common	Polyommatus icarus	Hauhechel-Bläuling	Icarusblauwtje
Blue, Eros	Polyommatus eros	Prächtiger Alpenbläuling	Vlaggewikkeblauwtje
Blue, Escher's	Polyommatus escheri	Escher-Bläuling	Groot tragantblauwtje
Blue, Furry	Polyommatus dolus	Dolus-Bläuling	Westelijk vachtblauwt
Blue, Iolas	Iolana iolas	Blasenstrauch-Bläuling	Blazenstruikblauwtje
Blue, Large	Maculinea arion	Schwarzgeflecktes Bläuling	Tijmblauwtje
Blue, Long-tailed	Lampides boeticus	Grosser Wander-Bläuling	Tijgerblauwtje
Blue, Mazarine	Polyommatus semiargus	Rotklee-Bläuling	Klaverblauwtje
Blue, Meleager's	Polyommatus daphnis	Zahnflügel-Bläuling	Getand blauwtje
Blue, Osiris	Cupido osiris	Kleiner Alpenbläuling	Zuidelijk dwergblauwt

Blue, Provençal Short-tailed	Cupido alcetas	Südlicher Kurzgeschwänzter Bläuling	Zuidelijk staartblauwtje
Blue, Provence Chalk-hill	Lysandra hispana	Provence Silbergrüner Bläuling	Provencaals bleek blauwtje
Blue, Ripart's Anomalous	Polyommatus ripartii	Südliche Esparsetten-Bläuling*	Zuidelijk esparcetteblauwtje
Blue, Turquoise	Polyommatus dorylas	Wundkleebläuling	Turkooisblauwtje
Blue-eye	Erythromma lindenii	Pokaljungfer	Kanaaljuffer
Bluet, Azure	Coenagrion puella	Hufeisen-Azurjungfer	Azuurwaterjuffer
Bluet, Common	Enallagma cyathigerum	Gemeine Becherjungfer	Watersnuffel
Bluet, Dainty	Coenagrion scitulum	Gabel-Azurjungfer	Gaffelwaterjuffer
Bluet, Mediterranean	Coenagrion caerulescens	Südliche Azurjungfer	Zuidelijke waterjuffer
Bluet, Mercury	Coenagrion mercuriale	Helm-Azurjungfer	Mercuurwaterjuffer
Bluet, Variable	Coenagrion pulchellum	Fledermaus-Azurjungfer	Variabele waterjuffer
Bluetail, Small	Ischnura pumilio	Kleine Pechlibelle	Tengere grasjuffer
Brown, Arran	Erebia ligea	Weissbindiger Mohrenfalter	Boserebia
Brown, Dusky Meadow	Hyponephele lycaon	Kleines Ochsenauge	Grauw zandoogje
Brown, Meadow	Maniola jurtina	Grosses Ochsenauge	Bruin zandoogje
Bush-cricket, Predatory	Saga pedo	Grosse Sägeschrecke	Grote roofsprinkhaan*
Bush-cricket, Provence Saddle	Ephippiger provincialis	Provence-Sattelschrecke	Provence Zadelsprinkhaan*
Bush-cricket, Southern Saw-tailed	Barbitistes fischeri	Südfranzösische Säbelschrecke	Zuidelijke zaagsprinkhaan*
Butterfly, Nettle-tree	Libythea celtis	Zürgelbaum-Schnauzenfalter	Snuitvlinder
Cardinal	Argynnis pandora	Kardinal	Kardinaalsmantel
Chaser, Blue	Libellula fulva	Spitzenfleck	Bruine korenbout
Cicada, Grey	Cicada orni	Mannazikade	Kraakcicade
Cleopatra	Gonepteryx cleopatra	Mittelmeer-Zitronenfalter	Cleopatra
Clubtail, Common	Gomphus vulgatissimus	Gemeine Keiljungfer	Beekrombout
Clubtail, Pronged	Gomphus graslinii	Französische Keiljungfer	Gevorkte rombout
Clubtail, Western	Gomphus pulchellus	Westliche Keiljungfer	Plasrombout
Clubtail, Yellow	Gomphus simillimus	Gelbe Keiljungfer	Gele rombout
Copper, Purple-shot	Lycaena alciphron	Violetter Feuerfalter	Violette vuurvlinder
Copper, Scarce	Lycaena virgaureae	Dukatenfalter	Morgenrood
Copper, Sooty	Lycaena tityrus	Brauner Feuerfalter	Bruine vuurvlinder
Darter, Banded	Sympetrum pedemontanum	Gebänderte Heidelibelle	Bandheidelibel
Darter, Red-veined	Sympetrum fonscolombii	Frühe Heidelibelle	Zwervende heidelibel
Darter, Southern	Sympetrum meridionale	Südliche Heidelibelle	Zuidelijke heidelibel
Darter, Spotted	Sympetrum depressiusculum	Sumpf-Heidelibelle	Kempense heidelibel
Demoiselle, Banded	Calopteryx splendens	Gebänderte Prachtlibelle	Weidebeekjuffer
Demoiselle, Beautiful	Calopteryx virgo	Blauflügel-Prachtlibelle	Bosbeekjuffer
Demoiselle, Copper	Calopteryx haemorrhoidalis	Bronzene Prachtlibelle	Koperen beekjuffer
Demoiselle, Western	Calopteryx xanthostoma	Südwestliche Prachtlibelle	Iberische beekjuffer
Dropwing, Violet	Trithemis annulata	Violetter Sonnenzeiger	Purperlibel
Duke of Burgundy	Hamearis lucina	Schlüsselblumen-Würfelfalter	Sleutelbloemvlinde
Emerald, Balkan	Somatochlora meridionalis	Balkan-Smaragdlibelle	Zuidelijke glanslibel
Emerald, Downy	Cordulia aenea	Falkenlibelle	Smaragdlibel
Emerald, Orange-spotted	Oxygastra curtisii	Gekielte Smaragdlibelle	Bronslibel
Emperor, Blue	Anax imperator	Grosse Königslibelle	Grote keizerlibel
Emperor, Lesser	Anax parthenope	Kleine Königslibelle	Zuidelijke keizerlibel
Emperor, Lesser Purple	Apatura ilia	Kleiner Schillerfalter	Kleine weerschijnvlinder

TOURIST INFORMATION & OBSERVATION TIPS

English	Scientific	German	Dutch
Emperor, Vagrant	Anax ephippiger	Schabrackenlibelle	Zadellibel
Featherleg, Blue	Platycnemis pennipes	Blaue Federlibelle	Blauwe breedscheenjuf
Featherleg, Orange	Platycnemis acutipennis	Orangerote Federlibelle	Oranje breedscheenjuf
Featherleg, White	Platycnemis latipes	Weisse Federlibelle	Witte breedscheenjuffe
Festoon, Southern	Zerynthia polyxena	Südlicher Osterluzeifalter	Zuidelijke pijpbloemvlinder
Festoon, Spanish	Zerynthia rumina	Spanischer Osterluzeifalter	Spaanse pijpbloemvlinder
Fritillary, Glanville	Melitaea cinxia	Wegerich-scheckenfalter	Veldparelmoervlinder
Fritillary, Knapweed	Melitaea phoebe	Flockenblumen-Scheckenfalter	Knoopkruidparelmoervlinder
Fritillary, Marsh	Euphydryas aurinia	Skabiosen-Scheckenfalter	Moerasparelmoervlinder
Fritillary, Pearl-bordered	Boloria euphrosyne	Frühlings-Perlmuttfalter	Zilvervlek
Fritillary, Provençal	Mellicta deione	Leinkraut-Scheckenfalter	Spaanse parelmoervlinder
Fritillary, Queen of Spain	Issoria lathonia	Kleiner Perlmutterfalter	Kleine parelmoervlinder
Fritillary, Spanish	Euphydryas desfontainii	Spanische Scheckenfalter	Mozaïekparelmoervlinder
Fritillary, Spotted	Melitaea didyma	Roter Scheckenfalter	Tweekleurige parelmoervlinder
Fritillary, Twin-spot	Brenthis hecate	Saumfleck-Perlmutterfalter	Dubbelstipparelmoervlinder
Fritillary, Weaver's	Boloria dia	Magerrasen-Perlmutterfalter	Akkerparelmoervlinder
Gatekeeper, Southern	Pyronia cecilia	Südliches Ochsenauge	Zuidelijk oranje zandoogje
Gatekeeper, Spanish	Pyronia bathseba	Spanischer Ochsenauge	Spaans oranje zandoog
Goldenring, Common	Cordulegaster boltonii	Zweigestreifte Quelljungfer	Gewone bronlibel
Goldenring, Sombre	Cordulegaster bidentata	Gestreifte Quelljungfer	Zuidelijke bronlibel
Grasshopper, Blue-winged	Oedipoda caerulescens	Blauflügelige Ödlandschrecke	Blauwvleugelsprinkhaan
Grasshopper, Crau	Prionotropis rhodanica	Crau-Schrecke*	Crau sprinkhaan*
Grasshopper, Red-winged	Oedipoda germanica	Rotflügelige Ödlandschrecke	Roodvleugelsprinkhaan
Grasshopper, Ventoux Mountain	Podisma amedegnatoae	Ventoux Gebirgsschrecke*	Ventoux bergsprinkhaan
Grasshopper, Western Band-winged	Oedipoda charpentieri	Charpentiers Ödlandschrecke	West-Mediterrane blauwvleugel sprinkhaan
Grayling, False	Arethusana arethusa	Rotbindiger Samtfalter	Oranje steppevlinder
Grayling, Great Banded	Brintesia circe	Weisser Waldportier	Witbandzandoog
Grayling, Tree	Neohipparchia statilinus	Eisenfarbiger Samtfalter	Kleine heivlinder
Grayling, Woodland	Hipparchia fagi	Grosser Waldportier	Grote boswachter
Hairstreak, Chapman's Green	Callophrys avis	Erdbeerbaum Zipfelfalter*	Aardbeiboomgroentje
Hairstreak, False Ilex	Satyrium esculi	Südlicher Eichen-Zipfelfalter	Spaanse eikenpage
Hairstreak, Green	Callophrys rubi	Grüner Zipfelfalter	Groentje
Hairstreak, Ilex	Satyrium ilicis	Brauner Eichen-Zipfelfalter	Bruine eikenpage
Hairstreak, Provence	Tomares ballus	Ballusbläuling	Groene klaverpage
Hairstreak, Spanish Purple	Laeosopis roboris	Spanischer Blauer Zipfelfalter	Essenpage
Hawker, Blue-eyed	Aeshna affinis	Südliche Mosaikjungfer	Zuidelijke glazenmaker
Hawker, Green-eyed	Aeshna isosceles	Keilfleck-Mosaikjungfer	Vroege glazenmaker
Hawker, Hairy	Brachytron pratense	Frühe Schilfjäger	Glassnijder
Hawk-moth, Broad-bordered Bee	Hemaris fuciformis	Hummelschwärmer	Glasvleugelpijlstaart
Hawk-moth, Hummingbird	Macroglossum stellatarum	Taubenschwänzchen	Kolibrievlinder
Hawk-moth, Spurge	Hyles euphorbiae	Wolfsmilchschwärmer	Wolfsmelkpijlstaart

Heath, Dusky	Coenonympha dorus	Dorus Wiesenvögelchen	Bleek hooibeestje
Heath, Pearly	Coenonympha arcania	Weissbindiges Wiesenvögelchen	Tweekleurig hooibeestje
Heath, Small	Coenonympha pamphilus	Kleines Wiesenvögelchen	Hooibeestje
Hermit	Chazara briseis	Berghexe	Heremiet
Insect, French Stick	Clonopsis gallica	Gallische Mittelmeerstabschrecke	Gallische wandelende tak
Mantis, European Dwarf	Ameles spallanzania	Kleine Fangschrecke	Dwergbidsprinkhaan
Mantis, Mediterranean	Iris oratoria	Mittelmeer-Gottesanbeterin	Mediterrane bidsprinkhaan*
Mantis, Praying	Mantis religiosa	Gottesanbeterin	Bidsprinkhaan
Orange-tip	Anthocharis cardamines	Aurorafalter	Oranjetipje
Orange-tip, Provence	Anthocharis euphenoides	Gelber Aurorafalter	Geel oranjetipje
Owlfly	Ascalaphidae	Schmetterlingshafte	Vlinderhaften
Pasha, Two-tailed	Charaxes jasius	Erdbeerbaumfalter	Aardbeiboomvlinder
Pincertail, Large	Onychogomphus uncatus	Grosse Zangenlibelle	Grote tanglibel
Pincertail, Small	Onychogomphus forcipatus	Kleine Zangenlibelle	Kleine tanglibel
Red-eye, Small	Erythromma viridulum	Kleines Granatauge	Kleine roodoogjuffer
Ringlet, Autumn	Erebia neoridas	Herbst-Mohrenfalter*	Herfsterebia
Ringlet, Larche	Erebia scipio	Blassbindiger Mohrenfalter	Provencaalse erebia
Ringlet, Piedmont	Erebia meolans	Gelbbindiger Mohrenfalter	Donkere erebia
Ringlet, Spring	Erebia epistygne	Provence-Mohrenfalter*	Lente-erebia
Satyr, Great Sooty	Satyrus ferula	Weisskernauge	Grote saterzandoog
Scarlet, Broad	Crocothemis erythraea	Feuerlibelle	Vuurlibel
Scolopendra	Scolopendra sp.	Riesenläufer/ Gürtelskolopender	Scolopendra*
Skimmer, White-tailed	Orthetrum albistylum	Östliche Blaupfeil	Witpuntoeverlibel
Skipper, Dingy	Erynnis tages	Kronwicken-Dickkopffalter	Bruin dikkopje
Skipper, Red Underwing	Spialia sertorius	Roter Würfel-Dickkopffalter	Kalkgraslanddikkopje
Skipper, Tufted	Carcharodus flocciferus	Heilziest-Dickkopffalter	Pluimdikkopje
Skipper, Yellow-banded	Pyrgus sidae	Graubrauner Dickkopffalter	Geelbandspikkeldikkopje
Spectre, Western	Boyeria irene	Westliche Geisterlibelle	Schemerlibel
Spreadwing, Common	Lestes sponsa	Gemeine Binsenjungfer	Gewone pantserjuffer
Spreadwing, Dark	Lestes macrostigma	Südliche Binsenjungfer	Grote pantserjuffer
Spreadwing, Migrant	Lestes barbarus	Südliche Binsenjungfer	Zwervende pantserjuffer
Spreadwing, Robust	Lestes dryas	Glänzende Binsenjungfer	Tangpantserjuffer
Spreadwing, Small	Lestes virens	Kleine Binsenjungfer	Tengere pantserjuffer
Swallowtail, Common	Papilio machaon	Schwalbenschwanz	Koninginnenpage
Swallowtail, Scarce	Iphiclides podalirius	Segelfalter	Koningspage
Swallowtail, Southern	Papilio alexanor	Südlicher Schwalbenschwanz	Zuidelijke koninginnenpage
Tortoiseshell, Large	Nymphalis polychloros	Grosser Fuchs	Grote vos
Wasp, Ichneumon	Ichneumonidae	Schlupfwespen	Sluipwespen
Wasp, Mammoth	Megascolia maculata	Gelbstirnige Dolchwespe	Reuzendolkwesp
White, Marbled	Melanargia galathea	Schachbrett	Dambordje

CROSSBILL GUIDES
IF YOU WANT TO SEE MORE

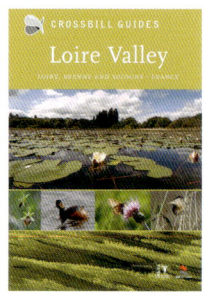
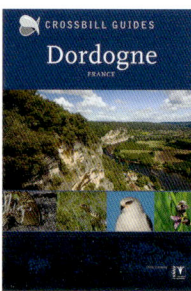
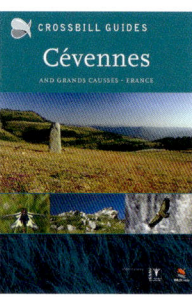
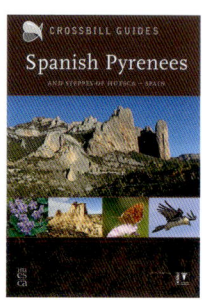
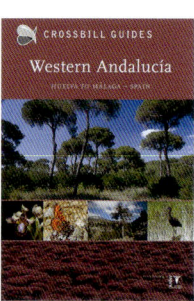
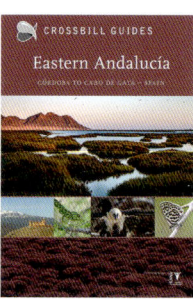
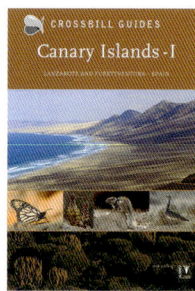
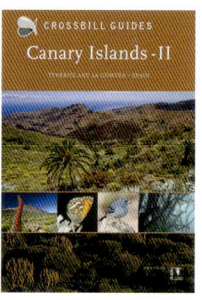
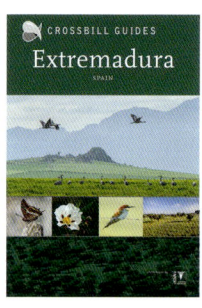
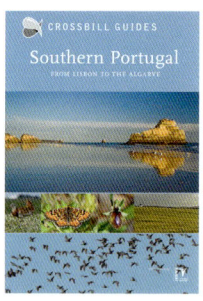
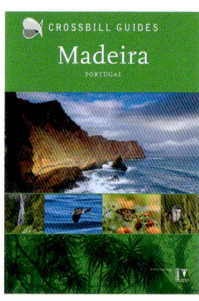
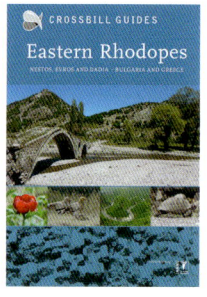
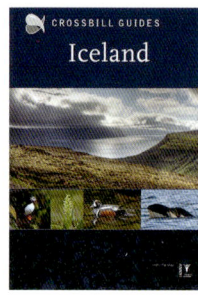
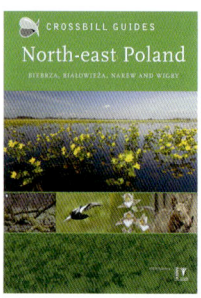
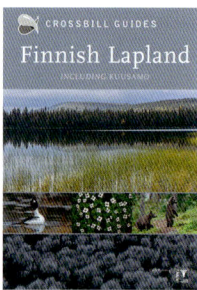
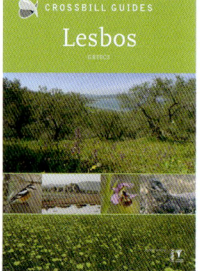

More titles are in preparation. Check our website for further details and updates.
WWW.CROSSBILLGUIDES.ORG